The Complete Book of
JUICING

YOUR DELICIOUS GUIDE TO HEALTHFUL LIVING

MICHAEL T. MURRAY, N.D.

Prima Publishing
P.O. Box 1260BK
Rocklin, CA 95677
(916) 632-4400

Copyediting by ANNE MONTAGUE

Composition by JANET HANSEN, ALPHATYPE

Production by E. A. PAUW, BOOKMAN PRODUCTIONS

Cover design by THE DUNLAVEY STUDIO

Illustrations by JIM STAUNTON

Library of Congress Cataloging-in-Publication Data

Murray, Michael T.
    The complete book of juicing / Michael T. Murray.
     p. cm.
    Includes index.
    ISBN 1–55958–268–5
    1. Fruit juices—Health aspects.   2. Vegetable juices—Health aspects. I. Title.
RA784.M84 1992
641.2'6—dc20   92–10188
                                      CIP

95 96 RRD 10 9 8 7 6 5 4 3

Printed in the United States of America

WARNING—DISCLAIMER

Prima Publishing has designed this book to provide information in regard to the subject matter covered. It is sold with the understanding that the publisher and the author are not liable for the misconception or misuse of information provided. Every effort has been made to make this book as complete and as accurate as possible. The purpose of this book is to educate. The author and Prima Publishing shall have neither liability nor responsibility to any person or entity with respect to any loss, damage, or injury caused or alleged to be caused directly or indirectly by the information contained in this book. The information presented herein is in no way intended as a substitute for medical counseling.

In memory of my grandmother, Pauline Meade Shier (1903–1991).

CONTENTS

FOREWORD

I've been sharing with people my personal story about juicing for more than 40 years. My message has been the connection between diet and health, and how by decreasing intake of meat and dairy products, and increasing consumption of fresh fruits, vegetables, grains, and legumes, people can help prevent diet-related diseases. Juicing is a great way to add more fresh fruits and vegetables to the diet, plus it's easy and delicious. I'm living proof that a good diet pays off in good health. I'm almost 70 years old and I've never felt better.

Michael Murray's *The Complete Book of Juicing* goes beyond the simple fact that juicing offers many health benefits; it takes an in-depth look at the scientific side of the juicing phenomenon. This book is a "must read" for anyone interested in juicing to improve or enhance the quality of life.

When I first started sharing my message, I was one of the very few people out there talking about how more fresh fruits and vegetables in the diet could help prevent diet-related disease and premature aging. Today health and medical professionals are accepting and acknowledging what I've been saying all along. The role of fresh fruit and vegetables as part of a low-fat, high-fiber diet does help promote health and prevent disease. Specifically, the American Cancer Society, the American Institute for Cancer Research, the U.S. Surgeon General's Office, heart disease specialist Dr. Dean Ornish, the American Heart Association, and many more all agree that various diet-related diseases may be prevented if the quality of

our diet is improved. Scientific studies show that cancer, heart disease, arthritis, diabetes, and stroke could be prevented, or lessened, if certain components found in a plant-based diet (fruits, vegetables, grains, and legumes) are consumed on a regular basis.

Dr. Michael Murray has gathered a wealth of information from respected scientific sources. His tireless research and practical experience working with patients prove that a preventive approach to health care, using nutrition as the basis, is the way to achieve optimum wellness. His recommendations are both clinically relevant and scientifically proven. The data he shares and the education he provides are eye-opening, fascinating, and completely support what I have been proposing all my life: including more fresh fruits and vegetables in your diet is one of the most important things you can do for your body, and juicing is one of the easiest ways to do this.

I feel this information is long overdue and deserves a space in each and every home in America.

Dr. Murray adds *The Complete Book of Juicing* to his impressive collection of health- and nutrition-oriented publications: *The Encyclopedia of Natural Medicine* and *The Healing Power of Herbs.*

Yours in health,

JAY KORDICH
The Juiceman

PREFACE

Health is a term that is difficult to define: a definition somehow tends to place unnecessary boundaries on its meaning. The World Health Organization defines health as "a state of complete physical, mental, and social well-being, not merely the absence of disease or infirmity." This definition provides a positive range of health well beyond the absence of sickness. Too many Americans live at the lower end of the spectrum. My life and this book are about helping people achieve a higher level of health.

Many of our health practices and lifestyle choices are based on habit and marketing hype. A great deal of time, energy, and money is spent to market bad health practices. The mass media constantly bombard us with messages urging us to make unhealthy choices regarding our health, diet, and lifestyle. In addition, the health practices and lifestyle of our parents usually become intricately woven into the fabric of our own lifestyles.

The first step in achieving and maintaining health is taking personal responsibility. In this context, responsibility means choosing a healthy alternative over a less healthy one. If you want to be healthy, simply make healthy choices. This may seem too simplistic, but if we look at the cumulative effects of our routine choices on attitude, diet, lifestyle, and exercise, it is quite apparent that we do in fact control the level of health we will experience. The reward for most people who maintain a positive mental attitude, eat a healthy diet, and exercise regularly is a life full of energy, joy, vitality, and a tremendous passion for living.

It is often difficult to "sell" people on health. It is usually not until the body fails us in some manner that we realize that we haven't taken care of it. Ralph Waldo Emerson said, "The first wealth is health." I urge you to take action now.

MICHAEL T. MURRAY, N.D.

ACKNOWLEDGMENTS

A special thanks to everyone at Trillium Health Products, especially Rick and Steve Cesari, the "Nutrition Hotline," and Cindy Peterson, as well as everyone at Prima, especially Ben, Jennifer, Laura, and Laurie.

I also would like to express sincere appreciation to Jay Kordich (The Juiceman) for his vision, untiring enthusiasm, and passion; and Cherie Calbom (The Juicewoman) for her support, knowledge, and charm.

And finally, I would like to thank my wife, Gina, not only for the tremendous impact she has made in my life, but also for the wonderful person that she truly is.

1
WHY JUICE?

T he quality of your life begins with the quality of the foods that sustain it. The surest path to a healthier, more energetic, and disease-free lifestyle begins with a diet rich in natural foods like whole grains, legumes, fruits and vegetables. Especially important on this path to health are fresh fruits and vegetable juices. Fresh juices provide the proteins, carbohydrates, essential fatty acids, vitamins, minerals and other food factors that are vital to your health.

The advantages of increased energy, strengthened immunity, reduced risk of disease, strong bones, and the glowing complexion that is the evidence of great health can all be yours when fresh fruit and vegetable juices form a substantial part of your daily diet. It is a well-known fact that the Surgeon General, the U.S. Department of Health and Human Services, the National Cancer Institute, and many other experts are all saying the same thing: "Eat more fresh fruits and vegetables!" Juicing provides nutritional advantages of plant foods in a concentrated form that is easily absorbed by the body, and is the most fun and efficient way to increase your consumption of these life-giving foods.

WHAT DO AMERICANS EAT?

The so-called Standard American Diet, or SAD, does not provide adequate levels of fruits and vegetables. According to several large surveys, including the U.S. Second National Health and Nutrition Examination, fewer than 10% of Americans met the minimum recommendation of two fruit servings and three vegetable servings a day, only 51% ate one garden vegetable a day, and 41% ate no fruit or fruit juice during the day.[1]

Instead of eating foods rich in vital nutrients, most Americans focus on refined foods high in calories, sugar, fat, and cholesterol, filling up on cheeseburgers, french fries, Twinkies, and chocolate chip cookies, and washing them down with artificially colored and flavored fruit drinks or

Estimated Total Deaths and % of Total Deaths for the 10 Leading Causes of Death: United States, 1987			
Rank	Cause of Death	Number	% of Total Deaths
1	**Heart diseases**	**759,400**	**35.7**
2	**Cancers**	**476,700**	**22.4**
3	**Strokes**	**148,700**	**7.0**
4	Unintentional injuries	92,500	4.4
5	Chronic obstructive lung disease	78,000	3.7
6	Pneumonia & influenza	68,600	3.2
7	**Diabetes mellitus**	**37,800**	**1.8**
8	Suicide	29,600	1.4
9	Chronic liver disease & cirrhosis	26,000	1.2
10	**Atherosclerosis**	**23,1000**	**1.1**
	All Causes	**2,125,100**	**100.0**

Causes of death in which diet plays a part are in bold.

From the Surgeon General's report on Nutrition and Health.
Source: National Center for Health Statistics, *Monthly
Vital Statistics Report,* vol. 37, no. 1, April 25, 1988.

colas. It is a "SAD" fact that the three leading causes of death in the United States—heart disease, cancer, and strokes—are diet-related and that over one-third of our adult population is overweight.

It has been estimated that in one year, the average American consumes 100 pounds of refined sugar and 55 pounds of fats and oils in the form of:

- 300 cans of soda pop
- 200 sticks of gum

- 18 pounds of candy
- 5 pounds of potato chips
- 7 pounds of corn chips, popcorn, and pretzels
- 63 dozen donuts and pastries
- 50 pounds of cakes and cookies
- 20 gallons of ice cream

On top of this, nearly one-third of our adult population smokes and at least 10% are alcoholics.

And what about the health effects of the over 4 billion pounds of additives, pesticides, and herbicides added to our foods each year? Is it any wonder we are sick? Is it any wonder that as a nation we rank lower in life expectancy than 16 other industrial nations, despite the fact that we spend more money on health care (a projected $813 billion for 1992) than any nation in the world?

THE ROLE OF THE DIET
IN DISEASE PREVENTION

An extensive body of research has clearly established the link between the SAD (high fat, high sugar, low fiber) and the development of the primary "diseases of civilization" (heart disease, several types of cancers, strokes, high blood pressure, diabetes, gallstones, arthritis, and more).[2]

The data confirming diet's role in chronic degenerative diseases are substantial. There are two basic facts that support this link: (1) a diet rich in plant foods (whole grains, legumes, fruits, and vegetables) protects against chronic degenerative diseases that are extremely common in so-called Western society; and (2) a diet providing a low intake of plant foods is a causative factor in the development of these diseases and creates conditions under which other causative factors are more active.

Much of the link between diet and chronic disease is based on the landmark work of two medical pioneers, Denis

Burkitt, M.D., and Hugh Trowell, M.D., authors of *Dietary Fibre, Fibre-depleted Foods and Disease.*[3] Burkitt formulated the following sequence of events, based on extensive studies examining the rate of diseases in various populations (epidemiological data) and his own observations of primitive cultures:

> First stage: The primal diet of plant eaters contains large amounts of unprocessed starch staples; there are few examples of chronic degenerative diseases like osteoarthritis, heart disease, diabetes, and cancer.
>
> Second stage: Commencing Westernization of diet, obesity and diabetes commonly appear in privileged groups.
>
> Third stage: With moderate Westernization of the diet, constipation, hemorrhoids, varicose veins, and appendicitis become common complaints.
>
> Fourth stage: Finally, with full Westernization of the diet, chronic degenerative diseases like diabetes, arthritis, gout, heart disease, and cancer are extremely common.

Based on Burkitt's work, as well as that of countless others, the recommendation of many medical organizations and experts is that the human diet focus primarily on plant-based foods: vegetables, fruits, grains, legumes, nuts, seeds. A diet rich in these foods will be high in dietary fiber and complex carbohydrates, low in fat, and low in refined sugars. Such a diet has been shown to offer significant protection against the development of chronic degenerative diseases like heart disease, cancer, arthritis, and osteoporosis.[2,3]

A diet based primarily on plant foods makes sense not only from a health standpoint, but from an environmental viewpoint as well. In *Diet for a New America,* John Robbins paints a graphic portrait of the consequences of typical American eating habits on individual health, on the environment,

on our natural resources, and on our planet as a whole.[4] Robbins's book is essential reading for anyone concerned about his or her health, the environment, or the earth.

The statistics in Figure 1.2, excerpted from *Diet for a New America,* clearly show the impacts of a diet based on the "New Four Food Groups" (fruits, vegetables, grains, and legumes), as promoted by the Physicians Committee for Responsible Medicine.[5] An increase in our consumption of fruits, vegetables, grains, and legumes means a decrease in America's dependence on meat and dairy products. This in turn leads to corresponding improvements in our health, environment, and natural resources.

At the bare minimum, Americans should follow the seven dietary recommendations given by the American Cancer Society, designed to significantly reduce the risk for cancer.[6] These recommendations are as follows:

- Avoid obesity.
- Reduce total fat intake to less than 30% total calories.
- Eat more high-fiber foods, such as whole-grain cereals, legumes, fruits, and vegetables.
- Emphasize fruits and vegetables for their carotene and vitamin C content.
- Include cruciferous vegetables, such as cabbage, broccoli, brussels sprouts, and cauliflower in the diet for their anticancer compounds.
- Be moderate in consumption of alcoholic beverages.
- Be moderate in the consumption of salt-cured, smoked, and nitrite-cured foods.

Where does juicing figure into these recommendations? Quite simply, without juicing it is extremely difficult to get the amount of nutrition we need to reduce our risk of not only cancer, but also heart disease and strokes. For example, recent studies indicate that to effectively reduce the risk of many cancers we would need to eat in a day the amount of beta-carotene equivalent to about two to three pounds of fresh

Effects of an Animal-Product Diet On:

Your Health

Risk of death from heart attack for average American man: **50%**

Risk of death from heart attack for American man who consumes no meat: **15%**

Increased risk of breast cancer for women who eat meat daily compared to less than once a week: **3.8 times higher**

Increased risk of fatal ovarian cancer for women who eat eggs three or more days a week compared to less than once a week: **3 times higher**

The Environment

A driving force behind the destruction of the tropical rain forests: **American meat habit**

Water pollution attributable to U.S. agriculture including runoff of soil, pesticides, and manure: **Greater than all municipal and industrial sources combined**

Our Natural Resources

Number of acres of U.S. forest that have been cleared to create cropland, pastureland, and rangeland currently producing a meat-centered diet: **260,000,000**

Number of acres of U.S. land that could be returned to forest if Americans adopted a meat-free diet and ceased exporting livestock feed: **204,000,000**

User of more than half of all water consumed for all purposes in the United States: **livestock production**

In California, gallons of water needed to produce 1 edible pound of:

Tomatoes	23	Milk	130
Lettuce	23	Egg	544
Wheat	24	Chicken	815
Carrots	33	Pork	1,630
Apples	49	Beef	5,214

Source: John Robbins, *Diet for a New America*
(Walpole, NH: Stillpoint Publishing, 1987).

carrots (roughly six large carrots).[7] To thoroughly chew one carrot takes about five minutes, so to eat six could take half an hour a day. Most Americans simply do not have the desire nor the time to do this. Juicing provides a quick, easy, and effective way to meet your daily quota of carotenes (discussed in the next chapter) and other valuable cancer-fighting nutrients. For example, 16 ounces of carrot juice provides the carotene equivalent of approximately three pounds of carrots.

MAKING JUICING A WAY OF LIFE

Juicing is extremely easy to incorporate into your life. Simply make a habit of drinking at least 16 ounces of juice each day. Fresh juice is a great way to start the morning—it's a tasty substitute for that cup of coffee. If you work away from home, make enough juice to fill your thermos and take it to work with you. A mid-morning or mid-afternoon juice pick-me-up is a healthy way to keep your energy level high. At lunch and dinner, start your meal with a "salad in a glass." Once you start experiencing some of the benefits of juicing, it will be easy to remember the importance of fresh fruit and vegetable juice in your daily routine.

FRESH JUICE VS. WHOLE FRUITS AND VEGETABLES

You may ask, "Why juice? Aren't we supposed to eat whole fruits and vegetables to get the fiber?" The answer: Of course you are, but you should juice too. Juicing fresh fruits and vegetables does provide some fiber, particularly the soluble fiber. And it is the soluble fiber that has been shown to lower cholesterol levels. Think about it—fiber refers to indigestible material found in plants. While this is very important for proper bowel function, it is the juice that nourishes us. Our body actually converts the food we eat into juice so that it can be absorbed. Juicing helps the body's digestive process and allows for quick absorption of high-quality nutrition. The result is increased energy levels. Juicing quickly provides the most easily digestible and concentrated nutritional benefits of fruits and vegetables.

FRESH JUICE VS. CANNED, BOTTLED, OR FROZEN JUICES

Fresh juice is far superior to canned, bottled, or frozen juices. Fresh juice not only contains greater nutritional values, it contains life. Specifically, fresh juice contains enzymes and other "living" ingredients. In contrast, canned, bottled, and packaged juices have been pasteurized, which keeps it on the shelf longer but causes the loss of identifiable nutrients like vitamins and minerals, as well as the loss of other factors not yet fully understood.

To illustrate this, a group of researchers designed a scientific study comparing the antiviral activity of fresh apple juice to commercial apple juice from concentrate, apple cider, and apple wine. The most potent antiviral activity was found in fresh apple juice.[8] Why? Commercial apple juices are produced using methods like pasteurization that destroy enzymes. In doing so, a great deal of the antiviral activity is lost as well.

Although the fresh juice was greatly superior in health benefits to the other products, it must be pointed out that it lost its potency during storage. To get the maximum benefit from apple juice's antiviral activity, or from any other fruit or vegetable, it is best to drink the freshest juice possible.

FRESH JUICE VS. PROCESSED FOOD PRODUCTS

There is a wide spectrum of products—from fresh whole foods to highly processed refined food products—offered in the American food supply. An excellent illustration is the

Modern Evolution of the Orange

**Raw, whole oranges or
freshly prepared orange juice**

**Refined, processed (pasteurized)
unsweetened orange juice**

**Refined, processed, sweetened
orange juice or concentrate**

**Refined, highly processed, sweetened,
artificially colored & flavored "orange" drinks**

**Completely fabricated products
never before known (such as Tang™)**

orange (see above). At each step in this modern evolution of the orange, there is a loss of nutritional value. For example, the vitamin C content of pasteurized orange juice is extremely unreliable. As with most processed juices, the total nutritional quality is substantially lower than that of fresh juice. This is

particularly true for juices stored in paperboard containers lined with wax or polyethylene. These products will lose up to 75% of their vitamin C content within three weeks.[9] Frozen juice concentrates fare no better, and orange drinks have no vitamin C unless it is added. This highlights the fact that in the latter stages listed on page 10, there is not only a decrease in nutritional value, there is also an increase in the number of synthetic additives.

More and more food additives (such as preservatives, artificial colors, artificial flavorings, and acidifiers) are being shown to be extremely detrimental to health. Although many food additives have been banned because they were found to cause cancer, a great number of synthetic food additives are still in use that are being linked to such diseases as depression, asthma and other allergies, hyperactivity and learning disabilities in children, and migraine headaches. Obviously the ingestion of synthetic food additives needs to be avoided.

Although the government has banned many synthetic food additives, it should not be assumed that the additives currently in our food supply are safe. For example, sulfites were considered harmless until 1986. Certain sulfite compounds that prevent fresh fruits and vegetables from browning were widely used on produce at restaurant salad bars. Since most people were not aware that sulfites were being added, and because most people were unaware that a sensitivity to sulfites was possible, many unsuspecting people experienced severe allergic or asthmatic reactions. For years, the FDA refused to consider a ban on sulfites, even while admitting these agents provoked attacks in an unknown number of people and in 5% to 10% of asthma victims. It was not until 1985, when sulfite sensitivity was linked to 15 deaths between 1983 and 1985, that the FDA agreed to review the matter. In 1986, the FDA finally banned sulfite use.

Clearly, the best way to reduce the need for such preservatives and other synthetic additives is to eat as many fresh and natural foods as possible. Juicing fresh fruits and

vegetables is not only a great way to increase your dietary intake of important nutritional components, it also helps you avoid the majority of harmful additives and preservatives. This is especially true if you juice only organic produce.

THE FRESHER THE JUICE, THE GREATER THE NUTRITION

Like commercial processing methods, home handling and cooking also means a loss of nutrients. For example, leafy vegetables will lose up to 87% of their vitamin C content upon cooking, while carrots, potatoes, and other root vegetables will lose up to 33% of vitamin B1, 45% of B2, 61% of B3, and 76% of vitamin C. Fruits and vegetables don't have to be cooked, however, to lose nutritional value. They will also lose nutritional value if exposed to air. For example, if you slice a cantaloupe and leave the slices uncovered in the refrigerator, they will lose 35% of their vitamin C content in 24 hours. Freshly sliced cucumbers, if left standing, will lose between 41% and 49% of their vitamin C content within the first three hours.[10] From this information we can conclude that it is best to drink fresh juice as soon as it is prepared. If this is not possible, juice should be stored in a thermos or in an airtight container in the refrigerator.

JUICING, OBESITY, AND HIGH BLOOD PRESSURE

Many Americans are overfed but undernourished. Estimates are that up to 50% of the adult population is overweight. Juice helps reset the body's appetite control by providing the body with the high-quality nutrition it needs. This is vitally important at all times, but especially during weight loss. If the body is not fed, it feels that it is starving. The result: Metabolism will slow down. This means less fat

will be burned. Juicing is an excellent way to supply key nutrients to the body in a fresh, raw, and natural way.

Diets containing a high percentage (up to 60% of the calories) of uncooked foods are associated with significant weight loss and lowering of blood pressure in overweight individuals.[11] Researchers seeking to determine why raw-food diets produce these effects have concluded that:

- *A raw-food diet is much more satisfying to the appetite.* Cooking can cause the loss of up to 97% of water-soluble vitamins (B vitamins and C) and up to 40% of the fat-soluble vitamins (A, D, E, and K). Since uncooked foods such as juices contain more vitamins and other nutrients, they are more satisfying to the body. The result is reduced calorie intake and thus weight loss in obese individuals.

- *The blood-pressure-lowering effect of raw foods is most likely due to healthier food choices, fiber, and potassium.* However, the effect of cooking the food cannot be ruled out. When patients are switched from a raw diet to a cooked diet (without a change in calorie or sodium content), there is a rapid increase of blood pressure back to prestudy levels.

- *A diet in which an average of 60% of the calories ingested comes from raw foods reduces the stress on the body.* Specifically, the presence of enzymes in raw foods, the reduced allergenicity of raw foods, and the effects of raw foods on our gut-bacteria ecosystem are thought to be much more healthful than the effects of cooked foods.

Juicing is a phenomenal way to reach the goal of ingesting 60% of total calories from raw foods. More and more experts are making this recommendation to encourage people to improve the nutritional quality of their diets. As a bonus, juice helps the body's digestive process and allows for quick absorption of high-quality nutrition. The result: increased energy

levels. This is one of the greatest advantages of utilizing fresh juice in a weight-loss plan.

Some juices are better than others for promoting weight loss. The most effective are those that are dense in nutrients but low in calories. Here in descending order are the most nutrient-dense fruits and vegetables suitable for juicing:

1. Bell peppers	11. Beets
2. Parsley	12. Pineapple
3. Kale	13. Cantaloupe
4. Broccoli	14. Watermelon
5. Spinach	15. Tomatoes
6. Celery	16. Apple
7. Brussels sprouts	17. Strawberries
8. Cauliflower	18. Pears
9. Carrots	19. Oranges
10. Cabbage	20. Grapes

The first eight vegetables listed are not only nutrient-dense, they are also quite strong-flavored. Mixing them with carrot, apple, or tomato juice will make them much more palatable. Notice that the fruits are further down on the scale than the vegetables. Although fruits are full of valuable nutrients, they contain more natural sugars than vegetables. This means they are higher in calories, so they should be used sparingly.

JUICING FOR HEALTH, LONGEVITY, AND RADIANT BEAUTY

Throughout this book, many key benefits of consuming fresh juices will be pointed out, but perhaps the greatest benefit is that it provides high levels of natural plant compounds known as antioxidants, which can protect the body against aging, cancer, heart disease, and many other degenerative conditions. The cells of the human body are constantly under

attack. The culprits? Free radicals and pro-oxidants. A free radical is a molecule that contains a highly reactive unpaired electron, while a pro-oxidant is a molecule that can promote oxidative damage. These highly reactive molecules can bind to and destroy other cellular components. Free-radical damage is a cause of aging, and is also linked to the development of cancer, heart disease, cataracts, Alzheimer's disease, arthritis, and virtually every other chronic degenerative disease.[2,12]

Where do these sinister agents come from? Believe it or not, most of the free radicals zipping through our bodies are actually produced during normal metabolic processes like energy generation, detoxification reactions, and immune defense mechanisms. Ironically, the major source of free-radical damage in the body is the oxygen molecule—the molecule that gives us life is also the molecule that can do the most harm! Just as oxygen can rust iron, when toxic oxygen molecules are allowed to attack our cells free-radical or oxidative damage occurs.

Although the body's own generation of free radicals is significant, the environment contributes greatly to the free-radical load of an individual. Cigarette smoking, for example, greatly increases an individual's free-radical load. Many of the harmful effects of smoking are related to the extremely high levels of free radicals being inhaled, depleting key antioxidant nutrients like vitamin C and beta-carotene. Other external sources of free radicals include ionizing radiation, chemotherapeutic drugs, air pollutants, pesticides, anesthetics, aromatic hydrocarbons, fried food, solvents, alcohol, and formaldehyde. These compounds greatly stress the body's antioxidant mechanisms. Individuals exposed to these factors need additional nutritional support.[12]

Our cells protect against free-radical and oxidative damage with the help of antioxidants and enzymes found in the plant foods we consume. The antioxidants include carotenes, flavonoids, vitamins C and E, and sulfur-containing compounds. Free radicals must be broken down by enzymes or

be chemically neutralized before they react with cellular molecules. Examples of the free-radical-scavenging enzymes produced by the body are catalase, superoxide dismutase, and glutathione peroxidase. Taking enzymes as an oral supplement has not been shown to increase enzyme tissue levels. However, ingesting antioxidant nutrients like manganese, sulfur-containing amino acids, carotenes, flavonoids, and vitamin C has been shown to increase tissue concentrations of the enzymes.[12,13]

The other way the cell can protect itself against free-radical or oxidative damage is via chemical neutralization, antioxidants binding to or neutralizing the free radical or pro-oxidant. For example, the nutritional antioxidants (vitamins C and E, beta-carotene, and selenium) block free-radical damage by chemically reacting with the free radical or pro-oxidant to neutralize it. Ingesting rich sources of these compounds from fresh juices can increase tissue concentrations of these nutrients, thereby supporting normal cellular protective mechanisms and blocking free-radical and oxidative damage.

SUMMARY

Many medical experts and departments of the U.S. government, including the National Academy of Science, the Department of Agriculture, and the Department of Health and Human Services, as well as the National Research Council and the National Cancer Institute, are recommending that Americans consume two to three servings of fruit and three to five servings of vegetables a day. Unfortunately, less than 10% of the population is meeting even the lowest recommendation of five servings of a combination of fruits and vegetables.

Juicing provides an easy and effective way to meet your dietary requirements for fresh fruits and vegetables, the most nutrient-packed form. One of the key benefits of fresh fruit and vegetable juices, beyond their nutritional superiority, is their

rich supply of antioxidant nutrients like vitamin C and beta-carotene. Since oxidative damage is a cause of aging, and is also linked to the development of cancer, heart disease, cataracts, Alzheimer's disease, arthritis, and virtually every other chronic degenerative disease, the consumption of fruits and vegetables is being shown to offer significant protection against the development of these diseases.

2

WHAT'S IN JUICE? THE NUTRIENTS

J uice is a source of natural water, and provides the body with easily absorbed protein, carbohydrates, essential fatty acids, vitamins, and minerals. Fresh juice also contains numerous accessory food components known as anutrients, including enzymes, and pigments such as carotenes, chlorophyll, and flavonoids, which are discussed in the next chapter. This chapter will describe the nutritional elements found in fresh fruit and vegetable juices and discuss their importance to our health.

WATER: VITAL FOR OPTIMAL PERFORMANCE

First, fresh juice provides natural water. Water is the most plentiful substance in the body. It constitutes over 60% of body weight. More than two-thirds of the body's water content is found inside the cells. The rest is found coursing through the body, carrying vital nutrients and blood cells. In addition, water functions in chemical reactions, serves as a lubricant in joints, aids in maintaining body temperature, and serves as an insulator and shock absorber in body temperature.

Each day your body requires an intake of over two quarts of water to function optimally. About one quart each day comes from the foods you eat. This means you need to drink at least one quart of liquids each day to maintain good water balance. More is needed in warmer climates and for physically active people.

Not drinking enough liquids or eating enough high-water-content foods puts a great deal of stress on the body. Kidney function is likely to be affected, gallstones and kidney stones are likely to form, and immune function will be impaired.

There is currently a great deal of concern about our water supply. Pure water is becoming increasingly difficult to find. Most of our water supply is full of chemicals, including not only chlorine and fluoride, which are routinely added, but

a wide range of toxic organic compounds and chemicals such as PCBs, pesticide residues, nitrates, and heavy metals like lead, mercury, and cadmium.[1] Drinking fresh fruit and vegetable juices (especially those derived from organic produce) is a fantastic way to give your body the natural, pure water it desires.

PROTEIN: ESSENTIAL TO GOOD HEALTH

After water, protein is the next most plentiful component of the body. The body manufactures proteins to make up muscles, tendons, ligaments, hair, nails, and other structures. Proteins also function as enzymes, hormones, and as important components to other cells, such as genes. Adequate protein intake is essential to good health. In fact, the meat and dairy industries have spent a great deal of money advertising the importance of protein. They have done such a good job that most Americans consume far greater amounts of protein than the body actually requires. The recommended daily allowance for protein is 44g for the average woman and 56g for the average man, or approximately 8% to 9% of total daily calories. Most Americans consume almost twice this amount.[2]

Proteins are composed of individual building blocks known as amino acids. The human body can manufacture most of the amino acids required for making body proteins. However, there are nine amino acids, termed "essential" amino acids, that the body cannot manufacture and must get from dietary intake: arginine, histadine, isoleucine, lysine, methionine, phenylalanine, threonine, tryptophan, and valine. The quality of a protein source is based on its level of these essential amino acids along with its digestibility and ability to be utilized by the body.

A complete protein source is one that provides all nine essential amino acids in adequate amounts. Animal products—meat, fish, dairy, poultry—are examples of complete

proteins. Plant foods, especially grains and legumes, often lack one or more of the essential amino acids, but become complete when they are combined. For example, combining grains with legumes (beans) results in a complete protein, as the two protein sources complement each other. With a varied diet of grains, legumes, fruits, and vegetables, a person is almost assured of complete proteins, as long as the calorie content of the diet is high enough.

Fresh fruits and vegetables often contain the full complement of amino acids. But because fruits and vegetables contain protein in lower quantities, they are generally considered poor protein sources. However, as previously mentioned, the nutritional qualities of fruits and vegetables become concentrated in their juice form, making juices an excellent source of easily absorbed amino acids and proteins. For example, 16 ounces of carrot juice (the equivalent of two to three pounds of fresh raw carrots) will provide nearly 5g of protein. Obviously, fresh juice should not be relied on to meet all your body's protein needs. You will need to eat other protein sources, such as grains and legumes. Or you can supplement your juice with the soy-based meal replacement formulas to meet all of your protein needs.

CARBOHYDRATES: THE BODY'S ENERGY SOURCE

Carbohydrates provide us with the energy we need for body functions. There are two groups of carbohydrates, simple and complex. Simple carbohydrates, or sugars, are quickly absorbed by the body for a ready source of energy. The natural simple sugars in fruits and vegetables have an advantage over sucrose (white sugar) and other refined sugars in that they are balanced by a wide range of nutrients that aid in the utilization of the sugars. Problems with carbohydrates begin when they are refined and stripped of these nutrients. Virtually all the vitamin content has been removed from white sugar, white breads and pastries, and many breakfast cereals.

Percentage of Calories as Protein

Legumes

Soybean sprouts	54%
Mung bean sprouts	43%
Soybean curd (tofu)	43%
Soy flour	35%
Soy sauce	33%
Broad beans	32%
Lentils	29%
Split peas	28%
Kidney beans	26%
Navy beans	26%
Lima beans	26%
Garbanzo beans	23%

Vegetables

Spinach	49%
Kale	45%
Broccoli	45%
Brussels sprouts	44%
Turnip greens	43%
Collards	43%
Cauliflower	40%
Mushrooms	38%
Parsley	34%
Lettuce	34%
Green peas	30%
Zucchini	28%
Green beans	26%
Cucumbers	24%
Green peppers	22%
Artichokes	22%
Cabbage	22%
Celery	21%
Eggplant	21%
Tomatoes	18%
Onions	16%
Beets	15%
Pumpkin	12%
Potatoes	11%

Grains

Wheat germ	31%
Rye	20%
Wheat, hard red	17%
Wild rice	16%
Buckwheat	15%
Oatmeal	15%
Millet	12%
Barley	11%
Brown rice	8%

Nuts and Seeds

Pumpkin seeds	21%
Peanuts	18%
Sunflower seeds	17%
Walnuts, black	13%
Sesame seeds	13%
Almonds	12%
Cashews	12%
Filberts	8%

Fruits

Lemons	16%
Honeydew melons	10%
Cantaloupe	9%
Strawberries	8%
Oranges	8%
Blackberries	8%
Cherries	8%
Grapes	8%
Watermelons	8%
Tangerines	7%
Papayas	6%
Peaches	6%
Pears	5%
Bananas	5%
Grapefruit	5%
Pineapple	3%
Apples	1%

Source: "Nutritive Value of American Foods in Common Units,"
U.S.D.A. Agriculture Handbook No. 456

When high-sugar foods are eaten alone, the blood sugar level rises quickly, producing a strain on blood sugar control.

Too much of any simple sugar, including the sugars found in fruit and vegetable juices, can be harmful—especially if you are hypoglycemic, diabetic, or prone to candida infection. Since fruit juices are higher in sugars than vegetable juices, their use should be limited. Sources of refined sugar should be limited even more. Read food labels carefully for clues on sugar content. If the words *sucrose, glucose, maltose, lactose, fructose, corn syrup,* or *white grape juice concentrate* appear on the label, extra sugar has been added.

Complex carbohydrates, or starches, are composed of many sugars (polysaccharides) joined together by chemical bonds. The body breaks down complex carbohydrates into simple sugars gradually, which leads to better blood sugar control. More and more research is indicating that complex carbohydrates should form a major part of the diet. Vegetables, legumes, and grains are excellent sources of complex carbohydrates.

FATS AND OILS: IMPORTANT CELLULAR COMPONENTS

There is very little fat in fresh fruit or vegetable juices, but the fats that are present are essential to human health. The essential fatty acids, linoleic acids, and linolenic acids provided by fruits and vegetables function in our bodies as components of nerve cells, cellular membranes, and hormonelike substances. Fats also help the body produce energy.

Animal fats are typically solid at room temperature and are referred to as saturated fats, while vegetable fats are liquid at room temperature and are referred to as unsaturated fats or oils. There is a great deal of research linking a diet high in saturated fat to numerous cancers, heart disease, and strokes. Both the American Cancer Society and the American Heart Association have recommended a diet containing less than 30% of calories as fat. The chart on page 25 makes it clear

Percentage of Calories as Fat

Eggs & Dairy Products

Butter	100%
Cream, light whipping	92%
Cream cheese	90%
Egg yolks	80%
Half-and-half	79%
Cheddar cheese	71%
Swiss cheese	66%
Eggs, whole	65%
Cow's milk	49%
Yogurt, plain	49%
Ice cream, regular	48%
Cottage cheese	35%
Lowfat (2%) milk/yogurt	31%

Meats

Sirloin steak*	83%
Pork sausage	83%
T-bone steak*	82%
Porterhouse steak*	82%
Bologna	81%
Spareribs	80%
Frankfurters	80%
Lamb rib chops*	79%
Salami	76%
Rump roast*	71%
Ham*	69%
Ground beef, fairly lean	64%
Veal breast*	64%
Leg of lamb	61%
Round steak*	61%
Chicken, dark meat[+]	56%
Chuck steak, lean only	50%
Turkey, dk. meat w/skin	47%
Chicken, light meat[+]	44%

* Lean, with fat
+ With skin, roasted

Fruits

Grapes	11%
Strawberries	11%
Apples	8%
Blueberries	7%
Lemons	7%
Pears	5%
Apricots	4%
Oranges	4%
Bananas	4%
Cantaloupe	3%
Pineapple	3%
Grapefruit	2%
Papayas	2%
Peaches	2%
Prunes	1%

Vegetables

Mustard greens	13%
Kale	13%
Beet greens	12%
Lettuce	12%
Turnip greens	11%
Cabbage	7%
Cauliflower	7%
Green beans	6%
Celery	6%
Cucumbers	6%
Turnips	6%
Zucchini	6%
Carrots	4%
Green peas	4%
Beets	2%
Potatoes	1%

Source: "Nutritive Value of American Foods in Common Units,"
U.S.D.A. Agriculture Handbook No. 456

that the easiest way for most people to achieve this goal is to eat fewer animal products and more plant foods.

VITAMINS: ESSENTIAL FOR LIFE

Vitamins are essential to good health; without them key body processes would halt. Vitamin and mineral deficiencies may be preventing many people from achieving optimal health. There are 15 different known vitamins, each with its own special role to play. The vitamins are classified into two groups: fat-soluble (A, D, E, and K) and water-soluble (the B vitamins and vitamin C).

Vitamins function along with enzymes in chemical reactions necessary for the body to function, including energy production. Vitamins and enzymes work together to act as catalysts in speeding up the making or breaking of chemical bonds that join molecules together. For example, vitamin C functions in the manufacture of collagen, the main protein substance of the body. Specifically, vitamin C is involved in the joining of a portion of a molecule of oxygen to the amino acid proline to form hydroxyproline, a very stable collagen ingredient. Since collagen is such an important protein for the structures that hold the body together (connective tissue, cartilage, tendons), vitamin C is vital for wound repair, healthy gums, and the prevention of easy bruising.

Fresh fruit and vegetable juices are rich sources of water-soluble vitamins and some fat-soluble vitamins (provitamin A carotenes, and vitamin K), as juicing allows for concentration of nutrition. Juicing provides key nutrients in their most natural form. Cooking destroys many of the B vitamins and vitamin C, so fresh fruit or vegetable juice is more nutritious than cooked fruits or vegetables.

While most people think of fruits as the best source of vitamin C, some vegetables also contain high levels, especially broccoli, peppers, potatoes, and brussels sprouts (see page 27). For the B vitamins (except vitamin B12), your best sources

Vitamin C Content of Selected Foods

Milligrams (mg) per 100 grams edible portion (100 grams = 3.5 oz.)

Acerola	1,300	Liver, calf	36
Peppers, red chili	369	Turnips	36
Guavas	242	Mangoes	35
Peppers, red sweet	190	Asparagus	33
Kale leaves	186	Cantaloupe	33
Parsley	172	Swiss chard	32
Collard leaves	152	Green onions	32
Turnip greens	139	Liver, beef	31
Peppers, green sweet	128	Okra	31
Broccoli	113	Tangerines	31
Brussels sprouts	102	New Zealand spinach	30
Mustard greens	97	Oysters	30
Watercress	79	Lima beans, young	29
Cauliflower	78	Black-eyed peas	29
Persimmons	66	Soybeans	29
Cabbage, red	61	Green peas	27
Strawberries	59	Radishes	26
Papayas	56	Raspberries	25
Spinach	51	Chinese cabbage	25
Oranges & juice	50	Yellow summer squash	25
Cabbage	47	Loganberries	24
Lemon juice	46	Honeydew melons	23
Grapefruit & juice	38	Tomatoes	23
Elderberries	36	Liver, pork	23

Source: "Nutritive Value of American Foods in Common Units,"
U.S.D.A Agriculture Handbook No. 456

are grains and the green leafy vegetables, such as spinach, kale, parsley, and broccoli.[3]

One vitamin that is often neglected is vitamin K. Vitamin K1, the form that is found in green leafy vegetables, has a role in converting inactive osteocalcin to its active form. Osteocalcin is the major noncollagen protein found in bone. Vitamin K is necessary for allowing the osteocalcin molecule to join with the calcium and hold it in place within the bone.

A deficiency of vitamin K leads to impaired mineralization of the bone due to inadequate osteocalcin levels. Very low blood levels of vitamin K1 have been found in patients with fractures due to osteoporosis.[4] The severity of the fracture strongly correlated with the level of circulating vitamin K. The lower the level of vitamin K, the more severe the fracture.

Vitamin K is found in green leafy vegetables and may be one of the protective factors of a vegetarian diet against osteoporosis. Juices are an excellent source of naturally occurring vitamin K.

MINERALS: NECESSARY FOR BLOOD, BONE, AND CELL FUNCTIONS

There are 22 different minerals important in human nutrition. Minerals function, along with vitamins, as components of body enzymes. Minerals are also needed for proper composition of bone, blood, and the maintenance of normal cell function. The minerals are classified into two categories, major and minor. The major minerals include calcium, phosphorus, potassium, sodium, chloride, magnesium, and sulfur. The minor, or trace, minerals include iron, iodine, zinc, chromium, vanadium, silicon, selenium, copper, fluoride, cobalt, molybdenum, manganese, tin, boron, and nickel.

Because plants incorporate minerals from the soil into their own tissues, fruits and vegetables are excellent sources for many minerals. The minerals as they are found in the earth are inorganic—lifeless. In plants, however, most minerals are complexed with organic molecules. This usually means better mineral absorption. Juice is thought to provide even better mineral absorption than the intact fruit or vegetable because juicing liberates the minerals into a highly absorbable form. The green leafy vegetables are the best plant source for many of the minerals, especially calcium.[5]

It has already been mentioned that vegetarians are at a lower risk for osteoporosis. In addition to vitamin K1, the high levels of many minerals found in plant foods, particularly vegetables, may also be responsible for this protective effect. A trace mineral gaining recent attention as a protective factor against osteoporosis is boron. Boron has been shown to have a positive effect on calcium and active estrogen levels in postmenopausal women, the group at highest risk for developing osteoporosis. In one study, supplementing the diet of postmenopausal women with 3mg of boron a day reduced urinary calcium excretion by 44% and dramatically increased the levels of 17-beta-estradiol, the most biologically active estrogen.[6] It appears boron is required to activate certain hormones, including estrogen and vitamin D. Since fruits and vegetables are the main dietary sources of boron, diets low in these foods may be deficient in boron. The high boron content of a vegetarian diet may be another protective factor against osteoporosis.

POTASSIUM: KEY TO BLOOD PRESSURE MAINTENANCE

One of the primary nutritional benefits of fresh fruit and vegetable juice is that it is very rich in potassium and very low in sodium.[7] The balance of sodium and potassium is extremely important to human health. Too much sodium in the diet can lead to disruption of this balance. Numerous studies have demonstrated that a low-potassium, high-sodium diet plays a major role in the development of cancer and cardiovascular disease (heart disease, high blood pressure, strokes).[8]

Conversely, a diet high in potassium and low in sodium is protective against these diseases, and in the case of high blood pressure it can be therapeutic.[9] Numerous studies have shown that sodium restriction alone does not improve blood pressure control in most people—it must be accompanied by a high potassium intake.[10]

Most Americans have a potassium-to-sodium (K:Na) ratio of less than 1:2. This means most people ingest twice as much sodium as potassium. Researchers recommend a dietary potassium-to-sodium ratio of greater than 5:1 to maintain health. This is ten times higher than the average intake. But even this may not be optimal. A natural diet rich in fruits and vegetables can produce a K:Na ratio greater than 100:1, as most fruits and vegetables have a K:Na ratio of at least 50:1. For example, here are the average K:Na ratios for several common fresh fruits and vegetables:

> carrots 75:1
> potatoes 110:1
> apples 90:1
> bananas 440:1
> oranges 260:1

FUNCTIONS OF POTASSIUM

Potassium is one of the electrolytes—mineral salts that can conduct electricity when they are dissolved in water. Electrolytes are always found in pairs; a positive molecule like sodium or potassium is always accompanied by a negative molecule like chloride. Potassium, as a major electrolyte, functions in the maintenance of:

- water balance and distribution
- acid-base balance
- muscle and nerve cell function
- heart function
- kidney and adrenal function

Potassium Content of Selected Foods

Milligrams (mg) per 100 grams edible portion (100 grams = 3.5 oz.)

Food	mg	Food	mg
Dulse	8,060	Cauliflower	295
Kelp	5,273	Watercress	282
Sunflower seeds	920	Asparagus	278
Wheat germ	827	Red cabbage	268
Almonds	773	Lettuce	264
Raisins	763	Cantaloupe	251
Parsley	727	Lentils, cooked	249
Brazil nuts	715	Tomato	244
Peanuts	674	Sweet potatoes	243
Dates	648	Papayas	234
Figs, dried	640	Eggplant	214
Avocados	604	Green peppers	213
Pecans	603	Beets	208
Yams	600	Peaches	202
Swiss chard	550	Summer squash	202
Soybeans, cooked	540	Oranges	200
Garlic	529	Raspberries	199
Spinach	470	Cherries	191
English walnuts	450	Strawberries	164
Millet	430	Grapefruit juice	162
Beans, cooked	416	Cucumbers	160
Mushrooms	414	Grapes	158
Potato with skin	407	Onions	157
Broccoli	382	Pineapple	146
Kale	378	Milk, whole	144
Bananas	370	Lemon juice	141
Meats	370	Pears	130
Winter squash	369	Eggs	129
Chicken	366	Apples	110
Carrots	341	Watermelon	100
Celery	341	Brown rice, cooked	70
Radishes	322		

Source: "Nutritive Value of American Foods in Common Units,"
U.S.D.A. Agriculture Handbook No. 456

Over 95% of the potassium in the body is found within cells. In contrast, most of the sodium in the body is located outside the cells in the blood and other fluids. How does this happen? Cells actually pump sodium out and potassium in via the "sodium-potassium pump." This pump is found in the membranes of all cells in the body. One of its most important functions is preventing the swelling of cells. If sodium is not pumped out, water accumulates within the cell, causing it to swell and ultimately burst.

The sodium-potassium pump also functions to maintain the electrical charge within the cell. This is particularly important to muscle and nerve cells. During nerve transmission and muscle contraction, potassium exits the cell and sodium enters, resulting in a change in electrical charge. This change is what causes a nerve impulse or muscle contraction. It is not surprising that a potassium deficiency affects muscles and nerves first.

Potassium is also essential for the conversion of blood sugar into glycogen, the storage form of blood sugar found in the muscles and liver. A potassium shortage results in lower levels of stored glycogen. Because glycogen is used by exercising muscles for energy, a potassium deficiency will produce great fatigue and muscle weakness. These are typically the first signs of potassium deficiency.

POTASSIUM DEFICIENCY

A potassium deficiency is characterized by mental confusion, irritability, weakness, heart disturbances, and problems in nerve conduction and muscle contraction. Dietary potassium deficiency is typically caused by a diet low in fresh fruits and vegetables but high in sodium. It is more common to see dietary potassium deficiency in the elderly. Dietary potassium deficiency is less common than deficiency due to excessive fluid loss (sweating, diarrhea, or urination) or the use of diuretics, laxatives, aspirin, and other drugs.

The amount of potassium lost in sweat can be quite significant, especially if the exercise is prolonged in a warm environment. Athletes or people who exercise regularly have higher potassium needs. Because up to 3g of potassium can be lost in one day by sweating, a daily intake of at least 4g of potassium is recommended for these individuals.

HOW MUCH POTASSIUM DO WE NEED?

The estimated safe and adequate daily dietary intake of potassium, as set by the Committee on Recommended Daily Allowances, is 1.9g to 5.6g. If body potassium requirements are not being met through diet, supplementation is essential to good health. This is particularly true for the elderly and the athlete. Potassium salts are commonly prescribed by physicians in the dosage range of 1.5g to 3g a day. However, potassium salts can cause nausea, vomiting, diarrhea, and ulcers. These effects are not seen when potassium levels are increased through the diet only. This highlights the advantages of using juices, foods, or food-based potassium supplements to meet the body's high potassium requirements. Most fruit and vegetable juices contain approximately 400mg of potassium per eight ounces.

Can you take too much potassium? Of course, but most people can handle any excess. The exception is people with kidney disease. They do not handle potassium in the normal way and are likely to experience heart disturbances and other consequences of potassium toxicity. Individuals with kidney disorders usually need to restrict their potassium intake and follow the dietary recommendations of their physicians.

SUMMARY

Fresh fruit and vegetable juices provide excellent nutrition in an easily absorbed form. They are rich in many vital nutrients, including pure water. Fresh juices are also nutrient-dense in that they provide a high amount of quality

nutrition per calorie. Proteins, carbohydrates, vitamins, and minerals are all found in natural forms in fresh juice. One of the key minerals provided by fresh juice is potassium, which is vital for many body functions and is especially important for heart, nerve, and muscle tissue.

3

WHAT'S IN JUICE? THE ANUTRIENTS

F resh juice contains a wide range of substances often collectively referred to as anutrients. Included in this category are enzymes; pigments like carotenes, chlorophyll, and flavonoids; and accessory food components. Nutrients are classically defined as substances that either provide nourishment or are necessary for body functions or structures. The designation "anutrient" signifies that these compounds are without nutritional benefit. But these substances do exert profound health benefits. The anutrients are responsible for many of the known as well as the unknown benefits of foods (see page 37).

This is perhaps best illustrated in population studies looking at diet and cancer. In these studies, consumption of higher levels of fresh fruits and vegetables is consistently associated with a reduced risk of cancers at most body sites.[1] Because this link has now been fully established, researchers are busy trying to understand exactly why such a diet protects against cancer.

Fruits and vegetables are known to contain a large number of potential anticancer substances, including both nutrients and anutrients. These plant substances have been shown to exert complementary and overlapping mechanisms of action in reducing risk of cancer, including antioxidant effects; inducing the manufacture of enzymes in the body that detoxify chemicals which cause cancer; blocking the chemical effects of cancer-causing compounds; and enhancing the immune system.[2]

A recent review of the role of fruits and vegetables in cancer prevention published in the medical journal *Cancer Causes and Control* concluded that humans appear to require a diet with a high intake of fruits and vegetables. These plant foods supply substances crucial to the maintenance of normal body functions, but only some of these substances are thought of as "essential nutrients." Cancer is viewed by many

Health Benefits of Selected Anutrients

Anutrient	Health Benefits	Food Sources
Allium compounds	Lower cholesterol levels, antitumor properties	Garlic and onions
Carotenes	Antioxidant, enhance immune system, anticancer properties	Darkly colored vegetables such as carrots, squash, spinach, kale, parsley; also cantaloupe, apricots, and citrus fruits
Coumarins	Antitumor properties, immune enhancement, stimulate antioxidant mechanisms	Carrots, celery, beets, citrus fruits
Dithiolthiones	Block the reaction of cancer-causing compounds within our cells	Cabbage-family vegetables
Flavonoids	Antioxidant, antiviral, and anti-inflammatory properties	Fruits, particularly darker fruits like cherries, blueberries; also vegetables, including tomatoes, peppers, and broccoli
Glucosinolates & Indoles	Stimulate enzymes that detoxify cancer-causing compounds	Cabbage, brussels sprouts, kale, radishes, mustard greens
Isothiocyanates & Thiocyanates	Inhibit damage to genetic material (DNA)	Cabbage-family vegetables
Limonoids	Protect against cancer	Citrus fruits
Phthalides	Stimulate detoxification enzymes	Parsley, carrots, celery
Sterols	Block the production of cancer-causing compounds	Soy products, whole grains, cucumbers, squash, cabbage-family vegetables

experts as a "maladaptation" to a reduced intake of compounds in foods (anutrients) that are required by the body's
metabolism for reasons other than nutritive effects. In other
words, cancer is the result of a deficiency of plant foods in
the diet. The review's final words are especially poignant:
"Vegetables and fruit contain the anticarcinogenic cocktail to
which we are adapted. We abandon it at our peril."[3]

More and more experts are realizing that it is not just the
"essential nutrients" that are important. In fact, the anutrients may possess the greater effect in protecting against cancer. Although some of the most potent anticancer effects
provided by fruits and vegetables are due to their high content
of antioxidants, the protective effects of fruits and vegetables
go far beyond antioxidant effects. For example, one of the
American Cancer Society's key dietary recommendations to
reduce the risk of cancer is to include cruciferous vegetables,
such as cabbage, broccoli, brussels sprouts, and cauliflower
in the diet.[4] These foods have been shown to exert a protective
effect against many types of cancer that is beyond the protective effect of their known nutrient content. The anticancer
compounds in cabbage-family vegetables include phenols,
indoles, isothiocyanates, and various sulfur-containing compounds. These compounds exhibit no real nutritional activity
and are therefore examples of anutrients. However, these cabbage-family compounds stimulate the body to detoxify and
eliminate cancer-causing chemicals: a very profound and
powerful effect in the war against cancer.

The study of foods is a dynamic and exciting field, especially in the area of anutrients. Every year, additional anutrients are discovered that produce remarkable health-promoting
effects. This emphasizes the importance of not relying on vitamin and mineral supplements for all your nutritional needs.
Supplements are designed as additions to a healthy diet. A
healthy diet must include not only adequate levels of known
nutrients, but also large quantities of fresh fruits and vegeta-

bles for their high content of "unknown" anutrients and accessory healing components.

ENZYMES: NECESSARY FOR LIFE

Fresh juice is referred to as a "live" food because it contains active enzymes. As mentioned earlier, enzymes often work with vitamins in speeding up chemical reactions. Without enzymes, there would be no life in our cells. Enzymes are far more prevalent in raw foods such as fresh juices because they are extremely sensitive to heat and are destroyed during cooking and pasteurization.

There are two major types of enzymes: synthetases and hydrolases. The synthetases help build body structures by making or synthesizing larger molecules. The synthetases are also referred to as metabolic enzymes. The hydrolases work to break down large molecules into smaller ones by adding water to the larger molecule. This process is known as hydrolysis. The hydrolases are also known as digestive enzymes.

Digestion is the body process that utilizes the greatest level of energy. That is why one of the key energy-enhancing benefits of fresh juice is its highly digestible form. When you eat, your body works very hard at separating out the juice from the fiber in your food. (Remember, it is the juice that nourishes our cells.) The juice extractor does this for the body, but that is not the only benefit to digestion with fresh juice. Fresh juice and other "live" foods contain digestive enzymes that help break down the foods in the digestive tract, thereby sparing the body's valuable digestive enzymes.

This sparing action is referred to as the "law of adaptive secretion of digestive enzymes."[5] According to this law, if some of the food is digested by the enzymes contained in the food, the body will secrete less of its own enzymes. This allows vital energy in the body to be shifted from digestion to other body functions, such as repair and rejuvenation. Fresh

juices require very little energy to digest. In as little as five minutes they begin to be absorbed. In contrast, a big meal of steak and potatoes may sit in the stomach for hours. If a meal is composed entirely from cooked (no-enzyme) foods, most of the body's energy is directed at digestion. What happened to your energy levels after your last large meal of cooked foods? If you are like most people, your energy levels fell dramatically. What would your life be like if you directed less energy toward digestion and more energy to other body functions? It would be a life full of increased energy, a life of passion, a life of vitality, a life of health.

For maximum energy levels, it is often recommended that 50% to 75% of your diet (by volume) come from raw fruits, vegetables, nuts, and seeds.[6] Juicing ensures that you can reach this percentage.

ENZYMES AND HUMAN HEALTH

Perhaps the best example of the beneficial effects of plant enzymes is offered by bromelain, the enzyme found in the pineapple plant. Bromelain was introduced as a medicinal agent in 1957, and since that time over 200 scientific papers on its therapeutic applications have appeared in the medical literature.[7,8]

Bromelain has been reported in these scientific studies to exert a wide variety of beneficial effects, including:

- assisting digestion
- reducing inflammation in cases of arthritis, sports injury, or trauma
- preventing swelling (edema) after trauma or surgery
- inhibiting blood platelet aggregation; enhancing antibiotic absorption
- relieving sinusitis
- inhibiting appetite
- enhancing wound healing

Although most studies have utilized commercially prepared bromelain, it is conceivable that drinking fresh pineapple juice could exert similar, if not superior, benefits. One
question that often comes up when talking about enzymes like
bromelain is whether the body actually absorbs enzymes in
their active form. There is definite evidence that, in both animals and man, up to 40% of bromelain given by mouth is absorbed intact, without being broken down.[9] This provides
some evidence that other plant enzymes may also be absorbed
intact and exert beneficial effects as well.

Conditions in which bromelain has documented clinical
efficacy include:

angina	maldigestion
arthritis	pancreatic insufficiency
athletic injury	phytobezoar
bronchitis	pneumonia
burn debridement	scleroderma
cellulitis	sinusitis
dysmenorrhea	staphylococcal infection
ecchymosis	surgical trauma
edema	thrombophlebitis

CAROTENES: REDUCING THE RISK OF CANCER AND HEART DISEASE

Carotenes or carotenoids represent the most widespread
group of naturally occurring pigments in nature. They are a
highly colored (red to yellow) group of fat-soluble compounds
that function in plants to protect against damage produced
during photosynthesis.[10] Carotenes are best known for their
capacity for conversion into vitamin A, their antioxidant activity, and their correlation with the maximum life-span potential of humans, other primates, and mammals.

Over 400 carotenes have been characterized, but only about 30 to 50 are believed to have vitamin A activity. These are referred to as "provitamin A carotenes." The biological effects of carotenes have historically been based on their corresponding vitamin A activity. Beta-carotene has been considered the most active of the carotenes, due to its higher provitamin A activity than other carotenes. However, recent research suggests that these vitamin A activities have been overemphasized, as there are other, nonvitamin A carotenes that exhibit far greater antioxidant and anticancer activities.[11]

The conversion of a provitamin A carotene into vitamin A depends on several factors: the level of vitamin A in the body, protein status, thyroid hormones, zinc, and vitamin C. The conversion diminishes as carotene intake increases, and when serum vitamin A levels are adequate. If vitamin A levels are sufficient, the carotene is not converted to vitamin A. Instead, it is delivered to body tissues for storage.[12]

Unlike vitamin A, which is stored primarily in the liver, unconverted carotenes are stored in fat cells, epithelial cells, and other organs (the adrenals, testes, and ovaries have the highest concentrations). Epithelial cells are found in the skin and the linings of the internal organs (including the respiratory tract, gastrointestinal tract, and genitourinary tract). Population studies have demonstrated a strong correlation between carotene intake and a variety of cancers involving epithelial tissues (such as lung, skin, cervix, gastrointestinal tract)[13] The higher the carotene intake, the lower the risk for cancer. Scientific studies are also showing that carotenes have antitumor and immune-enhancing activity.[14]

Cancer and aging share a number of common characteristics, including an association with free-radical damage, which has led to the idea that the prevention of cancer should also promote longevity. There is some evidence to support this claim, since it appears that tissue carotene content has a better correlation with maximal life-span potential (MLSP) of mammals, including humans, than any other factor that has been

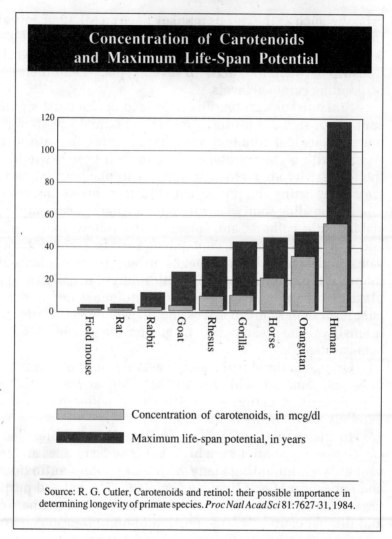

Concentration of Carotenoids and Maximum Life-Span Potential

Field mouse, Rat, Rabbit, Goat, Rhesus, Gorilla, Horse, Orangutan, Human

Concentration of carotenoids, in mcg/dl

Maximum life-span potential, in years

Source: R. G. Cutler, Carotenoids and retinol: their possible importance in determining longevity of primate species. *Proc Natl Acad Sci* 81:7627-31, 1984.

studied.[15] For example, the human MLSP of approximately 120 years correlates with serum carotene levels of 50–300 mcg/dl (micrograms per deciliter of blood), while other

primates such as the rhesus monkey have an MLSP of approximately 34 years, correlating with serum carotene levels of 6–12 mcg/dl. The figure on page 43 demonstrates the relationship between the MLSP of several species and their corresponding carotene levels.

Since tissue carotenoids appear to be the most significant factor in determining a species' maximal life-span potential, a logical conclusion is that individuals within the species with higher carotene levels in their tissues would be the longest-lived. Tissue carotene contents can best be increased by eating and juicing a diet high in mixed carotenes.

The leading sources of carotenes are dark green leafy vegetables (kale, collards, and spinach), and yellow-orange fruits and vegetables (apricots, cantaloupe, carrots, sweet potatoes, yams, and squash). The carotenes present in green plants are found in the chloroplasts with chlorophyll, usually in complexes with a protein or lipid. Beta-carotene is the predominant form in most green leaves and, in general, the greater the intensity of the green color, the greater the concentration of beta-carotene.

Orange-colored fruits and vegetables (carrots, apricots, mangoes, yams, squash) typically have higher concentrations of provitamin A carotenes. Again, the provitamin A content parallels the intensity of the color.

In the orange and yellow fruits and vegetables, beta-carotene concentrations are high, but other carotenes are present as well, including many with more potent antioxidant and anticancer effects than beta-carotene. The red and purple vegetables and fruits (such as tomatoes, red cabbage, berries, and plums) contain a large portion of non-vitamin A-active pigments, including flavonoids and carotenes. Legumes, grains, and seeds are also significant sources of carotenes.

Juicing provides greater benefit than beta-carotene supplements or intact carotene-rich foods because juicing ruptures cell membranes, thereby liberating important nutritional compounds like carotenes for easier absorption. Beta-carotene

Carotene Levels of Raw Fruits & Vegetables

Approximate total carotene, mcg per 100 grams (3.5 ounces)

Apples		Melons	2,100-6,200
Unpeeled	5,500-12,600	Oranges	2,400-2,700
Peeled	100-500	Papayas	1,100-3,000
Apricots	3,500	Peaches	2,700
Beet greens	10,000	Peppers	
Blackberries	600	Green bell	900-1,100
Broccoli	5,200	Spinach	37,000
Brussels sprouts	7,000	Squash	
Carrots	11,100	Acorn	3,900
Collard greens	20,000	Butternut	17,700
Grapes	200	Yellow	1,400
Kale	75,000	Zucchini	900
		Tomatoes	7,200

Sources: M. C. Linder, *Nutritional Biochemistry and Metabolism* (New York: Elsevier, 1991, p160); and M. S. Micozzi et al., Carotenoid analysis of selected raw and cooked foods associated with a lower risk for cancer, *J Natl Can Inst* 82:282-5, 1990.

supplementation, though beneficial, provides only one particular type of carotene, whereas juicing a wide variety of carotene-rich foods will provide a broad range of carotenes, many of which have properties more advantageous than those of beta-carotene.[16]

You cannot consume too many carotenes. Studies done with beta-carotene have not shown it to possess any

significant toxicity, even when used in very high doses in the treatment of numerous medical conditions.[17] However, increased carotene consumption can result in the appearance of slightly yellow- to orange-colored skin, because of the storage of carotenes in epithelial cells. This is known as carotenodermia, and is nothing to be alarmed about. In fact, it is probably a very beneficial sign. It simply indicates that the body has a good supply of carotenes.

FLAVONOIDS: NATURE'S BIOLOGICAL RESPONSE MODIFIERS

The flavonoids are another group of plant pigments providing remarkable protection against free-radical damage. These compounds are largely responsible for the colors of fruits and flowers. They serve more than aesthetic functions, however. In plants, flavonoids serve as protection against environmental stress. In humans, flavonoids appear to function as biological response modifiers; that is, they appear to alter the body's reaction to other compounds, such as allergens, viruses, and carcinogens, as evidenced by their anti-inflammatory, antiallergic, antiviral, and anticarcinogenic properties. Flavonoid molecules are unique in that they are active against a wide variety of oxidants and free radicals.

Recent research suggests that flavonoids may be useful in the support of many health conditions. In fact, many of the medicinal actions of foods, juices, herbs, pollens, and propolis are now known to be directly related to their flavonoid content. Over 4,000 flavonoid compounds have been characterized and classified according to chemical structure.

Different juices will provide different flavonoids and different benefits. For example, the flavonoids responsible for the red to blue colors of blueberries, blackberries, cherries, grapes, hawthorn berries, and many flowers are termed anthocyanidins and proanthocyanidins. These flavonoids are found in the flesh of the fruit as well as the skin and possess very strong

"vitamin P" activity.[18] (Flavonoids were originally termed vitamin P for their ability to prevent the permeability of the blood vessels in scurvy.) Among their effects are the abilities to increase vitamin C levels within cells, decrease the leakiness and breakage of small blood vessels, protect against free-radical damage, and support our joint structures.[19]

Flavonoids also have a very beneficial effect on collagen. Collagen is the most abundant protein of the body and is responsible for maintaining the integrity of "ground substance." Ground substance holds the tissues together. Collagen is also found in tendons, ligaments, and cartilage. Collagen is destroyed during inflammatory processes that occur in rheumatoid arthritis, periodontal disease, gout, and other inflammatory conditions involving bones, joints, cartilage, and other connective tissue. Anthocyanidins and other flavonoids affect collagen metabolism in many ways:

- They have the unique ability to actually crosslink collagen fibers, resulting in reinforcement of the natural crosslinking of collagen that forms the so-called collagen matrix of connective tissue (ground substance, cartilage, tendon, and so on).
- They prevent free-radical damage with their potent antioxidant and free-radical-scavenging action.
- They inhibit destruction to collagen structures by enzymes that our own white blood cells secrete during inflammation.
- They prevent the release and synthesis of compounds that promote inflammation, such as histamine.

These remarkable effects on collagen structures and their potent antioxidant activity make the flavonoid components of berries extremely useful in cases of arthritis and hardening of the arteries. Cherry juice has been shown to be of great benefit in gout, while feeding proanthocyanidin flavonoids from grape seeds to animals has resulted in reversal of the plaques

of atherosclerosis (hardening of the arteries), as well as decreases in serum cholesterol levels.[20] With atherosclerotic processes still the major killers of Americans, foods rich in anthocyanidins and proanthocyanidins appear to offer significant protection against as well as a potential reversal of the process.

Still other flavonoids are remarkable antiallergic compounds, modifying and reducing all phases of the allergic response. Specifically, they inhibit the formation and secretion of potent inflammatory compounds that produce the allergic response. Several prescription medications developed for allergic conditions like asthma, eczema, and hives were actually patterned after flavonoid molecules. An example of an antiallergy flavonoid is quercetin, which is found in many fruits and vegetables. Quercetin is a potent antioxidant that inhibits the release of histamine and other allergic compounds.[21]

CHLOROPHYLL: NATURE'S CLEANSING AGENT

Chlorophyll is the green pigment of plants found in the chloroplast compartment of plant cells. It is in the chloroplast that electromagnetic energy (light) is converted to chemical energy in the process known as photosynthesis. The chlorophyll molecule is essential for this reaction to occur.

The natural chlorophyll in green plants is fat-soluble. Most of the chlorophyll products found in health stores, however, contain water-soluble chlorophyll. Because water-soluble chlorophyll is not absorbed from the gastrointestinal tract, its use is limited to ulcerative conditions of the skin and gastrointestinal tract.[22] Its beneficial effect is largely due to its astringent qualities, coupled with an ability to stimulate wound healing. These healing properties have also been noted with the topical administration of water-soluble chlorophyll in the treatment of skin wounds. Water-soluble chlorophyll is

Flavonoid Content of Selected Foods

Milligrams (mg) per 100 grams edible portion (100 grams = 3.5 ounces)

Foods	4-Oxo-flavonoids[1]	Antho-cyanins	Catechins[2]	Biflavans
Fruits				
Grapefruit	50			
Grapefruit juice	20			
Orange, Valencia	50-100			
Orange juice	20-40			
Apple	3-16	1-2	20-75	50-90
Apple juice				15
Apricot	10-18		25	
Pear	1-5		5-20	1-3
Peach		1-12	10-20	90-120
Tomato	85-130			
Blueberry		130-250	10-20	
Cherry, sour		45		25
Cherry, sweet			6-7	15
Cranberry	5	60-200	20	100
Cowberry		100	25	100-150
Currant, black	20-400	130-400	15	50
Currant juice		75-100		
Grape, red		65-140	5-30	50
Plum, yellow		2-10		
Plum, blue		10-25	200	
Raspberry, black		300-400		
Raspberry, red		30-35		
Strawberry	20-100	15-35	30-40	
Hawthorn berry			200-800	
Vegetables				
Cabbage, red		25		
Onion	100-2,000	0-25		
Parsley	1,400			
Rhubarb		200		
Miscellaneous				
Beans, dry		10-1,000		
Sage	1,000-1,500			
Tea	5-50		10-500	100-200
Wine, red	2-4	50-120	100-150	100-250

[1] 4-Oxo-flavonoids: the sum of flavanones, flavones, and flavanols (including quercetin)
[2] Catechins include proanthocyanidins

Source: J. Kuhnau, The flavonoids: a class of semi-essential food components:
their role in human nutrition, *Wld Rev Nutr Diet* 24:117-91, 1976.

also used medically to help control body, fecal, and urinary odor.[23]

In order to produce a water-soluble chlorophyll, the natural chlorophyll molecule must be altered chemically. The fat-soluble form, the natural form of chlorophyll as found in fresh juice, offers several advantages over water-soluble chlorophyll. This is particularly true regarding chlorophyll's ability to stimulate hemoglobin and the production of red blood cells, and to relieve excessive menstrual blood flow.[24] In fact, the chlorophyll molecule is very similar to the heme portion of the hemoglobin molecule of our red blood cells.

Unlike water-soluble chlorophyll, fat-soluble chlorophyll is absorbed very well by the rest of the body, and contains other components of the chloroplast complex (including beta-carotene and vitamin K1) that possess significant health benefits. Water-soluble chlorophyll does not provide these additional benefits.

Like the other plant pigments, chlorophyll also possesses significant antioxidant and anticancer effects.[25] It has been suggested that chlorophyll be added to certain beverages, foods, chewing tobacco, and tobacco snuff to reduce cancer risk. A better recommendation would be to include fresh green vegetable juices regularly in the diet. Greens such as parsley, spinach, kale, and beet tops are rich not only in chlorophyll, but in minerals like calcium and carotenes. Parsley or some other green should be consumed whenever fried, roasted, or grilled foods are eaten, as parsley has been shown to reduce the cancer-causing risk of fried foods in human studies.[26] Presumably other greens would offer similar protection.

SUMMARY

Fresh juice contains a wide range of substances often collectively referred to as anutrients. Included in this category are enzymes; pigments like carotenes, chlorophyll, and flavonoids; and accessory food components. Although these substances possess little or no real "nutritional" value, they do exert profound health benefits.

Heme

Portion of Hemoglobin Molecule

Chlorophyll

More and more experts are realizing that it is not just the "essential nutrients" that are significant. This emphasizes the importance of not relying on vitamin and mineral supplements to supply all your nutritional needs. Supplements are designed as additions to a healthy diet. A healthy diet must include not only adequate levels of known nutrients, but large quantities of fresh fruits and vegetables for their high content of "unknown" anutrients and accessory healing components.

4

HOW TO JUICE: GETTING STARTED

The juicing craze sweeping the nation is largely the result of the dedication, perseverance, and vision of one man—Jay Kordich—better known as the Juiceman. It's Jay's vision that every home in America will one day have a juice extractor. The passion behind the vision is Jay's own experience with juicing. Jay believes he owes his life to juicing and has been telling people about it for nearly 50 years.

In his early twenties, Jay was stricken with a form of cancer that was not effectively treated by either surgery or chemotherapy. Determined to do all that he could to save his life, Jay became interested in some literature about a German doctor named Max Gerson who was treating patients in New York City with freshly made juices and other natural foods. Jay packed his bags and went to Dr. Gerson's clinic.

Jay began a regimen of 13 glasses of carrot-apple juice a day, beginning at 6 A.M. and drinking a glass every hour until early evening. After two and a half years, Jay was a well man. Having regained his health, Jay made a commitment to dedicate his life to spreading the word about the power of juicing.

After using hundreds of juicers over the years, in 1961 Jay helped design what was later to become the Juiceman juice extractor. Nearly 30 years of hard work and long hours later, Jay's vision looks like it will be realized.

BUYING A JUICER

In order to reap the rewards of juicing, you obviously need to choose a juicer from the wide variety available. Before we discuss some of the features of juicers, it is important to differentiate a juicer from a blender.

A juicer separates the liquid from the pulp. Remember, fiber is important, but it is the juice that nourishes our cells. It is the juice that we absorb. A blender is designed to liquefy all that is placed in it by chopping it up at high speeds. It doesn't separate the juice from the pulp, and thus the result

is a mushy, globby mess that really doesn't taste very good in most situations.

A blender can be quite useful in conjunction with a juicer. For example, bananas contain very little juice but taste delicious in drinks. You can mix freshly extracted juice, such as pineapple juice, along with banana or unsweetened frozen fruits to create a delicious "smoothie."

Juicers were once found only in health food stores; now they are everywhere. Most department stores usually offer only a selection of the lower-powered juicers, however. If you are serious about your health, get a serious juicer. The best selection of high-powered juicers is usually found at health food stores.

THE JUICEMAN JUICE EXTRACTORS

The Trillium Juiceman juice extractors are, in my opinion, the absolute best home juicers on the market. Trillium offers three different Juiceman juice extractors: the original Juiceman; the Juiceman II; and the Juiceman Jr. (see page 57). The first two are designed for the serious juice enthusiast, while the Juiceman Jr. is designed for the introductory market. I have personally owned and used several juicers, and the one that I happily own now is the Juiceman II, the most powerful, sophisticated, and easiest-to-use juicer currently available.

All of the Juiceman juice extractors feature a stainless steel cutting blade, stainless steel screen filters, and an aerodynamically designed pulp extraction system. The fruits and vegetables are cut by a rotating cutting blade so that all the juice is liberated. The centrifugal force pushes the pulp out the back of the machines into the pulp receptacle while the juice is strained through the stainless steel mesh and out to the front of the machine. This design allows for continuous juicing with no need to stop to clean or empty the machine during its use.

The differences in price and quality among juicers are largely based on the size of the motor and the sophistication of

the circuitry. Weak machines with low horsepower rating have to run at extremely high rpm (revolutions per minute) levels. But the rpm of a machine does not accurately reflect the ability of the juicer to juice effectively, because rpm is based on "free-wheeling stress-free performance." In simple terms, rpm is calculated when the machine is running at idle, not while it is juicing. When produce is fed into a low-powered machine, the number of revolutions will slow down dramatically or virtually stop. Most of the lower-priced machines (below $150) have difficulty handling one full-size carrot. Furthermore, the manual for one lower-priced juicer recommends that the machine should not be used for more than four minutes at a time.

All of Trillium's Juiceman juicers are built with powerful motors that provide an extra boost of torque. All of the machines feature high-tech electronic circuitry which sustains blade speed (rpm) during juicing. The comparison chart on page 57 outlines the main features of each model.

One of the things that impresses me most about the Juiceman juice extractors is their ability to juice both tough and hard fruits and vegetables like pineapple skins, watermelon rinds, carrots, and beets, while also being extremely effective with the more delicate greens like wheatgrass, parsley, and lettuce. If you have ever investigated or used juicers before, you know this is quite a feat.

RESULTS FROM AN INDEPENDENT STUDY

An independent professional engineering firm specializing in home appliances, Concept Consulting Services, based in Seattle, performed a limited study to evaluate how well nine popular juice extractors on the market prepared three fruit juices (orange, pineapple, and cantaloupe) and four vegetable juices (carrot, parsley, kale, and spinach). The results of the study are summarized on page 58.

A COMPARISON CHART:
JUICEMAN® JUICE EXTRACTORS

All of these household machines provide the benefits of continuous juicing with external pulp ejection through centrifugal force from a stainless steel cutting blade and basket.

	JUICEMAN® I	JUICEMAN® II	JUICEMAN JR.®
External pulp ejection basket	Yes	Yes	Yes
Top design	Clamp-top	Twist-top	Clamp-top
Power (wattage)	550W	690W	410W
Effective horsepower	.42 hp.	.50 hp.	.25 hp.
Revolutions per minute	6,300 rpm	6,300 rpm	9,000 rpm
Speed control	Yes (closed loop)	Yes (closed loop)	No*
Weight w/pulp bucket	7.7 lbs	8.4 lbs	6.9 lbs
Cutter blade diameter	3.0 inches	3.5 inches	3.0 inches
Blade basket diameter	5.5 inches	5.5 inches	5.5 inches
Blade basket frame	Hardened plastic	Stainless steel	Hardened plastic
Feed tube area	2.75 sq. inches	3.00 sq. inches	2.00 sq. inches
Safety switch (automatically turns off when disassembled)	No	Yes	Yes
30-Day unconditional money back guarantee	Yes	Yes	Yes
No-hassle 1-year warranty (repair or replace)	Yes	Yes	Yes
Extended (4 additional years) limited warranty (repair or replace except blade basket)	No	Yes	No

*The Juiceman Jr.® uses an open-loop feedback circuit to increase amperage to the motor when under stress. This overcomes severe rpm loss, but it is not equivalent to closed-loop speed control.

Independent Ratings Analysis

BETTER ● ◕ ◑ ◔ ○ WORSE

Listed in order of overall rating (best to worse)	Recovery-Carrots	Recovery-Parsley	Recovery-Spinach/Kale	Recovery-Cantaloupe/Pineapple	Recovery-Citrus	Juice Quality	Speed of Juicing	Motor Power	Cleaning Time	Ease of Use	Weight (lbs.)	Counter Space	Comments*
Juiceman II	●	●	●	◔	●	●	●	●	●	●	8.4	8 × 10	g, j
Juiceman (original)	◑	●	◕	●	●	◑	●	◕	◕	●	7.7	8 × 11	g, i
Juiceman Jr.	●	●	●	◔	◕	◑	◑	◑	◕	◑	6.9	7 × 11	
Oster 323-08	●	◕	●	◑	◔	●	◕	◔	◕	◑	7.5	7 × 11	a, f, h, i, k, o, p
Braun MP80	◕	◔	●	◔	◕	●	◕	◕	◕	◑	5.4	7 × 10	c, d, h, k, i, n, g
Moulinex M753	●	◑	◕	●	○	●	◑	◔	◕	◑	7.3	7 × 10	a, g, j, o, p
Juice Tiger	●	○	●	◕	◕	◕	○	◔	◑	○	4.4	7 × 10	r
Champion	◕	○	○	○	◕	◕	●	n/a	●	○	20.7	8 × 15	a, b, f, g, h, i, k
Acme 6001	◑	○	●	○	○	○	○	n/a	○	○	12.0	9 × 10	b, e, i, k, m

*See below for detailed comments.

1. **Recovery:** This was evaluated by comparing the weight of juice recovered to the weight of original product. Since different fruits and vegetables have different potential depending on the liquid-to-solid density, the criteria of evaluation were as follows: For carrots, spinach, kale, cantaloupe, and pineapple, the highest rating was given for more than 55% juice extracted (juice weight divided by original produce weight) and lowest rating given to machines that extracted less than 45%. For parsley, high was greater than 50% juice extracted and low was less than 30% juice extracted. For citrus, high was greater than 65% juice extracted and low was less than 55% juice extracted.

2. **Juice Quality:** This test compared the weight of strained juice to the weight of the juices tested: Carrots, parsley, spinach–kale, and cantaloupe–pineapple.

3. **Speed:** This was based on the average of the required times for processing during the juicing tests. Some juicers processed juice relatively quickly when operating but experienced pulp clogging quickly and had to be stopped and cleared before being able to finish an 8 oz. quantity of juice.

4. **Motor Power:** Each juicer was disassembled and the motor removed. A dynamometer was used to apply and measure the torque on each juicer motor. The torque and speed of the motor obtained from the dynamometer were used to calculate the horsepower output of each motor. Horsepower ranged from a high of .485 hp for Juiceman II to a low of .143 hp for Moulinex.

5. **Cleaning Time:** After each battery of juicing tests, each juicer was cleaned, removable parts were washed in hot running water with a cleaning brush, and motor bases wiped down. This time can be somewhat variable, but the results are a good reflection of the relative ease of cleaning.

6. **Ease of Use:** This is a qualitative evaluation of the characteristics of each juicer that are difficult if not impossible to quantify. We found this evaluation to be of considerable importance as the test progressed.

7. **Weight:** Some may feel this is an indication of quality, others may find it to be an ergonomic concern.

8. **Counter Space:** The size of some juicers makes this an important concern to those with limited space or numerous appliances.

9. **Note:** The design and construction of these juicers varied widely. There were many trade-offs and points well worth mentioning.

Comments

a. Has a feed tray, which makes it more convenient to process grapes, etc.

b. Does not process stringy vegetables well (parsley, kale, etc.).

c. Unit broke down during tests.

d. Pulp ejection is messy, not well contained.

e. Pineapple juice was nearly all foam.

f. Must use short juice container (under 5").

g. Has large opening for easy feeding and less preparation.

h. Some products tend to plug ejector chute.

i. No motor interlock to prevent motor start-up when cover off.

j. Has very little foam in juice.

k. Had to be disassembled and cleaned during one or more tests.

l. Has foam-separating juice container.

m. No pulp ejector.

n. Has pulp strainer for some additional juice recovery.

o. Tended to become off balance and vibrate excessively.

p. Constructed of lightweight, lower-quality plastic.

q. Has quick-stop safety feature; cutter stops rapidly when unit turned off.

r. Pulp container is small and pulp tended to plug up so that the machine had to be turned off and pulp cleaned out two to three times during 8 ounces of juicing.

Since the juice extractors differed in terms of motor power and sophistication of motor speed/torque control, a large number of variables were presented. For example, the juicers with less horsepower were often able to compete with some of the more powerful juicers in terms of juice recovery if the pieces of produce were quite small and fed through the machine very slowly. The result: Although the smaller juicers produced a similar yield, it would often take up to twice the amount of time. To control for these variables, a "speed of juicing" and "ease of juicing" analysis was added to the study design.

HOW TO JUICE

It is important to follow the instruction manual of the juicer you use. Although how to juice may appear pretty obvious, take the time to read through the manual or watch the instructional video if that is included with your juicer. Guidelines for individual fruits and vegetables will be discussed in Chapters 5 and 6.

BUY ORGANIC PRODUCE

Each year, over 1.2 billion pounds of pesticides and herbicides are sprayed on or added to crops in the United States. That is roughly ten pounds of pesticides for each man, woman, and child. Although the pesticides are designed to combat insects and other organisms, experts estimate that only 2% of the pesticide actually serves its purpose, while 98% is absorbed into the air, water, soil, or food supply. Most pesticides in use are synthetic chemicals of questionable safety. The major long-term health risks include cancer and birth defects; the major health risks of acute intoxication include vomiting, diarrhea, blurred vision, tremors, convulsions, and nerve damage.[1]

To get a glimpse of the scope of the problem, let's examine the case of the farmer. The lifestyle of a farmer is gen-

erally a healthy one if, as you would expect, a farmer eats fresh food, breathes clean air, works hard, and avoids such unhealthy habits as cigarette smoking and alcohol use. But several studies have shown that farmers are at greater risk for certain cancers, including lymphomas, leukemias, and cancers of the stomach, prostate, brain, and skin.

This leads to the question: Are pesticides, herbicides, and other synthetic chemicals responsible for this increased risk for certain cancers? The studies in farmers say yes. Large studies of farmers in Canada, Australia, Europe, New Zealand, and the United States have demonstrated that the greater the exposure to these chemicals, the greater the risk for non-Hodgkin's lymphoma.[2]

What is the government's position? Because the evidence for the cancer-causing capabilities of pesticides in animals is inadequate, the formal opinion of many "experts" is that they pose no significant risk for the public or the farmer. This opinion reflects a major dilemma to scientists. Which are more valid, studies in laboratory animals or population studies in humans? More and more human evidence is accumulating of increased cancer and birth defect rates after pesticide exposure that seems to indicate pesticides are not as safe as the "experts" would like us to believe.[3]

The history of pesticide use in this country is riddled with chemicals that were once widely used and then later banned due to health risks. Perhaps the best-known example is DDT. Widely used from the early 1940s to 1973, DDT was largely responsible for increasing farm productivity in this country, but at what cost? In 1962, Rachel Carson's classic *Silent Spring* detailed the full range of DDT's hazards, including its persistence in the food chain and its deadly effects, but it was another 10 years before the federal government banned the use of this deadly compound. Unfortunately, although DDT has been banned for nearly 20 years, it is still found in the soil and in root vegetables such as carrots and potatoes. Studies performed by the National Resources

Defense Council, a public-interest environmental group, found that 17% of the carrots analyzed still contained detectable levels of DDT.[4]

PESTICIDES IN USE TODAY

The majority of pesticides currently used in the United States today are probably less toxic than DDT and other banned pesticides, including aldrin, dieldrin, endrin, and heptachlor. However, many pesticides banned from use in the United States are shipped to other countries such as Mexico, which then send the food grown with it back to the United States. Although over 600 pesticides are currently used in the United States, most experts are concerned about only a relative few. The Environmental Protection Agency has identified 64 pesticides as potential cancer-causing compounds, while the National Research Council found that 80% of our cancer risk due to pesticides comes from 13 pesticides used widely on 15 important food crops. The pesticides are linuron, permethrin, chlordimeform, zineb, captafol, captan, maneb, mancozeb, folpet, chlorothalonil, metiram, benomyl, and O-phenylphenol. These pesticides are found in many crops, but those of greatest concern, in descending order, are tomatoes, beef, potatoes, oranges, lettuce, apples, peaches, pork, wheat, soybeans, beans, carrots, chicken, corn, and grapes.[5]

Pesticides Identified by the EPA as Potentially Causing Cancer

acephate (Orthene)
acifluorfen (Blazer)
alachlor (Lasso)
amitraz (Baam)
arsenic acid
asulam

azinphos-methyl (Guthion)
benomyl (Benlate)
calcium arsenate
captafol (Difolatan)
captan
chlordimeform (Galecron)
chlorobenzilate
chlorothalonil (Bravo)
copper arsenate
cypermethrin (Ammo, Cymbush)
cyromazine (Larvadex)
daminozide (Alar)
diallate
diclofop methyl (Hoelon)
dicofol (Kelthane)
ethalfluralin (Sonalan)
ethylene oxide
folpet
fosetyl al (Aliette)
glyphosate (Roundup)
lead arsenate
lindane
linuron (Lorox)
maleic hydrazine
mancozeb
maneb
methanearsonic acid
methomyl (Dual)
metiram
metolachlor (Dual)
O-phenylphenol

oryzalin (Surflan)
oxadiazon (Ronstar)
paraquat (Gramoxone)
parathion
PCNB
permethrin (Ambush, Pounce)
pronamide (Kerb)
sodium arsenate
sodium arsenite
terbutryn
tetrachlorvinphos
thiodicarb (Larvin)
thiophanate-methyl
toxaphene
trifluralin (Treflan)
zineb

Pesticide residue levels in food are monitored by both state and federal regulatory agencies in order to enforce legal tolerance levels. Public and governmental concern about the adequacy of the residue-monitoring programs has been increasing, however. In theory, here is how the monitoring system is designed to work. The EPA establishes a tolerance level for pesticides in raw or unprocessed foods utilizing the following key data:

1. Chemistry of the pesticide.
2. Expected quantity of residues present in food based on field trials.
3. Laboratory analytical procedures used for obtaining residue data.
4. Residues in animal feed derived from crop by-products or from forages and resulting residues, if any, in meat, milk, poultry, fish, and eggs.

5. Toxicity data on parent compound and any major impurities, degradation productions, or metabolites.

The Food and Drug Agency (FDA) is then responsible for enforcing the EPA limits. Individual state organizations, such as the departments of health and agriculture, may also be involved in the monitoring of food safety. This system falls short in the determination of the tolerance level, but more important are the facts that: (1) probably less than 1% of our domestic food supply is screened by the FDA; (2) the FDA does not test for all pesticides; and (3) the FDA does not prevent the marketing of the foods that it finds contain illegal residues.

A number of pesticide-poisoning epidemics have been reported over the years. The largest to date occurred in 1985. It involved the illegal use of aldicarb, an extremely toxic pesticide, on watermelons. Aldicarb is a systemic pesticide, which means it permeates the entire fruit. Over a thousand people in the western United States and Canada were stricken. Illness ranged from mild gastrointestinal upset to severe poisoning (vomiting, diarrhea, blurred vision, tremors, convulsions, and nerve damage).

While the EPA and FDA estimate that excessive pesticide residues are found on about 3% of domestic and 6% of foreign produce and acceptable levels are found in 13% of domestic produce, other organizations report much higher estimates. For example, the National Resources Defense Council tested fresh produce sold in San Francisco markets for pesticide residues and found 44% of 71 fruits and vegetables had detectable levels of 19 different pesticides; 42% of produce with detectable residues contained more than one pesticide. The sheer number and amount of pesticides showered on certain foods are astounding. For example, over 50 different pesticides are used on broccoli, 110 on apples, 70 on bell peppers, and so on. Many of the pesticides penetrate the entire fruit or vegetable and cannot be washed off, so it is obviously best to buy organic.

Many supermarket chains and produce suppliers are employing their own testing measures for determining the pesticide content of produce and are refusing to stock foods that have been treated with some of the more toxic pesticides such as alachlor, captan, and EBDCs (ethylene bisdithiocarbamates). In addition, many stores are asking growers to disclose all pesticides used on the foods as well as phase out the use of the 64 pesticides suspected of being capable of causing cancers. Ultimately it will be pressure from consumers that will influence food suppliers the most. Crop yield studies support the use of organic farming if the risk to human health is added to the equation.

WAXES

In addition to pesticides, consumers must also be aware of the waxes applied to many fruits and vegetables to seal in the water they contain, thereby keeping them looking fresh. According to FDA law, grocery stores must display a sign noting that waxes or postharvest pesticides have been applied. Unfortunately, most stores do not comply with the law and the FDA lacks the resources to enforce it. Currently, the FDA has approved six different waxes for use on produce. Approved compounds include shellac, paraffin, palm oil derivatives, and synthetic resins. These same items are used in furniture, floor, and car waxes. Foods to which these compounds can be applied include apples, avocados, bell peppers, cantaloupes, cucumbers, eggplants, grapefruits, lemons, limes, melons, oranges, parsnips, passion fruits, peaches, pineapples, pumpkins, rutabagas, squashes, sweet potatoes, tomatoes, and turnips.

One of the main reasons the waxes are added is to keep the produce from spoiling during the often lengthy time from harvest to the supermarket shelves. If grocery chains bought more local produce, chemicals would not be needed to keep the produce looking fresh. Instead, the large chains sign con-

tracts with large suppliers regardless of their location. This is why, for example, a grocery store in New York is stocked with Washington State apples and California broccoli.

The waxes themselves probably pose little health risk; however, most waxes have powerful pesticides or fungicides added to them. Since the waxes cannot be washed off with water, the fungicide or pesticide literally becomes cemented to the produce.

HOW TO REDUCE YOUR EXPOSURE

Here are some recommended methods of reducing exposure to pesticides as well as tips on removing the surface pesticide residues, waxes, fungicides, and fertilizers:

1. Buy organic produce. In the context of food and farming, the term *organic* is used to imply that the produce was grown without the aid of synthetic chemicals, including pesticides and fertilizers. In 1973, Oregon became the first state to pass laws that define labeling laws for organic produce. By 1989, 16 other states (California, Colorado, Iowa, Maine, Massachusetts, Minnesota, Montana, Nebraska, New Hampshire, North Dakota, Ohio, South Dakota, Texas, Vermont, Washington, and Wisconsin) had also adopted laws governing organic agriculture. Consumers should ask whether the produce is "certified organic." If so, by whom is it certified? Highly reputable certification organizations include: California Certified Organic Farmers, Demeter, Farm Verified Organic, Natural Organic Farmers Association, and the Organic Crop Improvement Association. Although more than 97% of the total produce grown in the United States is subjected to pesticides, organic produce *is* widely available.

2. If organic produce is not readily available, develop a good relationship with your local grocery store produce manager. Explain to him or her your desire to reduce your exposure to pesticides and waxes. Ask what measures the store takes to assure pesticide residues are within the tolerance limits. Ask where they get their produce, as foreign produce is much more likely to contain excessive levels of pesticides as well as pesticides that have been banned in the United States due to suspected toxicity. Try to buy local produce that is in season.

3. To remove surface pesticide residues, waxes, fungicides, and fertilizers, soak the produce in a mild solution of additive-free soap like Ivory or pure castille soap from the health food store. You can also use an all-natural, biodegradable cleanser like Nature's Wash from Trillium (1-800-800-8455). Simply spray the produce with Nature's Wash, gently scrub, and then rinse off.

4. Simply peel off the skin or remove the outer layer of leaves. The downside of this practice is that many of the nutritional benefits are concentrated in the skin and outer layers.

SUMMARY

In order to prepare fresh fruit and vegetable juices, you will need a good juicer. Of the wide selection of juicers on the market, the Juiceman juice extractors possess the most technologically advanced features. As for produce, it is best to buy organic. More and more evidence is accumulating on the dangerous health effects of pesticides. If you purchase nonorganic produce, it is important to take precautions to reduce exposure.

5

A JUICER'S GUIDE
TO FRUITS

Strictly speaking, a fruit is the ripened ovary of a female flower. This scientific definition covers both what the layperson calls fruit as well as nuts and some vegetables like squash, pumpkins, and tomatoes. However, we will deal only with the soft, succulent, fleshy fruits suitable for juicing in this chapter.

Since fruits contain a fair amount of natural fruit sugar, it is generally recommended to limit your intake to no more than two eight-ounce glasses of fresh fruit juice a day. The sugars in the fruit will be absorbed quite rapidly, which is great if you need some quick energy, but if you suffer from hypoglycemia, diabetes, candidiasis, or gout, it may aggravate your condition. Check with your doctor before incorporating fruit juices into your diet if you have any of these diseases. He or she will probably tell you to limit your consumption to four to eight ounces total for the day. Drink the juice with food; this will slow down the absorption of the sugar. And dilute the juice with pure water.

The more popular and readily available fruits will be discussed here in terms of origin, types, nutritional benefits, selection, and preparation for juicing. With modern transportation methods, a wide variety of fresh fruits are available to most people. A general rule of thumb when juicing fruits in recipes is to juice the softer fruits first, followed by the harder fruits, such as apples and pears. Please be sure to prepare the fruits according to the guidelines that follow and the recommendations from the owner's manual of your juice extractor.

APPLES

The apple originated in the Caucasus Mountains of western Asia and eastern Europe. It is often referred to as the king of fruits. In the United States, more than 25 varieties of apple

are available. The most popular variety is the Delicious. Good apples for juicing are Delicious (both red and golden yellow), Granny Smith, and Winesap varieties.

KEY BENEFITS

Apples are a good, but not great, source of many vitamins and minerals, particularly if they are unpeeled. Unpeeled apples are particularly high in non–provitamin A carotenes and pectin. Pectin is a remarkable type of fiber that has been shown to exert a number of beneficial effects. Because it is a gel-forming fiber, pectin can improve the intestinal muscle's ability to push waste through the gastrointestinal tract. Pectin can also bind to and eliminate toxins in the gut, as well as help reduce cholesterol levels. Since pectin is a water-soluble fiber, fresh juice still retains a portion of this beneficial fiber. Apple juice has also been shown to be antiviral.

Apples, as well as other soft fruits and vegetables, contain ellagic, chlorogenic, and caffeic acids, anutrients with significant anticancer actions.[1] Fresh whole apples and fresh apple juice contain approximately 100–130mg per 100g (roughly 3½ ounces) of these valuable compounds. The content of these compounds in canned, bottled, or frozen apple juice is at or near zero. Another strong case for drinking your apple juice fresh.

A great deal of exciting research has been done on ellagic acid, which has been referred to as a "new breed of anticancer drugs." One of its prime actions is to protect against damage to chromosomes and block the cancer-causing actions of many pollutants.[2] Specifically, ellagic acid has been shown to block the cancer-causing effects of several compounds in cigarette smoke known collectively as polycyclic aromatic hydrocarbons (PAH). Ellagic acid is a potent antioxidant and has also shown an ability to increase many of the body's antioxidant compounds, including glutathione.[3]

Ellagic acid is just one more example of an anutrient with powerful anticancer properties, and it is one more example of why we need to consume foods fresh.

From this discussion it is obvious fresh apple juice has benefits of its own, but one of the key uses of apples is to mix it with other fruits as well as vegetables because of its sweet but not overpowering flavor.

NUTRITIONAL ANALYSIS

1 medium raw apple, with skin (138g)

Nutrients and Units

Water	115.83	g
Calories	81	kcal
Protein	0.27	g
Fat	0.49	g
Carbohydrate	21.05	g

VITAMINS

Vitamin A	*7	RE
Vitamin C	7.8	mg
Thiamine	0.023	mg
Riboflavin	0.019	mg
Niacin	0.1	mg

MINERALS

Potassium	159	mg
Calcium	10	mg
Iron	0.25	mg
Magnesium	6	mg
Phosphorus	10	mg
Sodium	1	mg

*RE = retinol equivalents

SELECTION

You should definitely buy organic apples if you can. The recent publicity about the dangerous chemical known as alar that is sprayed on apples curtailed its use to an extent, but apples are still treated with many other chemicals. In addition, apples will often be waxed to keep them fresher longer. Be aware that even organic apples will appear "waxy," because apples have a natural coating of a waxlike substance.

Fresh apples should be firm, crisp, and well-colored. If an apple lacks color, it has likely been picked before it was fully mature and has been ripened artificially. Apples picked when mature will have more color and better flavor, and will store longer than apples picked too early. Check out the hardness of the apple. A fresh apple will produce a characteristic snap when you apply pressure to the skin with a finger. Overripe apples will not give you a crisp snap; they will feel softer.

PREPARATION FOR JUICING

Wash organic apples; soak or spray nonorganic ones with a biodegradable wash, then rinse. Since the seeds of apples contain very small amounts of cyanide, many people recommend that you core the apples to remove the seeds. Cut the apples into wedges that the juicer will accommodate.

APPLE JUICE RECIPES

Apple juice is delicious on its own, or it can be mixed with both fruits and vegetables. See the following recipes in Chapter 7: Apple Spice, Basic Carrot-Apple, Bone Builder's Cocktail, Bowel Regulator, Cherry Pop, Cholesterol-Lowering Tonic, Cruciferous Surprise, Everything but the Kitchen Sink, Femme Fatale, Ginger Ale, Ginger Hopper, Green Drink, High C, Immune Power Vegetable, Iron Plus, Jicama-Carrot-Apple, Liver Mover, Liver Tonic, Mint Foam,

Purple Cow, Tummy Tonic, Waldorf Salad, and Zesty Cran-Apple.

Apple-Apricot

2 apples, cut into wedges
2 apricots, pitted

Apple-Apricot-Peach

1 apple, cut into wedges
1 apricot, pitted
1 peach, pitted

Apple-Berry

1 cup berries (such as strawberries, blueberries, raspberries)
2 apples, cut into wedges

Apple-Cherry

1 cup pitted cherries
2 apples, cut into wedges

Apple-Grape-Lemon

2 apples, cut into wedges
1 cup grapes
¼ lemon with the skin

Apple-Grapefruit

1 apple, cut into wedges
1 grapefruit, peeled

Apple-Kiwi

2 Golden Delicious apples, cut into wedges
4 kiwifruits

Apple-Mint

4 apples, cut into wedges
½ handful of fresh mint

Apple-Orange

2 apples, cut into wedges
2 oranges, peeled

Apple-Papaya

2 apples, cut into wedges
½ papaya, seeded, sliced

Apple-Peach

2 apples, cut into wedges
2 peaches, pitted, sliced

Apple-Pear-Ginger

3 apples, cut into wedges
1 pear, sliced
¼-inch slice of fresh ginger

APRICOTS

The apricot is technically classified as a drupe, a fleshy, one-seeded fruit with the seed enclosed in a stony pit. The apricot is in the same family as the almond, cherry, peach, and plum. Apricots originated in China. Alexander the Great is believed to have brought the apricot to Greece and ultimately the rest of Western civilization.

KEY BENEFITS

Apricots are a good source of potassium, magnesium, iron, and carotenes. Dried apricots are quite popular, but

most contain high levels of sulfur dioxide, which is added during the drying process to inactivate enzymes that would cause the fruit to spoil. Alternative preservation methods, such as blanching, do not necessitate the use of sulfur.

NUTRITIONAL ANALYSIS

3 raw apricots, pitted (107mg)

Nutrients and Units

Water	88	g
Calories	55	kcal
Protein	2	g
Fat	trace	
Carbohydrate	12.8	g

VITAMINS

Vitamin A	90	RE
Vitamin C	10	mg
Thiamine	0.03	mg
Riboflavin	0.04	mg
Niacin	0.6	mg

MINERALS

Potassium	115	mg
Calcium	20	mg
Iron	0.6	mg
Magnesium	7	mg
Phosphorus	23	mg
Sodium	1	mg

SELECTION

Fresh, ripe apricots should be a uniform golden-orange color, round, and about two inches in diameter. Ripe apricots

yield to a gentle pressure on the skin. If the fruit is quite hard or more yellow in appearance, it is unripe; if it is quite soft or mushy, it is overmature. Fresh apricots are in season June through August.

PREPARATION FOR JUICING

Wash organic apricots; soak or spray nonorganic ones with a biodegradable wash, then rinse. Slice them in half and remove the pit.

APRICOT JUICE RECIPES

Apricots are drier (85% water) than most other fleshy fruits and therefore do not work well as the sole component of a juice. Apricots mix quite deliciously with other fruits, especially apples, oranges, and peaches. See the Apricot-Mango Ambrosia recipe in Chapter 7.

Apricot-Orange

    4 apricots, pitted
    2 oranges, peeled

Apricot-Pear

    4 apricots, pitted
    1 pear, sliced

BANANAS

Although it looks like a tree, bananas actually grow on a plant. The difference between a tree and a plant is that in order to be a tree, there must be wood in the stem above the ground. Bananas are thought to have originated in Malaysia and spread to India, the Philippines, and New Guinea. The most popular type of banana is the large, yellow, smooth-skinned variety familiar to most Americans. This banana is known as the Manque or Gros Michel (Big Mike). Other

varieties familiar to many are the smaller red-skinned type known as the Red Jamaican and the larger green bananas known as plaintains. Plaintains are used like a vegetable in that they are usually fried or cooked. Bananas are the second leading fruit crop in the world, after grapes.

KEY BENEFITS

Bananas are packed full of nutrition, especially potassium. An averaged-size banana contains a whopping 440mg potassium and only 1mg sodium. Bananas are showing some promise in the treatment of peptic ulcers.[4]

NUTRITIONAL ANALYSIS

1 banana (114g)

Nutrients and Units

Water	85	g
Calories	105	kcal
Protein	1.18	g
Fat	0.55	g
Carbohydrate	26.71	g

VITAMINS

Vitamin A	9	RE
Vitamin C	10.3	mg
Thiamine	0.051	mg
Riboflavin	0.014	mg
Niacin	0.616	mg

MINERALS

Potassium	451	mg
Calcium	7	mg

Iron	0.35mg
Magnesium	33 mg
Phosphorus	22 mg
Sodium	1 mg

SELECTION

Bananas are best when they are yellow with no green showing and speckled with brown. Bananas with green tips are not quite ripe, but they will continue to ripen if stored at room temperature. After ripening, bananas can be stored in the refrigerator, and though the skin will turn dark brown, they will remain fresh for three to five days. Bananas that are bruised, discolored, or soft have deteriorated and should not be used.

PREPARATION FOR JUICING

Bananas do not lend themselves to juicing, but you can make fresh juice from other fruits and mix it with a banana in a blender. In the summer, try freezing a banana and blending it with fresh apple-strawberry juice to make a delicious smoothie.

BANANA SMOOTHIE RECIPES

See the following recipes in Chapter 7: Enzymes Galore, Immune Power Fruit, Mike's Favorite, Monkey Shake, and Potassium Punch. Here is another great smoothie.

Banana-Cantaloupe Smoothie

½ cantaloupe with skin, sliced

1 banana, peeled

Juice cantaloupe, pour juice into blender, add banana, and liquefy.

BERRIES

Blackberries, blueberries, raspberries, strawberries, currants, and other berries will be discussed as a group. Berries flourish in many parts of the world, especially in the Northern Hemisphere. Hundreds of varieties of berries now exist as a result of accidental and intenational crossbreeding (hybridization).

KEY BENEFITS

Berries are rich in vital nutrients, yet low in calories. Hence berries are excellent foods for those who have a sweet tooth and are attempting to improve their quality of nutrition without increasing the caloric content of their diet. Juices prepared from fresh berries typically contain less than 100 calories per eight ounces and provide a rich source of potassium, pure water, water-soluble fibers, and flavonoids. It is the flavonoids, mainly a group known as anthocyanidins, that are responsible for berries' color. For example, the purplish black of blackberries comes from the anthocyanidin known as cyanidin, while the red of strawberries is due to pelargonidin. The beneficial effects of flavonoids are discussed in Chapter 3.

Berries have long been used for a wide range of medicinal effects; now more and more research is supporting many of the folk uses of berries. For example, during World War II, British Royal Air Force pilots consumed bilberry (a variety of blueberry) preserves before their night missions, believing the folk wisdom that bilberries improve night vision. After the war, numerous studies demonstrated that blueberry extracts do in fact improve nighttime visual acuity and lead to quicker adjustment to darkness and faster restoration of visual acuity after exposure to glare.

Bilberry extracts have been used by physicians for medical purposes in Europe since 1945. Most of the therapeutic

applications have involved eye complaints. Results have been most impressive in individuals with retinitis pigmentosa, sensitivity to bright lights, diabetic retinopathy, and macular degeneration. Additional research also points out that bilberries may protect against cataracts and glaucoma, and can be quite therapeutic in the treatment of varicose veins, hemorrhoids, and peptic ulcers.[5]

Most of the clinical studies have utilized a variety of berry extracts, but primarily bilberry and black currants, concentrated for anthocyanoside content. To achieve a similar concentration using fresh fruit would require a daily intake of at least 16 ounces (one pint) of fresh juice daily.

Berries, especially strawberries, are good sources of the anticancer compound ellagic acid (see Apples). In one study, strawberries topped a list of eight foods most linked to lower rates of cancer deaths among a group of 1,271 elderly people in New Jersey. Those eating the most strawberries were three times less likely to develop cancer than those eating few or no strawberries.

NUTRITIONAL ANALYSIS

1 cup blackberries (144g)

Nutrients and Units

Water	123	g
Calories	74	kcal
Protein	1.04g	
Fat	0.65g	
Carbohydrate	18.38g	

VITAMINS

Vitamin A	24	RE
Vitamin C	30.2	mg

Thiamine	0.043mg
Riboflavin	0.058mg
Niacin	0.576mg

MINERALS

Potassium	282	mg
Calcium	46	mg
Iron	0.83	mg
Magnesium	29	mg
Phosphorus	30	mg
Sodium	0	mg

SELECTION

Buy the freshest berries possible. When berries are not in season, you can purchase unsweetened frozen berries and use them to make smoothies in the blender with fresh juice.

PREPARATION FOR JUICING

Wash organic berries; soak or spray nonorganic ones with a biodegradable wash, then rise.

BERRY JUICE RECIPES

Mixing one cup of berries with two apples is a good way to dilute some of the strong berry flavor if desired (as in the Apple-Berry recipe above). See the following recipes in Chapter 7: Color Me Pink, Immune Power Fruit, Kids' Favorite, and Mike's Favorite.

Berry-Orange

1 cup strawberries or other berries
2 oranges, peeled

Berry-Pear

1 cup berries

2 pears, sliced

Berry-Pineapple

1   cup berries

½ pineapple with skin, sliced

Triple-Berry

½ cup blackberries

½ cup strawberries

½ cup other berry

1   apple or pear, sliced

CANTALOUPES OR MUSKMELONS

In the United States, what we commonly refer to as a cantaloupe is actually a muskmelon; true cantaloupes are seldom grown here. Cantaloupes are thought to have originated in either Africa or the Middle East and are now grown all over the world.

KEY BENEFITS

Cantaloupes are extremely nutrient-dense, as defined by quality of nutrition per calorie. One pound of cantaloupe is seldom over 150 calories, yet provides excellent levels of carotenes, potassium, and other valuable nutrients, especially if the skin is also juiced. Cantaloupe has been shown to contain the compound adenosine, which is currently being used in patients with heart disease to keep the blood thin and relieve angina attacks.[6]

NUTRITIONAL ANALYSIS

½ cantaloupe, without skin (267g)

Nutrients and Units

Water	240	g
Calories	94	kcal
Protein	2.34	g
Fat	0.74	g
Carbohydrate	22.33	g

VITAMINS

Vitamin A	861	RE
Vitamin C	112.7	mg
Thiamine	0.096	mg
Riboflavin	0.056	mg
Niacin	1.53	mg

MINERALS

Potassium	825	mg
Calcium	28	mg
Iron	0.57	mg
Magnesium	28	mg
Phosphorus	45	mg
Sodium	23	mg

SELECTION

The three principal signs of a ripe cantaloupe are: (1) no stem, but a smooth, shallow basin where the stem was once attached; (2) thick, coarse, and corky netting or veining over the surface; and (3) a yellowish-buff skin color under the netting. Overripeness is characterized by a pronounced yellow-

ing with a soft, watery, and insipid flesh. Small bruises will do no harm, but large bruised areas should be cut away. Examine the stem scar to make sure that no mold is growing. Keep them at room temperature if a little hard, in the refrigerator if fully ripe.

PREPARATION FOR JUICING

Wash organic cantaloupes; soak or spray nonorganic ones with a biodegradable wash, then rinse. Slice the cantaloupe in half, remove the seeds, and then cut it into strips that will feed through the juicer. There is no need to remove the skin if your juicer will handle it.

CANTALOUPE JUICE RECIPES

Cantaloupe juice is fantastic on its own. For recipes that use cantaloupe, see Banana-Cantaloupe above and Kids' Favorite in Chapter 7. Here is another great-tasting cantaloupe recipe.

Cantaloupe-Watermelon

½ cantaloupe with skin, sliced
Add as much watermelon as desired

CHERRIES

Cherries are grown in every state and throughout most parts of the world. Where the cherry comes from is not known. There are basically two types of cherries: sweet and sour. The 500 varieties of sweet cherries include Bing, black, Windsor, and Napoleon. There are over 270 varieties of sour cherries. Sometimes sour cherries are referred to as tart, pie, or red cherries. The sweet cherries are best for juicing. In general, the darker the cherry, the better it is for you.

KEY BENEFITS

Consuming the equivalent of a half pound of fresh cherries a day has been shown to be very effective in lowering uric acid levels and preventing attacks of gout. Cherries, like berries, are rich sources of flavonoids. The anthocyanidins and proanthocyanidins that give these fruits their deep red-blue color are remarkable in their ability to prevent collagen destruction (see Chapter 3).

NUTRITIONAL ANALYSIS

1 cup cherries, pitted (145g)

Nutrients and Units

Water	117.09	g
Calories	104	kcal
Protein	1.74	g
Fat	1.39	g
Carbohydrate	24	g

VITAMINS

Vitamin A	31	RE
Vitamin C	10.2	mg
Thiamine	0.073	mg
Riboflavin	0.087	mg
Niacin	0.58	mg

MINERALS

Potassium	325	mg
Calcium	21	mg
Iron	0.56	mg
Magnesium	16	mg

| Phosphorus | 28mg |
| Sodium | 1mg |

SELECTION

Good cherries have bright, glossy, plump-looking sur-faces and fresh-looking stems. They should be firm, but not hard. Overmature cherries are usually easy to spot. Soft, leaking flesh, brown discoloration, and mold growth are all indications of decay.

PREPARATION FOR JUICING

Wash organic cherries; soak or spray nonorganic ones with a biodegradable wash, then rinse. Remove the stems and use a cherry-pitter or cut the cherries in half to remove the pit.

CHERRY JUICE RECIPES

Fresh cherry juice is delicious on its own, but can also be mixed with apples and other fruits. See Apple-Cherry above, and Cherry Pop in Chapter 7.

Cherry-Peach

1 cup pitted cherries
1 peach, pitted
1 apple or pear, sliced

Cherry-Pear

1 cup pitted cherries
2 pears, sliced

Cherry-Pineapple

1 cup pitted cherries
½ pineapple with skin, sliced

CRANBERRIES

Cranberries grow wild in Europe, North America, and Asia. Almost all of the world cranberry crop is produced in the United States, however. Most Americans associate cranberries with Thanksgiving and Christmas dinner, but more and more individuals are eating and drinking these berries throughout the year.

KEY BENEFITS

Cranberries are quite bitter and have been used more for their medicinal rather than their nutritional benefits. Several clinical studies have shown cranberries and cranberry juice to be quite effective in treating bladder infections. In one study, 16 ounces of cranberry juice a day was shown to produce beneficial effects in 73% of the subjects (44 females and 16 males) with active urinary tract infections. Furthermore, withdrawal of the cranberry juice in the people who benefited resulted in recurrence of bladder infection in 61%.[7]

Many people believe the action of cranberry juice is due to acidifying the urine and the antibacterial effects of a cranberry component, hippuric acid. However, these are probably not the major mechanisms of action. In order to acidify the urine, at least one quart of cranberry juice would have to be consumed. And the concentration of hippuric acid in the urine as a result of drinking cranberry juice is not sufficient to inhibit bacteria. Since a positive effect on bladder infection was noted when patients drank only 16 ounces of cranberry juice a day, another mechanism is more likely.

Recent studies have shown components in cranberry juice to reduce the ability of the common bacteria *E. coli* to adhere to the lining of the bladder and urethra. In order for bacteria to infect, they must first adhere to the mucosa. By interfering with adherence, cranberry juice greatly reduces the likelihood of infection and helps the body fight off infection.

This is the most likely explanation of cranberry juice's positive effects in bladder infections.

Of seven juices studied (cranberry, blueberry, grapefruit, guava, mango, orange, and pineapple), only cranberry and blueberry contained this inhibitor.[8] Blueberry juice is a suitable alternative to cranberry juice in bladder infections.

It must be pointed out that most cranberry juices on the market contain one-third cranberry juice mixed with water and sugar. Fresh cranberry juice naturally sweetened with apple or grape juice is preferable.

NUTRITIONAL ANALYSIS

1 cup cranberries (145g)

Nutrients and Units

Water	122.68	g
Calories	82	kcal
Protein	1	g
Fat	0.55	g
Carbohydrate	20.49	g

VITAMINS

Vitamin A	15	RE
Vitamin C	18.9	mg
Thiamine		0.070mg
Riboflavin		0.073mg
Niacin		0.521mg

MINERALS

Potassium	129	mg
Calcium	9	mg
Iron	0.24	mg

Magnesium	7mg
Phosphorus	15mg
Sodium	9mg

SELECTION

Cranberries that are ripe are plump, red, shiny, and firm. Poor quality is indicated by shriveling, dull appearance, and softness. Fresh cranberries can be stored in the refrigerator for several months with only minimal loss of moisture and nutritional value.

PREPARATION FOR JUICING

Wash organic cranberries; soak or spray nonorganic ones with a biodegradable wash, then rinse.

CRANBERRY JUICE RECIPES

Again, since cranberries are quite bitter, it is best to mix them with a sweeter fruit, such as apple or grapes. Try the Cranberry Crush and Zesty Cran-Apple recipes in Chapter 7, as well as this one:

Cranberry-Pear

> 1 cup cranberries
> 2 pears, sliced

GRAPE

Grapes have been eaten since prehistoric times and cultivated as far back as 5000 B.C. The grape is the leading fruit crop in the world. There are three basic types: Old World, North American, and hybrids. The versatile Old World variety accounts for over 95% of the grapes grown in the world and is used for table grapes, raisins, and wine. North American

grapes, including the Concord and Niagara, are available in seedless varieties and are well suited for juice and as table grapes, but not for raisins. The hybrid, a cross between Old World and North American grapes, is used primarily in the production of wine.

KEY BENEFITS

Grapes provide nutritional benefits similar to those of other berries. The nutritional quality can be enhanced by juicing grapes containing seeds. In Europe, a grape seed extract rich in flavonoids known as procyanolic oligomers or leukocyanidins is widely used in treating varicose veins and other venous disorders. These flavonoids are extremely powerful antioxidants and have also been shown to reverse atherosclerosis.[9]

NUTRITIONAL ANALYSIS

1 cup North American type grapes (92g)

Nutrients and Units

Water	75	g
Calories	58	kcal
Protein	0.58	g
Fat	0.32	g
Carbohydrate	15.78	g

VITAMINS

Vitamin A	9	RE
Vitamin C	3.7	mg
Thiamine	0.085	mg
Riboflavin	0.052	mg
Niacin	0.276	mg

MINERALS

Potassium	176	mg
Calcium	13	mg
Iron	0.27	mg
Magnesium	5	mg
Phosphorus	9	mg
Sodium	2	mg

SELECTION

Grapes do not ripen after harvesting, so look for grapes that are well colored, firmly attached to the stem, firm, and wrinkle-free. Green grapes are usually the sweetest. After purchase, the grapes should be stored in the refrigerator, where they will maintain their freshness for several days.

PREPARATION FOR JUICING

Wash organic grapes; soak or spray nonorganic ones with a biodegradable wash, then rinse.

GRAPE JUICE RECIPES

Pure grape juice is pretty sweet; you may want to dilute it with water or use it as a base for lemonade or cranberry juice. See the Apple-Grape-Lemon recipe above, and in Chapter 7, Gina's Sweet Sunshine and Zesty Cran-Apple.

Grape-Grapefruit

 1 cup grapes
 1 grapefruit, peeled

Grape-Lemon-Pineapple

 1 cup grapes
 ¼ lemon with skin
 ½ pineapple with skin, sliced

GRAPEFRUIT

The grapefruit was first noticed on Barbados in 1750; by 1880 it had become an important commercial crop in Florida. The best grapefruits are grown in Florida and Texas. For juicing purposes, grapefruits with a red-pink meat, such as the Ruby Red and Star Ruby, are best.

KEY BENEFITS

Fresh grapefruit is low in calories and is a good source of flavonoids, water-soluble fibers, potassium, vitamin C, and folic acid. Grapefruit, like other citrus fruits, has been shown to exert some anticancer effects in human population studies as well as in animal studies. Grapefruit pectin has been found to possess cholesterol-lowering action similar to that of other fruit pectins.

Recently, grapefruit consumption has been shown to normalize hematocrit levels. The hematocrit refers to the percentage of red blood cells per volume of blood. The normal hematocrit level is 40%–54% for men and 37%–47% for women. Low hematocrit levels usually reflect anemia. High hematocrit levels may reflect severe dehydration or an increased number of red blood cells. A high hematocrit reading is associated with an increased risk of heart disease, because it means that the blood is too viscous (thick).

Naringin, a flavonoid isolated from grapefruit, has been shown to promote the elimination of old red blood cells. This prompted researchers to evaluate the effect on hematocrit levels of eating a half to one grapefruit a day. As expected, the grapefruit was able to lower high hematocrit levels. However, researchers were surprised to find that it had no effect on normal hematocrit levels and actually increased low hematocrit levels.[10]

This balancing action is totally baffling to most drug scientists, but not to experienced herbalists, who have used terms such as alterative, amphiteric, adaptogenic, or tonic to describe this effect. Many foods as well as herbs seem to

possess actions that are not at all consistent with modern understanding. For example, many natural compounds in herbs and foods appear to alter body control mechanisms to aid in the normalization of many of the body's processes. When there is an elevation in a certain body function the herb or food will have a lowering effect, and when there is decrease in a certain body function it will have a heightening effect. Grapefruit appears to have this effect on hematocrit levels.

NUTRITIONAL ANALYSIS

1 grapefruit (230g)

Nutrients and Units

Water	209	g
Calories	74	kcal
Protein	1.5	g
Fat	0.24	g
Carbohydrate	18.58	g

VITAMINS

Vitamin A	29	RE
Vitamin C	79	mg
Thiamine	0.083	mg
Riboflavin	0.046	mg
Niacin	0.575	mg

MINERALS

Potassium	321	mg
Calcium	27	mg
Iron	0.2	mg
Magnesium	19	mg
Phosphorus	20	mg
Sodium	1	mg

SELECTION

Fresh grapefruits of good quality are firm but springy to the touch, well shaped, and heavy for their size. Grapefruits that are soft, wilted, flabby, or have green on the skin should not be consumed.

PREPARATION FOR JUICING

Some people are allergic to citrus peels, so when such allergies are suspected, caution must be employed. Grapefruits should always be peeled in any case. Citrus peels contain some beneficial oils, but these oils can interfere with some body functions, so they must not be consumed in any significant quantity. For example, citrus peels contain a compound known as citral that antagonizes some of the effects of vitamin A. After the fruit is peeled, it should be cut into wedges small enough to feed through the juicer.

GRAPEFRUIT JUICE RECIPES

See the Apple-Grapefruit and Grape-Grapefruit recipes above, and in Chapter 7, Color Me Pink.

Grapefruit-Orange

½ grapefruit, peeled
2 oranges, peeled

Grapefruit-Papaya

1 grapefruit, peeled
½ papaya, seeded, sliced

Grapefruit-Pineapple

1 grapefruit, peeled
½ pineapple with skin, sliced

KIWIFRUITS

The kiwifruit was developed in New Zealand from a smaller, less tasty fruit, the Chinese gooseberry. Since it is now grown in California, more and more Americans are discovering this deliciously nutritious fruit. The kiwifruit is a small oval that is brown and fuzzy on the outside; inside, it contains a sherbet-green meat surrounding small jet-black edible seeds.

KEY BENEFITS

Kiwifruits are rich in enzymes if juiced unpeeled and with the seeds. They are also rich in vitamin C and potassium.

NUTRITIONAL ANALYSIS

1 large kiwifruit (91g)

Nutrients and Units

Water	75.58	g
Calories	55	kcal
Protein	0.9	g
Fat	0.4	g
Carbohydrate	13.54	g

VITAMINS

Vitamin A	16	RE
Vitamin C	89	mg
Thiamine	0.018	mg
Riboflavin	0.046	mg
Niacin	0.455	mg

MINERALS

Potassium	302	mg
Calcium	24	mg
Iron	0.37	mg
Magnesium	27	mg
Phosphorus	37	mg
Sodium	4	mg

SELECTION

Kiwifruits should feel firm, but not rock-hard. They should give slightly when pressed.

PREPARATION FOR JUICING

Simply cut them up unpeeled or peeled. Kiwifruit mixes deliciously with most other fruits, especially grapes and oranges.

KIWI JUICE RECIPES

See the Apple-Kiwi recipe above, and the Digestive Delight and Mint Foam recipes in Chapter 7.

Kiwi-Orange

   3 kiwifruits
   2 oranges, peeled

Kiwi-Papaya

   3 kiwifruits
   ½ papaya, seeded, sliced

LEMONS

The lemon originated somewhere in Southeast Asia. Since the lemon tree is more sensitive to freezing temperatures than other citrus trees, it has been the most difficult to cultivate. But, unlike other citrus trees, the lemon tree bears fruit continuously. California and Florida lead the United States in the production of lemons.

KEY BENEFITS

Lemons are rich in vitamin C and potassium. The vitamin C content and storage capacity of lemons made them useful for sailors in the battle against scurvy during long voyages. Lemons also contain a substance known as limonene, which is being used to dissolve gallstones and is showing extremely promising anticancer properties.[11] The highest content of limonene is found in the white spongy inner parts.

NUTRITIONAL ANALYSIS

1 medium lemon without peel (58g)

Nutrients and Units

Water	51.61	g
Calories	17	kcal
Protein	0.64	g
Fat	0.17	g
Carbohydrate	5.41	g

VITAMINS

Vitamin A	2	RE
Vitamin C	30.7	mg
Thiamine	0.023	mg

Riboflavin	0.012mg	
Niacin	0.058mg	

MINERALS

Potassium	80	mg
Calcium	15	mg
Iron	0.35	mg
Magnesium	4	mg
Phosphorus	9	mg
Sodium	1	mg

SELECTION

A ripe lemon should have a fine-textured skin with a deep yellow color and be firm to the touch. Deep-yellow-colored lemons are usually less acidic than the lighter or greenish-yellow varieties. They are also usually thinner-skinned and yield a larger proportion of juice. Avoid dried-out, shriveled, or hard-skinned fruit.

PREPARATION FOR JUICING

Wash organic lemons; soak or spray nonorganic ones with a biodegradable wash, then rinse. You can use the peel if you are juicing less than half a lemon; otherwise, it is a good idea to peel it (see Grapefruit).

LEMON JUICE RECIPES

Lemon juice is usually too sour on its own; it must be mixed with other juices. Jay Kordich has a recipe for lemonade that is outstanding: juice 4 apples and ¼ lemon with the skin and serve over crushed ice. See the Apple-Grape-Lemon and Grape-Lemon-Pineapple recipes above, and the following recipes in Chapter 7: Gina's Sweet Sunshine, Ginger Ale, Kill the Cold, and Zesty Cran-Apple.

LIMES

The lime is similar to the lemon, only smaller and greener. Like the lemon, the lime originated somewhere in Southeast Asia. Like lemons, limes were used by sailors to combat scurvy during long voyages, especially British sailors, hence the term "limeys."

KEY BENEFITS

Limes do not differ much in nutritional value from lemons.

SELECTION

Limes should be green in color and heavy for their size. If limes show purple to brown spots, this is a sign that they are decaying.

PREPARATION FOR JUICING

Wash organic limes; peel, then soak or spray nonorganic ones with a biodegradable wash, then rinse. You can use the peel if you are juicing less than half a lime; otherwise, it is a good idea to discard the peel (see Grapefruit). Lime juice is usually too sour on its own and must be mixed with other juices. The addition of lime seems to have a "cooling" effect.

LIME JUICE RECIPES

Limes can be substituted for lemons in any recipe.

MANGOES

Mangoes originated in India, and are now grown in many tropical locations, including California, Hawaii, and Florida. Mangoes are one of the leading fruit crops of the world. In fact, more mangoes are consumed by more people on a regular basis than apples.

KEY BENEFITS

Mangoes are a good source of potassium, vitamin C, carotenes, and flavonoids. Mangoes provide a rich assortment of antioxidants and are delicious when ripe.

SELECTION

A ripe mango will yield to pressure in a fashion similar to an avocado. Mangoes should be yellowish-green with a smooth skin and emit a sweet fragrance. Avoid fruit that is too hard or soft, bruised, and smells of fermentation. Although they come in all sizes, the larger ones are the easiest to use for juicing.

PREPARATION FOR JUICING

Wash organic mangoes; soak or spray nonorganic ones with a biodegradable wash, then rinse. Mangoes have a pit at the center, so you will need to cut this away and then cut the fruit into strips or wedges.

MANGO JUICE RECIPES

Mangoes yield a thicker juice, so you'll want to juice them with fruits like apples, pears, and oranges that have a high water content. See the Apricot-Mango Ambrosia and Enzymes Galore recipes in Chapter 7.

Mango-Orange

    1 mango, pitted, sliced
    2 oranges, peeled

Mango-Papaya

    1 mango, pitted, sliced
    ½ papaya, seeded, sliced

Mango-Pear

1 mango, pitted, sliced
2 pears, sliced

Mango-Pineapple

1 mango, pitted, sliced
½ pineapple with skin, sliced

NECTARINES (SEE PEACHES AND NECTARINES)

ORANGES

The modern-day orange evolved from varieties native to southern China and Southeast Asia. Oranges are by far the leading fruit crop of the United States. Personally, I prefer the California orange (the Valencia) to the Florida variety, although the latter will typically generate more juice. Mandarin oranges, tangerines, tangelos, and citron provide benefits similar to those of the orange.

KEY BENEFITS

Everyone knows that oranges are an excellent source of vitamin C. Equally important is their supply of flavonoids. The combination of vitamin C and flavonoids makes orange juice a very valuable drink in strengthening the immune system, supporting connective tissues such as the joints, gums, and ground substance, and promoting overall good health.

The consumption of oranges and orange juice has been shown to protect against cancer, support the immune system, and help fight viral infections.[12] In addition to vitamin C and flavonoids, oranges also have good amounts of carotenes, pectin, potassium, and folic acid.

NUTRITIONAL ANALYSIS

1 raw California orange (121g)

Nutrients and Units

Water	104.5	g
Calories	59	kcal
Protein	1.26	g
Fat	0.36	g
Carbohydrate	14.49	g

VITAMINS

Vitamin A	28	RE
Vitamin C	58.7	mg
Thiamine	0.205	mg
Riboflavin	0.048	mg
Niacin	0.332	mg

MINERALS

Potassium	217	mg
Calcium	48	mg
Iron	0.11	mg
Magnesium	12	mg
Phosphorus	21	mg
Sodium	0	mg

SELECTION

Fresh oranges are of the best quality when they are well colored, heavy, firm, and have a fine-textured skin. Look out for moldy, severely bruised, and soft-puffy oranges. Oranges keep well in the refrigerator for more than a week.

PREPARATION FOR JUICING

Peel the oranges, trying to retain as much of the white spongy portion as possible. Cut into wedges and feed into the juicer.

ORANGE JUICE RECIPES

Orange juice is delicious on its own. Three oranges will usually yield more than eight ounces of juice. See the Apple-Orange, Apricot-Orange, Berry-Orange, Kiwi-Orange, and Mango-Orange recipes above, and the following recipes in Chapter 7: Apricot-Mango Ambrosia, Cranberry Crush, Enzymes Galore, Gina's Sweet Sunshine, Immune Power Fruit, Monkey Shake, Orange Aid, and Potassium Punch.

Orange-Papaya

> 2　oranges, peeled
> ½ papaya, seeded, sliced

Orange-Peach

> 2 oranges, peeled
> 1 peach, pitted

PAPAYAS

The papaya originated in Central America. The green unripe papaya is the source of papain, a protein-digesting enzyme similar to bromelain. Papain is used commercially in many meat tenderizers.

KEY BENEFITS

Papayas are rich in antioxidant nutrients such as carotenes, vitamin C, and flavonoids. Papayas also contain good amounts of many minerals, especially potassium and magnesium. Although the ripe fruit does not contain as much papain

as the unripe fruit, nonetheless it does contain some. In addition to its commercial uses, papain has been applied to a number of medicinal conditions, such as indigestion, chronic diarrhea, hay fever, sports injuries and other causes of trauma, and allergies. Basically, papain is used in a manner similar to bromelain.[13]

NUTRITIONAL ANALYSIS

1 papaya, peeled (304g)

Nutrients and Units

Water	270	g
Calories	117	kcal
Protein	1.86	g
Fat	0.43	g
Carbohydrate	29.82	g

VITAMINS

Vitamin A	612	RE
Vitamin C	187.8	mg
Thiamine	0.082	mg
Riboflavin	0.097	mg
Niacin	1.028	mg

MINERALS

Potassium	780	mg
Calcium	72	mg
Iron	0.3	mg
Magnesium	31	mg
Phosphorus	16	mg
Sodium	8	mg

SELECTION

Papayas should be yellow-green in color and firm, but not rock-hard, to the touch. Overmature papayas will be soft and will usually show signs of decay.

PREPARATION FOR JUICING

Wash organic papayas; soak or spray nonorganic ones with a biodegradable wash, then rinse. Papayas contain small black seeds, which are edible but quite bitter. I recommend that you cut the papaya in half, remove the seeds, and then cut it into slices.

PAPAYA JUICE RECIPES

Papaya juice is good on its own. See the recipes for Apple-Papaya, Grapefruit-Papaya, Kiwi-Papaya, Mango-Papaya, and Orange-Papaya, above, and Enzymes Galore, Monkey Shake, and Potassium Punch in Chapter 7.

Papaya-Pear

½ papaya, seeded, sliced
2 pears, sliced

Papaya-Pineapple

½ papaya, seeded, sliced
½ pineapple with skin, sliced

PEACHES AND NECTARINES

The peach, like many other fruits, is native to China. There are numerous varieties of peaches, but there are basically two types: freestone and clingstone. This refers to how easy it is to remove the pit from the fruit. Popular freestone varieties include Elberta, Hale, and Golden Jubilee. Popular

clingstone varieties are the Fortuna, Johnson, and Sims. Nec-
tarines are essentially peaches without the fuzz.

KEY BENEFITS

Eight ounces of pure peach or nectarine juice contains
fewer than 100 calories, yet provides some important nutrients like potassium, carotenes, flavonoids, and natural
sugars.

NUTRITIONAL ANALYSIS

1 peach (87g)

Nutrients and Units

Water	76.26	g
Calories	37	kcal
Protein	0.61	g
Fat	0.08	g
Carbohydrate	9.65	g

VITAMINS

Vitamin A	47	RE
Vitamin C	5.7	mg
Thiamine	0.025	mg
Riboflavin	0.036	mg
Niacin	0.861	mg

MINERALS

Potassium	171	mg
Calcium	5	mg

Iron	0.1mg
Magnesium	6 mg
Phosphorus	11 mg
Sodium	0

SELECTION

Fresh peaches and nectarines should be fairly firm. They will ripen at home at room temperature if they are not fully ripe. The color indicates the variety of the peach rather than ripeness; hence it should not be used as a gauge for ripeness. Be on the lookout for bruises and signs of spoilage. Once they are ripe, store peaches in the refrigerator.

PREPARATION FOR JUICING

Wash organic peaches; soak or spray nonorganic ones with a biodegradable wash, then rinse. Cut in half, remove the stone, being careful to get all of it, then slice into wedges.

PEACH JUICE RECIPES

Peaches yield a thicker juice, so you'll want to juice them with apples or pears. See the Apple-Apricot-Peach, Cherry-Peach, and Orange-Peach recipes above, and the Potassium Punch recipe in Chapter 7.

Peach-Pear

    1 peach, pitted, sliced
    2 pears, sliced

PEARS

The pear originated in western Asia, but is now cultivated throughout much of the world. There are numerous varieties of pears. The best varieties for juicing include the Bosc, Anjou, Bartlett, and Comice.

KEY BENEFITS

Pears are an excellent source of water-soluble fibers, including pectin. In fact, pears are actually higher in pectin than apples. Pears, like apples, can be added to vegetable-based juices to improve their flavor.

NUTRITIONAL ANALYSIS

1 pear (166g)

Nutrients and Units

Water	139	g
Calories	98	kcal
Protein	0.65	g
Fat	0.66	g
Carbohydrate	25	g

VITAMINS

Vitamin A	3	RE
Vitamin C	6.6	mg
Thiamine	0.033	mg
Riboflavin	0.066	mg
Niacin	0.166	mg

MINERALS

Potassium	208	mg
Calcium	19	mg
Iron	0.41	mg
Magnesium	9	mg
Phosphorus	18	mg
Sodium	1	mg

SELECTION

As pears ripen, their skin color changes from green to the color characteristic for the variety. Bosc pears turn brown, Anjou and Bartlett pears turn yellow, and Comice pears have a green mottled skin. Fresh pears are best when they yield to pressure like an avocado does. Unripe pears will ripen at home if stored at room temperature. Once ripe, they should be refrigerated. For juicing, firm pears are much easier to juice than soft pears.

PREPARATION FOR JUICING

Wash organic pears; soak or spray nonorganic ones with a biodegradable wash, then rinse. Cut the pear into slices or wedges.

PEAR JUICE RECIPES

Pear juice is delicious on its own, and it also mixes quite well with many fruits and vegetables. See the recipes above for Apple-Pear-Ginger, Apricot-Pear, Berry-Pear, Cherry-Pear, Cranberry-Pear, Mango-Pear, Papaya-Pear, and Peach-Pear.

Pear-Plum

2 plums, pitted
2 pears, sliced

PINEAPPLES

The pineapple is native to South America. The United States ranks as one of the world's leading suppliers of pineapples, although the only state that produces them is Hawaii. The edible flesh of the pineapple has a characteristic flavor often described as a mixture of apple, strawberry, and peach.

KEY BENEFITS

The virtues of bromelain, the protein-digesting enzyme complex of pineapple, have already been discussed (see pages 40–41). Briefly, bromelain has been shown to be useful in a number of health conditions, including angina, arthritis, indigestion, upper respiratory tract infections, athletic injuries, and trauma.

In a study conducted at the Cancer Research Center of Hawaii at the University of Hawaii, an extract of pineapple significantly inhibited the growth of tumor cells in cell cultures.[14] In this study, an enzyme known as peroxidase was indicated to be the major antitumor component. This would indicate that fresh pineapple may have effects beyond its bromelain content. Fresh pineapple juice is rich in enzymes, vitamin C, and potassium.

NUTRITIONAL ANALYSIS

1 cup diced pineapple without skin (155g)

Nutrients and Units

Water	135	g
Calories	77	kcal
Protein	0.6	g
Fat	0.66	g
Carbohydrate	19.21	g

VITAMINS

Vitamin A	4	RE
Vitamin C	23.9	mg
Thiamine	0.143	mg
Riboflavin	0.056	mg
Niacin	0.651	mg

MINERALS

Potassium	175	mg
Calcium	11	mg
Iron	0.57	mg
Magnesium	21	mg
Phosphorus	11	mg
Sodium	1	mg

SELECTION

The main thing to be concerned about is the presence of decayed or moldy spots. Check the bottom stem scar. Ripe pineapples have a fruity, fragrant aroma, are more yellow than green in color, and are heavier for their size.

PREPARATION FOR JUICING

Twist or cut off the top. Wash and scrub organic pineapples; soak or spray nonorganic ones with a biodegradable wash, then scrub and rinse. If your juicer will handle it, simply cut up the pineapple, skin and all, into pieces that can be fed into the juicer.

PINEAPPLE JUICE RECIPES

Pineapple is low in calories and makes a fantastic base for fruit drinks, especially when mixed with berries. See the recipes above for Berry-Pineapple, Cherry-Pineapple, Grape-Lemon-Pineapple, Grapefruit-Pineapple, Mango-Pineapple, and Papaya-Pineapple. See the following recipes in Chapter 7: Digestive Delight, The Don Juan, Enzymes Galore, Immune Power Fruit, Mike's Favorite, Orange Aid, and Pineapple-Ginger Ale.

PLUMS AND PRUNES

Like peaches and apricots, plums are classified as a drupe because of their hard pit or stone surrounded by soft,

pulpy flesh with a thin skin. Plums originated in Europe and Asia. There are five main types: European, Japanese, American, Damson, and Ornamental. A prune is a dried plum, just like a raisin is a dried grape.

KEY BENEFITS

Plums and prunes are often used for their laxative effects. Prunes are more effective than plums in this capacity. Plums are good sources of carotenes, flavonoids, potassium, and iron.

NUTRITIONAL ANALYSIS

1 plum (66g)

Nutrients and Units

Water	56.23	g
Calories	36	kcal
Protein	0.52	g
Fat	0.41	g
Carbohydrate	8.6	g

VITAMINS

Vitamin A	21	RE
Vitamin C	6.3	mg
Thiamine		0.028mg
Riboflavin		0.063mg
Niacin	0.33	mg

MINERALS

Potassium	113	mg
Calcium	2	mg
Iron	0.07	mg

Magnesium	4mg
Phosphorus	7mg
Sodium	0

SELECTION

Plums vary in color and size. They can be as small as a cherry or as large as a peach, and their skin can be green, yellow, blue, or purple. Select fresh plums based on the color characteristic to the variety. Ripe plums are firm to slightly soft. Avoid plums that have skin breaks or brownish discolorations, or are overly soft.

PREPARATION FOR JUICING

Wash organic plums; soak or spray nonorganic ones with a biodegradable wash, then rinse. Prunes can be rehydrated by soaking them in water (2–4 prunes per 1 cup of water) for 24 hours and then added, along with the soaking water, to the blender.

PLUM JUICE RECIPES

See the recipes Pear-Plum above and Bowel Regulator in Chapter 7.

RASPBERRIES (SEE BERRIES)

STRAWBERRIES (SEE BERRIES)

TANGERINES (SEE ORANGES)

WATERMELON

Watermelons originated in Africa, but have been cultivated since ancient times in Europe and Asia. Today water-

melons are grown worldwide in tropical, semitropical, and temperate climates. The most common watermelon consumed in the United States is light to dark green with stripes or mottling on the outside covering a bright red flesh with dark brown or black seeds. The flesh can also be pink, orange, yellow, or white.

KEY BENEFITS

Watermelon, as its name would imply, is an excellent source of pure water. It is very low in calories. If watermelon juice is prepared using the rind and all, the nutritional quality improves dramatically, as the nutrients are highly concentrated in the rind and seeds. Watermelon is an excellent diuretic.

NUTRITIONAL ANALYSIS

1 cup diced watermelon without rind (160g)

Nutrients and Units

Water	146.42	g
Calories	50	kcal
Protein	0.99	g
Fat	0.68	g
Carbohydrate	11.5	g

VITAMINS

Vitamin A	58	RE
Vitamin C	15.4	mg
Thiamine	0.128	mg
Riboflavin	0.032	mg
Niacin	0.32	mg

MINERALS

Potassium	186	mg
Calcium	13	mg
Iron	0.28	mg
Magnesium	17	mg
Phosphorus	14	mg
Sodium	3	mg

SELECTION

People tap on watermelons to determine if they sound hollow and are therefore ripe; however, this practice does not mean success. Look for watermelons that have a smooth surface and a cream-colored underbelly. Despite the best precautions, it is difficult to judge the quality of a watermelon without cutting it in half. When cut, indicators of a good watermelon include firm, juicy red flesh with dark brown to black seeds. The presence of white streaks in the flesh or white seeds usually indicates immaturity.

PREPARATION FOR JUICING

Wash, scrub, and rinse organic watermelon; soak or spray nonorganic watermelon with a biodegradable wash, then scrub and rinse. Cut the watermelon (rind and all) into long strips that will feed into the juicer.

WATERMELON JUICE RECIPES

Watermelon juice is best consumed alone or in combination with other melon juices. See Cantaloupe-Watermelon above.

6

A JUICER'S GUIDE
TO VEGETABLES

What is the difference between a vegetable and a fruit? In 1893, this question came before the U.S. Supreme Court, which ruled a vegetable refers to a plant grown for an edible part that is generally eaten as part of the main course, while a fruit is a plant part generally eaten as an appetizer, as a dessert, or out of hand. Some typical parts of plants used as vegetables are: bulbs (garlic and onion), flowers (broccoli and cauliflower), fruits (pumpkins and tomatoes), leaves (spinach and lettuce), roots (carrots and beets), seeds (beans, peas, and corn), stalks (celery), stems (asparagus), and tubers (potatoes and yams).

The U.S. Department of Agriculture has established voluntary grade standards for fruits and vegetables. The official USDA grades are:

U.S. Fancy: premium quality, the top quality range.

U.S. No. 1: the chief trading grade; good quality.

U.S. No. 2: intermediate quality.

U.S. No. 3: low quality.

The grading is largely visual, based not only on the external qualities but also the internal appearance. Models, color guides, and color photographs are available for graders to check samples for shape, degree of coloring, and degree of defects or damage.

Vegetables should play a major role in the diet. The U.S. National Academy of Science, the Department of Health and Human Services, and the National Cancer Institute are recommending that Americans consume three to five servings of vegetables a day. Drinking a minimum of two eight-ounce glasses of fresh vegetable juice each day appears to be an extremely healthy recommendation.

Please be sure to prepare the vegetables according to the guidelines given below and the recommendations from the owner's manual of your juice extractor.

ASPARAGUS

The asparagus is a member of the lily family native to the Mediterranean. It has been used as a medicinal plant in the treatment of arthritis and rheumatism, and as a diuretic. Asparagus is now grown all over the world.

KEY BENEFITS

Asparagus is low in calories and carbohydrates, but very rich in protein. In fact, a four-ounce glass of asparagus juice contains more protein than one cup of cooked rice or corn. Asparagus is also a good source for many vitamins and minerals, including vitamin C, riboflavin, and folic acid. Asparagus contains the amino acid asparagine, which when excreted in the urine can give off a strong odor. Don't be alarmed; this is short-lived.

NUTRITIONAL ANALYSIS

6 raw asparagus spears (100g)

Nutrients and Units

Water	92	g
Calories	32	kcal
Protein	2.5	g
Fat	0.2	g
Carbohydrate	5	g

VITAMINS

Vitamin A	16	RE
Vitamin C	33	mg
Thiamine	0.18	mg
Riboflavin	0.5	mg

Niacin	1.5	mg
Vitamin B6	0.18	mg
Folic acid	104	mcg

MINERALS

Potassium	278	mg
Calcium	22	mg
Iron	1	mg
Magnesium	18	mg
Phosphorus	62	mg
Sodium	2	mg

SELECTION

The best-quality asparagus will be firm and fresh, and the tips will be closed. The greener the stalk, the higher the concentration of nutrients.

PREPARATION FOR JUICING

Wash organic asparagus; soak or spray nonorganic asparagus with a biodegradable wash, then rinse. Feed the asparagus into the juicer with the head end going in first.

ASPARAGUS JUICE RECIPES

Asparagus is pretty strong on its own. Add it to the Basic Carrot-Apple (see Chapter 7), or try the following recipes.

Asparagus-Carrot-Celery

4 asparagus spears
3 carrots
2 celery ribs

Asparagus-Celery
6 asparagus spears
4 celery ribs

BEANS, STRING OR SNAP

The string or snap bean originated in Mexico and Peru. Native Americans cultivated the plant northward and southward, and Spanish explorers took it to Europe.

KEY BENEFITS

String beans are an excellent source of protein and water-soluble fiber compounds, including gums and pectins. Legumes, in general, provide exceptional nutritional benefit to the diabetic. Numerous studies have shown a diet high in legumes will lead to better blood sugar control in diabetics. Presumably a great deal of the beneficial effects would exist in the juice.

NUTRITIONAL ANALYSIS

1 cup raw string beans (135g)

Nutrients and Units

Water	124	g
Calories	36	kcal
Protein	1.84g	
Fat	0.18g	
Carbohydrate	8.26g	

VITAMINS

Vitamin A	71	RE
Vitamin C	11	mg

Thiamine	0.065	mg
Riboflavin	0.1	mg
Niacin	0.5	mg
Vitamin B6	0.28	mg
Folic acid	63.2	mcg

MINERALS

Potassium	151	mg
Calcium	61	mg
Iron	1.11	mg
Magnesium	29	mg
Phosphorus	33	mg
Sodium	17	mg

SELECTION

The beans should be fresh-looking and green in color, and snap when broken. Avoid string beans that are dry and wrinkled in appearance.

PREPARATION FOR JUICING

Wash organic beans; soak or spray nonorganic ones with a biodegradable wash, then rinse.

BEAN JUICE RECIPES

String bean juice on its own is quite thick and not very tasty; a cup of beans can be juiced and added to the Basic Carrot-Apple recipe.

BEETS

Beets belong to the same family as spinach, chard, and kale. Both the root and the leaves are eaten. Beets were orig-

inally cultivated in Europe and Asia, but are now cultivated worldwide, both for food and as a source for sugar production.

KEY BENEFITS

The beet greens are higher in nutritional value than the roots, especially in calcium, iron, vitamin A, and vitamin C. Beet roots have long been used for medicinal purposes, primarily focusing on disorders of the liver. Beets have gained recognition for their reported anticancer properties.[1]

NUTRITIONAL ANALYSIS

2 beets, without tops (163g)

Nutrients and Units

Water	142.22	g
Calories	77	kcal
Protein	2.41	g
Fat	0.23	g
Carbohydrate	16.3	g

VITAMINS

Vitamin A	3	RE
Vitamin C	17.9	mg
Thiamine	0.082	mg
Riboflavin	0.033	mg
Niacin	0.652	mg
Vitamin B6	0.08	mg
Folic acid	151	mcg

MINERALS

Potassium	528	mg
Calcium	25	mg
Iron	1.5	mg
Magnesium	34	mg
Phosphorus	78	mg
Sodium	118	mg

SELECTION

Good-quality beets should have their greens intact. The greens should be fresh-looking, with no signs of spoilage. Slightly flabby greens can be restored to freshness if stored in the refrigerator in water. If it is too late, simply cut off the greens. The beet root should be firm, smooth, and vibrant red-purple vs. soft, wrinkled, and dull-colored. The smaller beets are generally better for juicing.

PREPARATION FOR JUICING

Wash organic beet roots or greens; soak or spray non-organic ones with a biodegradable wash, then rinse.

BEET JUICE RECIPES

Beet juice tends to be irritating to the throat and esophagus if consumed alone. Try the recipes below, and see these recipes in Chapter 7: Better Red than Dead, Cleansing Cocktail, Iron Plus, Liver Mover, and Liver Tonic.

Beet-Carrot

½ beet with top
4 carrots

Beet-Carrot-Celery

½ beet with top
3 carrots
2 celery ribs

Beet-Carrot-Parsley

½ beet with top
4 carrots
½ handful of parsley

Beet-Carrot-Pepper

½ beet with top
3 carrots
½ green or red bell pepper

Beet-Carrot-Spinach

½ beet with top
3 carrots
½ cup spinach

Beet–Sweet Potato

½ beet with top
1 sweet potato
1 apple, cut into wedges (optional)

BITTER MELON

Bitter melon, also known as balsam pear, is a tropical fruit widely cultivated in Asia, Africa, and South America. Usually the bitter-flavored unripe fruit is used as a vegetable. In addition to being part of the diet, unripe bitter melon has

been used extensively in folk medicine as a remedy for diabetes. The ripe fruit is showing promise in the treatment of leukemia, but the ripe fruit is not readily available in the United States. Unripe bitter melon is available primarily at Asian grocery stores.

KEY BENEFITS

Bitter melon is composed of several compounds with proven antidiabetic properties; science has confirmed the blood-sugar-lowering action of the fresh juice of the unripe bitter melon in both experimental and clinical studies. Although bitter melon has been shown to stimulate insulin release, its main mechanism of action is thought to be increasing the uptake of glucose by the cells. This indicates a direct as well as an indirect effect. Bitter melon contains a compound known as charantin that is more potent than the drug tolbutamide which is often used in the treatment of diabetes to lower blood sugar levels. Bitter melon also contains an insulinlike compound referred to as polypeptide-P, or vegetable insulin, which lowers blood sugar levels when injected into insulin-dependent diabetics. Since it appears to have fewer side effects than insulin, it has been suggested as a replacement for some patients. However, it may not be necessary to inject the material, as the oral administration of as little as two ounces of the juice has shown good results in clinical trials in patients with diabetes.[2]

SELECTION

The bitter melon is a green, cucumber-shaped fruit with gourdlike bumps all over it. It looks like an ugly cucumber. Choose smaller fruit, as you will not need, nor want, much of the juice. The fruit should be firm, like a cucumber.

PREPARATION FOR JUICING

Wash organic bitter melon; soak or spray nonorganic bitter melon with a biodegradable wash, then rinse. Slice it into

strips that can be fed into the juicer. It is called "bitter" melon with good reason. But remember, in the clinical studies the dose was only two ounces. I would recommend just taking it on its own, because its flavor is extremely difficult to mask. However, you can try combining it with eight ounces carrot-apple juice (see Basic Carrot-Apple).

BITTER MELON JUICE RECIPES

It is called "bitter" melon with good reason. But remember, in the clinical studies the dose was only 2 ounces. I would recommend just taking it on its own, because its flavor is extremely difficult to mask. However, you can try combining it with 8 ounces of the Basic Carrot-Apple in Chapter 7.

BROCCOLI

A member of the cruciferous, or cabbage, family of vegetables, broccoli developed from wild cabbage native to Europe, was improved by the Romans and later-day Italians, and is now cultivated throughout the world.

KEY BENEFITS

Broccoli is one of the most nutrient-dense foods. A one-cup serving provides about the same amount of protein as a cup of corn or rice, but less than one-third the calories. Broccoli is one of the richest sources of vitamin C. Like the other members of the cabbage family, broccoli is demonstrating remarkable anticancer effects (see Cabbage), particularly in breast cancer. Compounds in broccoli known as indoles (specifically indole-3-carbinol) increase the excretion of the form of estrogen (2-hydroxyestrone) linked to breast cancer.

NUTRITIONAL ANALYSIS

⅔ cup raw broccoli (100g)

Nutrients and Units

Water	91.46	g
Calories	26	kcal
Protein	2.81	g
Fat	0.29	g
Carbohydrate	4.76	g

VITAMINS

Vitamin A	207	RE
Vitamin C	56.4	mg
Thiamine	0.053	mg
Riboflavin	0.096	mg
Niacin	0.47	mg
Vitamin B6	0.13	mg
Folic acid	67	mcg

MINERALS

Potassium	212	mg
Calcium	56	mg
Iron	0.81	mg
Magnesium	18	mg
Phosphorus	50	mg
Sodium	24	mg

SELECTION

Broccoli should be dark green, deep sage green, or purplish-green, depending on the variety. The stalks and stems should be tender and firm. Yellowed or wilted leaves indicate loss of much of the nutritional value. Avoid wilted, soft, and noticeably aged broccoli.

PREPARATION FOR JUICING

Wash organic broccoli; soak or spray nonorganic broccoli with a biodegradable wash, then rinse. Slice the broccoli into strips. Feed the broccoli into the juicer headfirst.

BROCCOLI JUICE RECIPES

Broccoli juice needs to be mixed with other juices to make it more palatable. Juice ½ cup broccoli and add it to the Basic Carrot-Apple recipe in Chapter 7. Also try the recipes below and these recipes in Chapter 7: Cruciferous Surprise, Everything but the Kitchen Sink, High C, and Iron Plus.

Broccoli-Carrot

> 1 broccoli spear
> 3 carrots

Broccoli-Carrot-Celery

> 1 broccoli spear
> 3 carrots
> 1 celery rib

Broccoli-Carrot-Parsley

> 1 broccoli spear
> 3 carrots
> ½ cup parsley

BRUSSELS SPROUTS

Like broccoli, brussels sprouts evolved from the wild cabbage. It was developed to its present form near Brussels; hence its name. It is cultivated throughout the world. In the United States, almost all brussels sprouts come from California.

KEY BENEFITS

Brussels sprouts are similar in nutritional quality to broccoli. As a member of the cabbage family, brussels sprouts are being investigated for their anticancer properties (see Cabbage).

NUTRITIONAL ANALYSIS

1 cup raw brussels sprouts (150g)

Nutrients and Units

Water	136	g
Calories	60	kcal
Protein	4	g
Fat	0.8	g
Carbohydrate	13.5	g

VITAMINS

Vitamin A	112	RE
Vitamin C	96	mg
Thiamine	0.16	mg
Riboflavin	0.124	mg
Niacin	0.92	mg
Vitamin B6	0.28	mg
Folic acid	94	mcg

MINERALS

Potassium	494	mg
Calcium	56	mg
Iron	1.88	mg

Magnesium	32mg
Phosphorus	88mg
Sodium	34mg

SELECTION

Brussels sprouts should be firm and fresh in appearance, with a good green color. Avoid ones with dull, wilted, or yellow leaves.

PREPARATION FOR JUICING

Wash organic brussels sprouts; soak or spray nonorganic ones with a biodegradable wash, then rinse.

BRUSSELS SPROUTS JUICE RECIPES

The phosphorus content of brussels sprouts is nearly twice as high as their calcium content, and high phosphorus consumption has been linked to osteoporosis, because it will reduce the utilization and promote the excretion of calcium. Therefore, it is wise to juice brussels sprouts with foods higher in calcium, like kale, spinach, and parsley. Brussels sprouts are pretty strong on their own; add ½ cup or 4 sprouts to the Basic Carrot-Apple in Chapter 7.

Brussels Sprouts–Carrot-Spinach
    4   brussels sprouts
    3   carrots
    ½ cup spinach

CABBAGE

The cabbage, or cruciferous, family of vegetables includes cabbage, broccoli, cauliflower, brussels sprouts, kale, collard, mustard, radishes, rutabagas, turnips, and other common vegetables. This family of vegetables is receiving

much attention for their impressive anticancer properties (discussed below).

The modern-day cabbage developed from wild cabbage brought to Europe from Asia by roving bands of Celtic people around 600 B.C. Cabbage spread as a food crop throughout northern Europe (Germany, Poland, Russia, Austria) because it was well adapted to cooler climates, had high yields per acre, and could be stored over the winter in cold cellars.

There are numerous types of cabbage, including different varieties of red and green cabbage. Varieties of cabbage are now cultivated throughout much of the northern latitudes of the Northern Hemisphere.

KEY BENEFITS

The cabbage family of vegetables offers numerous health benefits. From a nutrient standpoint, cabbage provides excellent levels of many known nutrients, including vitamin C, potassium, iron, and calcium. But perhaps more important than the nutrient content of cabbage is the anutrient level. The cabbage family contains more anutrients with demonstrable anticancer properties than any other vegetable family. In fact, one of the American Cancer Society's key dietary recommendations to reduce the risk of cancer is to include on a regular basis cruciferous vegetables, such as cabbage, broccoli, brussels sprouts, and cauliflower, in the diet.[3]

ANUTRIENT COMPOUNDS IN CABBAGE WITH ANTICANCER PROPERTIES

COMPOUND	METHOD OF ACTION
Dithioltiones	Induce antioxidant and detoxification mechanisms
Glucosinolates	Induce antioxidant and detoxification mechanisms

Indoles	Induce antioxidant and detoxification mechanisms; improve metabolism of estrogen
Isothiocyanates	Inhibit cancer development and tumor growth
Coumarins	Block reaction of cancer-causing compounds at key sites
Phenols	Induce detoxification enzymes and prevent the formation of carcinogens

As is evident above, the anutrient components in cabbage work primarily by increasing antioxidant defense mechanisms as well as improving the body's ability to detoxify and eliminate harmful chemicals and hormones. The anticancer effects of cabbage-family vegetables have been noted in population studies. Consistently, the higher the intake of cabbage-family vegetables, the lower the rates of cancer, particularly colon and breast cancer.[4]

Fresh cabbage juice has also been shown to be extremely effective in the treatment of peptic ulcers, usually in less than seven days (see Chapter 8).[5]

Cabbage-family vegetables contain goitrogens, compounds that can interfere with thyroid hormone action in certain situations (low iodine levels, primarily). The goitrogens are largely isothiocyanates that block the utilization of iodine; however, there is no evidence that these compounds in cruciferous vegetables interfere with thyroid function to any significant degree when dietary iodine levels are adequate. Therefore, it is a good idea if large quantities of cruciferous vegetables (more than four servings a day) are being consumed that the diet also contain adequate amounts of iodine. Iodine is found in kelp and other seaweeds, vegetables grown near the sea, seafood, iodized salt, and food supplements. Rutabagas and turnips contain the highest concentration of the goitrogens.

NUTRITIONAL ANALYSIS

½ head raw cabbage

Nutrients and Units

Water	420	g
Calories	108	kcal
Protein	5.5	g
Fat	0.82	g
Carbohydrate	24.4	g

VITAMINS

Vitamin A	57	RE
Vitamin C	215	mg
Thiamine	0.23	mg
Riboflavin	0.14	mg
Niacin	1.4	mg
Vitamin B6	0.43	mg
Folic acid	207	mcg

MINERALS

Potassium	1,116	mg
Calcium	212	mg
Iron	2.5	mg
Magnesium	67	mg
Phosphorus	110	mg
Sodium	82	mg

SELECTION

Cabbage should appear fresh and crisp with no evidence of decay or worm injury.

PREPARATION FOR JUICING

Wash organic cabbage; soak or spray nonorganic cabbage with a biodegradable wash, then rinse. Cut the cabbage into slender wedges that can be fed into the juicer.

CABBAGE JUICE RECIPES

Cabbage juice is pretty strong on its own. See the recipes below and Cruciferous Surprise, Purple Cow, and Vitamin U for Ulcer in Chapter 7.

Cabbage-Carrot

½ head of cabbage, cut into wedges
3   carrots

Cabbage-Carrot-Celery

½ head of cabbage, cut into wedges
3   carrots
2   celery ribs

Cabbage-Carrot-Parsley

½ head of cabbage, cut into wedges
3   carrots
½ cup parsley

CARROTS

Carrots are believed to have originated in the Middle East and Asia. The earlier varieties were mostly purple and black. Apparently the modern-day carrot was originally a mutant variety lacking certain purple or black pigments. Carrots are now cultivated worldwide.

KEY BENEFITS

The carrot is the king of vegetables. Of the commonly consumed vegetables, it is the highest source of provitamin A carotenes. In fact, as shown below, two carrots provide roughly 4,050 retinol equivalents, or roughly four times the RDA (recommended daily allowance) for vitamin A. But, unlike vitamin A, beta-carotene and other carotenes in carrots do not cause toxicity. Carrots are full of many other nutrients and anutrients, but it is their carotene content that is most talked about. Judging from extensive human studies, as little as one carrot a day could conceivably cut the rate of lung cancer in half.[6]

NUTRITIONAL ANALYSIS

2 raw carrots (144g)

Nutrients and Units

Water	126	g
Calories	62	kcal
Protein	1.5	g
Fat	0.28	g
Carbohydrate	14.6	g

VITAMINS

Vitamin A	4,050	RE
Vitamin C	13.4	mg
Thiamine	0.14	mg
Riboflavin	0.84	mg
Niacin	1.3	mg
Vitamin B6	0.2	mg
Folic acid	20	mcg

MINERALS

Potassium	466	mg
Calcium	38	mg
Iron	0.72	mg
Magnesium	22	mg
Phosphorus	64	mg
Sodium	50	mg

SELECTION

Carrots should be fresh-looking, firm, smooth, and vibrantly colored. Avoid carrots that have cracks, are bruised, or have mold growing on them.

PREPARATION FOR JUICING

Wash organic carrots; soak or spray nonorganic ones with a biodegradable wash, then scrub and rinse. It is recommended that you cut off the carrot greens (tops). At the very least, do not juice more than a few carrot greens, as they are a rich source of compounds that once absorbed into the body can react with sunlight to produce a severe sunburn or rash. Feed the carrots into the juicer fat end first to avoid getting the carrot stuck.

CARROT JUICE RECIPES

Carrot juice is one of the most popular juices because it is delicious on its own. Its sweet flavor makes it a valuable addition to many bitter-tasting vegetable juices. See these recipes in this chapter: Asparagus-Carrot-Celery, Beet-Carrot, Beet-Carrot-Celery, Beet-Carrot-Parsley, Beet-Carrot-Pepper, Beet-Carrot-Spinach, Broccoli-Carrot, Broccoli-Carrot-Celery, Broccoli-Carrot-Parsley, Brussels Sprouts–Carrot-Spinach, Cabbage-Carrot, Cabbage-Carrot-Celery, and Cabbage-Carrot-Parsley.

See the following recipes in Chapter 7: Basic Carrot-Apple, Better Red than Dead, Bone Builder's Cocktail, Cholesterol-Lowering Tonic, Cleansing Cocktail, Cruciferous Surprise, Diuretic Formula, The Energizer, Everything but the Kitchen Sink, Ginger Hopper, Immune Power Vegetable, Iron Plus, Jicama-Carrot-Apple, Liver Tonic, Popeye's Power Drink, Potassium Power, Super V-7, and Vitamin U for Ulcer.

Carrot-Cauliflower

4 carrots

1 cup cauliflower

Carrot-Celery

4 carrots

4 celery ribs

Carrot-Celery-Parsley

4 carrots

3 celery ribs

½ cup parsley

Carrot-Cucumber-Parsley

4 carrots

½ cucumber

½ cup parsley

Carrot–Dandelion Greens

5 carrots

½ cup dandelion greens

Carrot–Dandelion Root

4 carrots

1 dandelion root

Carrot-Dandelions-Spinach

4   carrots
1   dandelion root
½ cup spinach

Carrot-Fennel

4   carrots
½ fennel bulb

Carrot–Jerusalem Artichoke

4 carrots
1 cup Jerusalem artichoke

Carrot-Jicama

5   carrots
½ cup jicama

Carrot-Kale

5 carrots
3 kale leaves

Carrot-Leek-Parsley

4 carrots
1 leek
1 cup parsley

Carrot-Lettuce

4 carrots
1 head of lettuce, cut into wedges

Carrot-Onion-Parsley

4   carrots
½ onion
1   cup parsley

Carrot-Pepper

5 carrots
½ green or red bell pepper

Carrot-Radish

4 carrots
2 radishes with greens

Carrot-Spinach

5 carrots
1 cup spinach

Carrot-Turnip

4 carrots
1 turnip with greens

Carrot-Wheatgrass

5 carrots
½ cup wheatgrass

Carrot–Sweet Potato

4 carrots
½ sweet potato

CAULIFLOWER

Like broccoli and brussels sprouts, cauliflower also evolved from the wild cabbage. It is thought that the original variety may have originated in Asia, but it was in Italy that it was developed to its present form. Because cauliflower is susceptible to both frost and hot weather, over 80% of the U.S. crop is produced in California.

KEY BENEFITS

Cauliflower is not as nutrient-dense as many of the other cabbage-family vegetables. Its white color is a sign that it has much less of the beneficial carotenes and chlorophyll. Cauliflower is a good source of boron (see page 29), as it will not grow well in boron-deficient soil. For the anticancer properties of cauliflower, see Cabbage.

NUTRITIONAL ANALYSIS

1 cup raw cauliflower, cut into 1-inch pieces (100g)

Nutrients and Units

Water	92.26	g
Calories	24	kcal
Protein	2	g
Fat	0.18	g
Carbohydrate	4.9	g

VITAMINS

Vitamin A	2	RE
Vitamin C	71.5	mg
Thiamine	0.76	mg
Riboflavin	0.057	mg
Niacin	0.63	mg
Vitamin B6	0.231	mg
Folic acid	66	mcg

MINERALS

Potassium	355	mg
Calcium	29	mg

Iron	0.58	mg
Magnesium	14	mg
Phosphorus	46	mg
Sodium	15	mg

SELECTION

Cauliflower should be fresh-looking, with clean, white-colored flower heads and crisp fresh leaves. Avoid cauliflower with wilted leaves, dirty flower heads, or obvious signs of decay.

PREPARATION FOR JUICING

Wash organic cauliflower; soak or spray nonorganic cauliflower with a biodegradable wash, then scrub and rinse. Cut the cauliflower into pieces that will easily fit into the juicer.

CAULIFLOWER JUICE RECIPES

Straight cauliflower juice is pretty strong; mix ½ cup of it with the Basic Carrot-Apple or The Energizer in Chapter 7.

CELERY

Celery is a member of the umbelliferous family along with carrots, parsley, and fennel. Modern celery evolved from wild celery native to the Mediterranean, where its seeds were once widely used as a medicine, particularly as a diuretic.

KEY BENEFITS

Celery is rich in potassium and sodium. Celery juice after a workout serves as a great electrolyte replacement drink.

Celery contains anutrient compounds known as coumarins, which are being shown to help in preventing cancer and enhancing the activity of certain white blood cells. Coumarin compounds also tone the vascular system, lower blood pressure, and may be useful in cases of migraine.

NUTRITIONAL ANALYSIS

3 raw celery ribs (120g)

Nutrients and Units

Water	114	g
Calories	18	kcal
Protein	0.8	g
Fat	1.4	g
Carbohydrate	4.4	g

VITAMINS

Vitamin A	16	RE
Vitamin C	7.6	mg
Thiamine	0.04	mg
Riboflavin	0.04	mg
Niacin	0.36	mg
Vitamin B6	0.036	mg
Folic acid	10.6	mcg

MINERALS

Potassium	340	mg
Calcium	44	mg
Iron	0.6	mg
Magnesium	14	mg
Phosphorus	32	mg
Sodium	106	mg

SELECTION

The best celery is light-green, fresh-looking, and crisp. The ribs should snap, not bend. Limp, pliable celery should be avoided.

PREPARATION FOR JUICING

Cut off the bottom portion to separate the ribs and allow for complete cleaning. Wash organic celery; soak or spray nonorganic celery with a biodegradable wash, then rinse.

CELERY JUICE RECIPES

Celery juice can be quite satisfying on its own, but it is usually mixed with other juices. See these recipes above: Asparagus-Carrot-Celery, Asparagus-Celery, Beet-Carrot-Celery, Broccoli-Carrot-Celery, Cabbage-Carrot-Celery, and Carrot-Celery. See the following recipes in Chapter 7: Cleansing Cocktail, Cucumber Cooler, Diuretic Formula, Everything but the Kitchen Sink, Femme Fatale, Potassium Power, Super V-7, Vitamin U for Ulcer, and Waldorf Salad.

Celery-Cabbage
4 celery ribs
½ head of cabbage, cut into wedges

Celery-Cucumber
4 celery ribs
½ cucumber

Celery-Cucumber-Kale
4 celery ribs
½ cucumber
3 kale leaves

Celery-Cucumber-Parsley

  4 celery ribs
  ½ cucumber
  ½ cup parsley

Celery-Cucumber-Parsley-Spinach

  4 celery ribs
  ½ cucumber
  ½ cup parsley
  ½ cup spinach

Celery–Dandelion Greens

  4 celery ribs
  1 cup dandelion greens

Celery-Fennel

  4 celery ribs
  ½ fennel bulb

Celery-Fennel-Parsley

  4 celery ribs
  ½ fennel bulb
  ½ cup parsley

Celery-Lettuce-Spinach

  4 celery ribs
  1 head of lettuce, cut into wedges
  ½ cup spinach

CHARD, SWISS (SEE KALE)

COLLARDS (SEE KALE)

CUCUMBERS

The cucumber is a tropical plant that originated in Southeast Asia. Cucumbers are refreshing vegetables in their fresh form; unfortunately, over 70% of the U.S. cucumber crop is used to make pickles.

KEY BENEFITS

Fresh cucumbers are composed primarily of water. The hard skin of the cucumber is an excellent source of some important minerals like silica. Silica contributes to the strength of connective tissue, which holds the body together. It includes the intracellular cement, muscles, tendons, ligaments, cartilage, and bone. Without silica, connective tissue would not be properly constructed. Cucumber juice is often recommended as a source of silica and as a way to improve the complexion and the health of the skin.

NUTRITIONAL ANALYSIS

1 raw cucumber (301g)

Nutrients and Units

Water	289	g
Calories	39	kcal
Protein	1.63g	
Fat	0.39g	
Carbohydrate	8.76g	

VITAMINS

Vitamin A	14	RE
Vitamin C	0.09mg	
Thiamine	0.06mg	

Riboflavin	0.9	mg
Niacin	0.752	mg
Vitamin B6	0.156	mg
Folic acid	42	mcg

MINERALS

Potassium	448	mg
Calcium	42	mg
Iron	0.84	mg
Magnesium	33	mg
Phosphorus	51	mg
Sodium	6	mg

SELECTION

Cucumbers should be fresh-looking, well shaped, and medium to dark green in color. Avoid withered, shriveled, and yellow ones. Try to buy cucumbers that have not been waxed.

PREPARATION FOR JUICING

Wash organic cucumbers; soak or spray nonorganic ones with a biodegradable wash, then rinse. Waxed cucumbers should be peeled.

CUCUMBER JUICE RECIPES

Cucumber juice on its own is not that satisfying; it's best mixed with other juices. See these recipes above: Carrot-Cucumber-Parsley, Celery-Cucumber, Celery-Cucumber-Parsley, Celery-Cucumber-Parsley-Spinach, and Celery-Cucumber-Kale. See the following recipes in Chapter 7: Cucumber Cooler, Everything but the Kitchen Sink, Salad in a Glass, and Super V-7.

Cucumber-Tomato-Parsley

½ cucumber

2   tomatoes, quartered

½ cup parsley

Cucumber-Tomato-Watercress

½ cucumber

2   tomatoes, quartered

1   bunch of watercress

DANDELIONS

The dandelion is a perennial plant with an almost worldwide distribution. While many individuals consider the dandelion an unwanted weed, herbalists all over the world have revered this valuable herb. Its name is a corruption of the French for "tooth-of-the-lion" (dent-de-lion), which describes the herb's leaves with their several large, pointed teeth. Its scientific name, *Taraxacum,* is from the Greek *taraxos* (disorder) and *akos* (remedy). This alludes to dandelions' ability to correct a multitude of disorders.

Dandelions have a long history of folk use throughout the world. In Europe, dandelions were used in the treatment of fevers, boils, eye problems, diarrhea, fluid retention, liver congestion, heartburn, and various skin problems. In China, dandelions have been used in the treatment of breast problems (cancer, inflammation, lack of milk flow), liver diseases, appendicitis, and digestive ailments. Its use in India, Russia, and other parts of the world revolved primarily around its action on the liver.

KEY BENEFITS

Dandelions are a rich source of nutrients and other compounds that may improve liver functions, promote weight loss, and possess diuretic effects. The dandelion contains

greater nutritional value than many other vegetables. It is particularly high in vitamins and minerals, protein, choline, inulin, and pectins. Its carotenoid content is extremely high as reflected by its higher vitamin A content than carrots: dandelions have 14,000 I.U. (international units) of vitamin A per 100g compared to 11,000 I.U. for carrots. Dandelions should be thought of as an extremely nutritious food and rich source of medicinal compounds that have a toning effect on the body. Both the greens and the roots can be used for this purpose.

Dandelion root is regarded as one of the finest liver remedies, both as food and medicine. Studies in humans and laboratory animals have shown that dandelion root enhances the flow of bile, improving such conditions as liver congestion, bile duct inflammation, hepatitis, gallstones, and jaundice. Dandelions' action on increasing bile flow is twofold: They have a direct effect on the liver, causing an increase in bile production and flow to the gallbladder (choleretic effect), and a direct effect on the gallbladder, causing contraction and release of stored bile (cholagogue effect). Dandelions' historical use in such a wide variety of conditions is probably closely related to their ability to improve liver function.

Dandelions have also been used historically in the treatment of obesity. This fact prompted researchers to investigate dandelions' effect on the body weight of experimental animals. When these animals were administered a fluid extract of dandelion greens for one month, they lost as much as 30% of their initial weight. Much of the weight loss appeared to be a result of significant diuretic activity.

SELECTION

Wild dandelions are plentiful in most parts of the United States. Dandelion greens are often available commercially as well, especially at open markets and health food stores. The fresher the dandelions, the better.

PREPARATION FOR JUICING

Dandelion greens and roots should be washed thoroughly and be prepared to feed into the juicer.

DANDELION JUICE RECIPES

You will want to mix the dandelion with other vegetables. See these recipes above: Carrot–Dandelion Greens, Carrot-Dandelion Root, Carrot-Dandelions-Spinach, and Celery–Dandelion Greens. See the Diuretic Formula and Liver Tonic recipes in Chapter 7.

FENNEL

Fennel is a member of the umbelliferous family along with celery, carrots, and parsley. Like many vegetables, modern-day fennel was developed in Italy. It has a long history as a medicinal plant in the Mediterranean region. Fennel has a licorice flavor.

KEY BENEFITS

Fennel does offer some good nutrition, but it is largely used for its more medicinal effects. Among herbalists, fennel is referred to as: (1) an intestinal antispasmodic; (2) a carminative, or compound that relieves or expels gas; (3) a stomachic, or compound that tones and strengthens the stomach; and (4) an anodyne, or compound that relieves or soothes pain. Fennel also contains substances known as phytoestrogens, making it useful in many conditions specific to women, especially menopause. Fennel is even higher in coumarin compounds than celery or carrots.

SELECTION

Fennel should be bought with both the bulb and stems attached. It should be fresh-looking and, like celery, its branches should snap with pressure as opposed to bending.

PREPARATION FOR JUICING

Wash organic fennel; soak or spray nonorganic fennel with a biodegradable wash, then rinse. Cut up the bulb and branches so that they can be fed into the juicer.

FENNEL JUICE RECIPES

Fennel is pretty strong on its own unless you really love licorice. Otherwise, mix it with carrots, apples, pears, or celery. See the recipes for Carrot-Fennel, Celery-Fennel, and Celery-Fennel-Parsley above, and Femme Fatale and Tummy Tonic in Chapter 7.

GARLIC

Garlic is a member of the lily family that is cultivated worldwide. The garlic bulb is composed of individual cloves enclosed in a papery skin. Garlic has been used throughout history to treat a wide variety of conditions. Sanskrit records document garlic remedies approximately 5,000 years ago; the Chinese have been using it for at least 3,000 years. The Codex Ebers, an Egyptian medical papyrus dating to about 1550 B.C., mentions garlic as an effective remedy for a variety of ailments. Hippocrates, Aristotle, and Pliny cited numerous therapeutic applications for garlic. In general, garlic has been used throughout the world to treat coughs, toothache, earache, dandruff, hypertension, atherosclerosis, hysteria, diarrhea, dysentery, diphtheria, vaginitis, and many other conditions.

Stories, verse, and folklore (such as its alleged ability to ward off vampires) give historical documentation to garlic's power. Sir John Harrington in *The Englishman's Doctor,* written in 1609, summarized garlic's virtues and faults:

> Garlic then have power to save from death
> Bear with it though it maketh unsavory breath,
> And scorn not garlic like some that think
> It only maketh men wink and drink and stink.

KEY BENEFITS

The therapeutic uses of garlic are quite extensive. Its consumption should be encouraged, despite its odor, especially in individuals with elevated cholesterol levels, heart disease, high blood pressure, diabetes, candidiasis, asthma, infections (particularly of the respiratory tract), and gastrointestinal complaints.

Many studies have found that garlic decreases total serum cholesterol levels while increasing serum HDL-cholesterol levels. HDL cholesterol, often termed the "good" cholesterol, is a protective factor against heart disease. Garlic has also demonstrated blood-pressure-lowering action in many studies. Garlic has been shown to decrease the systolic pressure by 20–30mm Hg (millimeters mercury) and the diastolic by 10–20mm Hg in patients with high blood pressure.

In a 1979 study of three populations of vegetarians in the Jain community in India who consumed differing amounts of garlic and onions, numerous favorable effects on blood lipids were observed in the group that consumed the largest amount (see below).[7] The study is quite significant because the subjects had nearly identical diets, except for garlic and onion ingestion.

EFFECTS OF GARLIC AND ONION CONSUMPTION ON SERUM LIPIDS UNDER CAREFULLY MATCHED DIETS

GARLIC ONION CONSUMPTION	CHOLESTEROL LEVEL	TRIGLYCERIDE LEVEL
Garlic 50g/wk onion 600g/wk	159mg/dl	52mg/dl
Garlic 10g/wk onion 200g/wk	172mg/dl	75mg/dl
No garlic or onions	208mg/dl	109mg/dl

Garlic has also been found to:

- lower blood sugar levels in diabetes
- help eliminate heavy metals like lead
- promote detoxification reactions
- enhance the immune system
- protect against cancer
- be an antibacterial
- be an antifungal
- be an anthelmintic (kills worms)

It is beyond the scope of this book to detail all the wonderful properties of this truly remarkable medicinal plant. There are whole books on garlic, and in my book *The Healing Power of Herbs,* garlic receives much attention, if you are interested.

Much of garlic's therapeutic effect is thought to result from its volatile factors, composed of sulfur-containing compounds: allicin, diallyl disulfide, diallyl trisulfide, and others. Other constituents of garlic include additional sulfur-containing compounds, high concentrations of trace minerals (particularly selenium and germanium), glucosinolates, and enzymes. The compound allicin is mainly responsible for the pungent odor of garlic.

Many of the therapeutic compounds in garlic have not been found in cooked, processed, and commercial forms, so the broad range of beneficial effects attributed to garlic are best obtained from fresh, raw garlic, although limited, specific effects can be obtained from the other forms. For medicinal purposes, at least three cloves of garlic a day is recommended; for protective measures, at least three cloves a day is a good idea.

SELECTION

Buy fresh garlic. Do not buy garlic that is soft, shows evidence of decay such as mildew or darkening, or is beginning to sprout.

PREPARATION FOR JUICING

Remove the garlic clove from the bulb and wrap it in a green vegetable, such as parsley. This accomplishes two things: (1) it prevents the garlic from popping out of the juicer and (2) the chlorophyll helps bind some of the odor. It is a good idea to juice the garlic first, as the other vegetables will remove the odor from the machine.

GARLIC JUICE RECIPES

You can add garlic to The Energizer in Chapter 7. Also see the Cholesterol-Lowering Tonic and Immune Power Vegetable recipes in Chapter 7.

GINGER

Ginger is an erect perennial herb that has thick tuberous rhizones (underground stems and root). It originated in southern Asia, although it is now extensively cultivated throughout the tropics (for example, in India, China, Jamaica, Haiti, and Nigeria). Exports from Jamaica to all parts of the world amount to more than 2 million pounds annually. Ginger has been used for thousands of years in China to treat numerous health conditions.

KEY BENEFITS

Historically, the majority of complaints for which ginger was used concerned the gastrointestinal system. Ginger is generally regarded as an excellent carminative (a substance that promotes the elimination of intestinal gas) and intestinal spasmolytic (a substance that relaxes and soothes the intestinal tract).

A clue to ginger's success in eliminating gastrointestinal distress is offered by recent double-blind studies that showed ginger to be very effective in preventing the symptoms of mo-

tion sickness, especially seasickness.[8] In fact, in one study ginger was shown to be far superior to Dramamine, a commonly used over-the-counter and prescription drug for motion sickness. Ginger reduces all symptoms associated with motion sickness, including dizziness, nausea, vomiting, and cold sweating.

Ginger has also been used to treat the nausea and vomiting associated with pregnancy. Recently, the benefit of ginger was confirmed in hyperemesis gravidarum, the most severe form of morning sickness.[9] This condition usually requires hospitalization. Gingerroot powder at a dose of 250mg four times a day brought about a significant reduction in both the severity of the nausea and the number of attacks of vomiting.

Ginger has also been shown to be a very potent inhibitor of the formation of the inflammatory compounds prostaglandin and thromboxanes. This could explain some of ginger's historical use as an anti-inflammatory agent. However, ginger also has strong antioxidant properties and contains a protease (a protein-digesting enzyme) that may have action similar to bromelain on inflammation.

In one clinical study, seven patients with rheumatoid arthritis, for whom conventional drugs had provided only temporary or partial relief, were treated with ginger. One patient took 50g a day of lightly cooked ginger, while the remaining six took either 5g fresh or 0.1–1g powdered ginger daily. All patients reported substantial improvement, including pain relief, joint mobility, and decrease in swelling and morning stiffness.[10] Ginger, like garlic, has also been shown to significantly reduce serum and improve liver function.

Although most scientific studies have used powdered gingerroot, fresh gingerroot at an equivalent dosage is believed to yield even better results because it contains active enzymes. Most studies used 1g powdered gingerroot. This would be equivalent to about 10g or one-third ounce fresh gingerroot, roughly a quarter-inch slice.

SELECTION

Fresh ginger can now be purchased in the produce section at most supermarkets. The bronze root should be fresh-looking, with no signs of decay like soft spots, mildew, or a dry, wrinkled skin. Store fresh ginger in the refrigerator.

PREPARATION FOR JUICING

Slice the amount of ginger desired and feed into the juicer. It's best to feed the ginger in first, before whatever you are juicing it with.

GINGER JUICE RECIPES

See the following recipes in Chapter 7: Apple Spice, Cholesterol-Lowering Tonic, Digestive Delight, The Don Juan, Ginger Ale, Ginger Hopper, Immune Power Vegetable, Kill the Cold, Pineapple-Ginger Ale, and Tummy Tonic. And see Apple-Pear-Ginger in Chapter 5.

JERUSALEM ARTICHOKE

The Jerusalem artichoke, often referred to as a "sunchoke," is native to North America. It is not part of the artichoke family; in fact, it belongs to the daisy family (Compositae) and is closely related to the sunflower. The name *Jerusalem* is thought to be an English corruption of Ter Neusen, the place in The Netherlands from which the plant was introduced into England. Alternatively, Webster says *Jerusalem* is a corruption of *girasole,* the Italian word for sunflower. The plants were cultivated by the Native Americans.

KEY BENEFITS

Jerusalem artichokes are full of a sugar known as inulin. Inulin is a polysaccharide, or starch, that is handled by the body differently than other sugars. In fact, inulin is not used by the body for energy metabolism. This makes Jerusalem ar-

tichokes extremely beneficial to diabetics. Inulin has actually been shown to improve blood sugar control. Since the body does not utilize the primary carbohydrate of the Jerusalem artichoke, the calorie content is virtually nil, only seven per 100g (roughly 3½ ounces).

Inulin also has the ability to enhance a component of our immune system known as complement.[11] Specifically, inulin is an activator of the alternative complement pathway, which is responsible for increasing host defense mechanisms such as neutralization of viruses; destruction of bacteria; and increasing the movement of white blood cells to areas of infection. Many medicinal plants, such as echinacea and burdock, owe much of their immune-enhancing effect to inulin. Jerusalem artichokes are one of the richest sources of inulin available.

SELECTION

Fresh Jerusalem artichokes should be firm, with fresh-looking skin.

PREPARATION FOR JUICING

Wash organic Jerusalem artichokes; soak or spray nonorganic ones with a biodegradable wash, then rinse.

JERUSALEM ARTICHOKE JUICE RECIPES

The juice is pretty harsh by itself; it is best to mix it with carrot, apple, or pear. Also see the Carrot–Jerusalem Artichoke recipe above and Immune Power Vegetable in Chapter 7.

JICAMA

Jicama, pronounced "HEE-ka-ma," is a turnip-shaped root vegetable native to Mexico and Central America.

KEY BENEFITS

Jicama's high water content makes it a fantastic vegetable to juice. Like most root vegetables, it is especially high in potassium. Its flavor is very similar to that of water chestnut. In fact, many Oriental restaurants will substitute jicama for the more expensive water chestnut.

SELECTION

High-quality jicama should be firm and heavy for its size. Jicama that is shriveled, soft, or particularly large is likely to be tough, woody, and contain less water.

PREPARATION FOR JUICING

Wash organic jicama; soak or spray nonorganic jicama with a biodegradable wash, then scrub and rinse. Cut up the jicama into pieces that will feed into the juicer.

JICAMA JUICE RECIPES

Jicama is too potent to drink on its own. See the Carrot-Jicama recipe above, and Jicama-Carrot-Apple in Chapter 7.

KALE AND OTHER GREENS

Kale is probably the closest relative of wild cabbage in the whole cabbage family. Kale and collards are essentially the same vegetable, but kale has leaves with curly edges and is less tolerant of heat. Kale is native to Europe, where it has been cultivated for many centuries as food for people as well as animals. In the United States, kale is grown primarily on the East Coast from Delaware to Florida. Other greens of the cabbage family such as mustard greens, turnip greens, kohl-

rabi, and watercress offer benefits similar to those of kale and collards and can be used similarly.

KEY BENEFITS

Greens are rich in essential vitamins and minerals, especially calcium, potassium, and iron. A cup of kale or collards actually has more calcium than a cup of milk. Furthermore, they contain almost three times as much calcium as phosphorus. High phosphorus consumption has been linked to osteoporosis, as it will reduce the utilization and promote the excretion of calcium.

As members of the cabbage family, greens exhibit the same sort of anticancer properties (see Cabbage). They are excellent sources of many anutrients, especially pigments like carotenes and chlorophyll. Greens are among the most highly nutritious vegetables.

NUTRITIONAL ANALYSIS

1 cup raw kale (100g)

Nutrients and Units

Water	88g
Calories	45kcal
Protein	5g
Fat	1g
Carbohydrate	7g

VITAMINS

Vitamin A	1,066RE
Vitamin C	102mg

Thiamine	0.11	mg
Riboflavin	0.2	mg
Niacin	1.8	mg
Vitamin B6	0.18	mg
Folic acid	183	mcg

MINERALS

Potassium	243	mg
Calcium	206	mg
Iron	1.8	mg
Magnesium	12	mg
Phosphorus	64	mg
Sodium	2	mg

SELECTION

High-quality greens are fresh, tender, and dark green. Avoid greens that show dry or yellowing leaves, evidence of insect injury, or decay.

PREPARATION FOR JUICING

Rinse organic greens; soak or spray nonorganic greens with a biodegradable wash, then rinse. A salad spinner is a great way to dry the leaves and prepare them for juicing. Usually the leaves can be fed into the juicer intact; large leaves may need to be cut.

KALE JUICE RECIPES

The juice of kale and other greens is difficult to drink on its own, but can be added to other juices for a delicious and healthy drink. See the Carrot-Kale and Celery-Cucumber-Kale recipes above, and the following recipes in Chapter 7: Bone Builder's Cocktail, Cruciferous Surprise, Green Drink, Iron Plus, and Purple Cow.

LEEKS

Leeks are related to onions and garlic. While the bulbs of garlic and onions are typically the edible portion, it is the leaves and stems of leeks that are eaten rather than the long, narrow bulb.

KEY BENEFITS

Leeks share many of the qualities of onions and garlic, only they are less dense. This means that larger quantities of leeks would need to be consumed in order to produce effects similar to those of onions and garlic. Presumably, leeks can lower cholesterol levels, improve the immune system, and fight cancer in a way similar to onions and garlic.

NUTRITIONAL ANALYSIS

½ cup raw leeks (100g)

Nutrients and Units

Water	82	g
Calories	90	kcal
Protein	2.2	g
Fat	0.3	g
Carbohydrate	11.2	g

VITAMINS

Vitamin A	60	RE
Vitamin C	17	mg
Thiamine	0.11	mg
Riboflavin	0.06	mg
Niacin	0.5	mg

Vitamin B6	0.05	mg
Folic acid	20	mcg

MINERALS

Potassium	347	mg
Calcium	50	mg
Iron	1.1	mg
Magnesium	6	mg
Phosphorus	50	mg
Sodium	5	mg

SELECTION

Leeks should have broad, dark, solid leaves and a thick white neck with a base about one inch in diameter. Those with yellowing, wilted, or discolored leaves should be avoided.

PREPARATION FOR JUICING

Wash organic leeks; soak or spray nonorganic ones with a biodegradable wash, and then rinse. Slice lengthwise into pieces that can be fed into the juicer.

LEEK JUICE RECIPES

Leek juice is quite potent on its own, so it is best to mix it with more palatable bases such as Basic Carrot-Apple (Chapter 7), or in Carrot-Leek-Parsley, above.

LETTUCE

Lettuce is native to the Mediterranean region and is a member of the daisy or sunflower family (Compositae). The ancient Greeks and Romans hailed lettuce as a medicinal plant. Augustus Caesar went so far as to erect a statue in its

honor, believing it had aided his recovery from illness. Lettuce is a major salad crop of the United States. There are numerous types of lettuce, such as iceberg, romaine, butterhead, and looseleaf varieties.

KEY BENEFITS

In general, the darker the lettuce the greater the nutrient content: romaine > looseleaf > butterhead > iceberg.

NUTRITIONAL ANALYSIS

1 head raw iceberg

Nutrients and Units

Water	517	g
Calories	70	kcal
Protein	5.4	g
Fat	1	g
Carbohydrate	11.26	g

VITAMINS

Vitamin A	178	RE
Vitamin C	21	mg
Thiamine	0.25	mg
Riboflavin	0.16	mg
Niacin	1	mg
Vitamin B6	0.22	mg
Folic acid	301	mcg

MINERALS

Potassium	852	mg
Calcium	102	mg

Iron	2.7mg
Magnesium	48 mg
Phosphorus	108 mg
Sodium	48 mg

SELECTION

Good-quality lettuce will appear fresh, crisp, and free from any evidence of decay. Avoid lettuce that has a rusty appearance and signs of decay.

PREPARATION FOR JUICING

Rinse organic lettuce; soak or spray nonorganic lettuce with a biodegradable wash, then rinse. A salad spinner is a great way to dry the leaves and prepare them for juicing. Cut the lettuce into wedges or feed the leaves into the juicer intact, folding them if necessary. The darker lettuce varieties are the best to juice.

LETTUCE JUICE RECIPES

Lettuce can be added to a number of the recipes in Chapter 7: Basic Carrot-Apple, The Energizer, and Salad in a Glass, to name a few. Also see the Carrot-Lettuce and Celery-Lettuce-Spinach recipes above.

MUSTARD GREENS (SEE KALE)

ONIONS

Onions, like garlic, are members of the lily family. Onions originated in the central part of Asia, from Iran to Pakistan, and moved northward into the southern part of Russia. Numerous forms and varieties of onion are cultivated worldwide. Common varieties are white globe, yellow globe, red globe, and green (shallots or scallions). With the globe onions, the part used is the fleshy bulb, while with green

onions, both the long slender bulb and the green leaves are used.

KEY BENEFITS

Onions, like garlic, contain a variety of organic sulfur compounds. Onion also has the enzyme alliinase, which is released when the onion is cut or crushed, resulting in the so-called crying factor (propanethial S-oxide). Other constituents include flavonoids (primarily quercetin), phenolic acids, sterols, saponins, pectin, and volatile oils.

Although not nearly as valued a medicinal agent as garlic, onion has been used almost as widely. Onions possess many of the same effects as garlic (see Garlic). There are, however, some subtle differences that make one more advantageous than the other in certain conditions.

Like garlic, onions and onion extracts have been shown to decrease blood lipid levels, prevent clot formation, and lower blood pressure in several clinical studies. Onions have been found to have significant blood-sugar-lowering action, comparable to that of the prescription drugs tolbutamide and phenformin often given to diabetics. The active blood-sugar-lowering principle in onions is believed to be allyl propyl disulphide (APDS), although other constituents, such as flavonoids, may play a significant role as well. Experimental and clinical evidence suggests that APDS lowers glucose by competing with insulin (also a disulfide molecule) for breakdown sites in the liver, thereby increasing the life span of insulin. Other mechanisms, such as increased liver metabolism of glucose or increased insulin secretion, have also been proposed.

Onion has been used historically to treat asthma. Its effectiveness in asthma is due to its ability to inhibit the production of compounds that cause the bronchial muscle to spasm, along with its ability to relax the bronchial muscle.

An onion extract was found to destroy tumor cells in test tubes and to arrest tumor growth when tumor cells were implanted in rats. The onion extract was shown to be unusually nontoxic, since a dose as high as 40 times the dose required to kill the tumor cells had no adverse effect on the host. In addition, green onions have been shown to exhibit significant activity against leukemia in mice.

Again, the liberal use of the *Allium* species (garlic, onions, leeks, and so on) appears particularly indicated considering the major disease processes (such as atherosclerosis, diabetes, and cancer) of the 20th century.

NUTRITIONAL ANALYSIS

½ onion, raw (100g)

Nutrients and Units

Water	90	g
Calories	34	kcal
Protein	1.18	g
Fat	0.26	g
Carbohydrate	7.3	g

VITAMINS

Vitamin A	0	
Vitamin C	8.4	mg
Thiamine	0.06	mg
Riboflavin	0.01	mg
Niacin	0.1	mg
Vitamin B6	0.157	mg
Folic acid	19.9	mcg

MINERALS

Potassium	155	mg
Calcium	25	mg

Iron	0.37mg
Magnesium	10 mg
Phosphorus	29 mg
Sodium	2 mg

SELECTION

Globe onions should be clean and hard, with dry, smooth skins. Avoid onions in which the seed stem has developed, as well as those that are misshaped and show evidence of decay.

Green onions should have fresh-looking green tops and a white neck. Yellowing, wilted, or discolored tops should be avoided.

PREPARATION FOR JUICING

Peel and wash organic onions; peel, then soak or spray nonorganic ones with a biodegradable wash, then rinse.

ONION JUICE RECIPES

Onion juice is too strong to be consumed straight. You can substitute onion for garlic. And see the Carrot-Onion-Parsley recipe above.

PARSLEY

Parsley, like carrots and celery, is a member of the umbelliferous family. It is native to the Mediterranean. Unfortunately, most parsley is now used as a garnish instead of in foods.

KEY BENEFITS

Parsley is extremely rich in a wide number of nutrients, chlorophyll, and carotenes. The high chlorophyll content of parsley can help mask the odor and taste of many other

foods, such as garlic. Ingesting parsley has been shown to inhibit the increase in urinary mutagenicity following the ingestion of fried foods. This is most likely due to the chlorophyll (see Chapter 3), but other compounds in parsley such as vitamin C, flavonoids, and carotenes have also been shown to inhibit the cancer-causing properties of fried foods.

Parsley has benefits well beyond its chlorophyll content. It has long been used for medicinal purposes and is regarded as an excellent "nerve stimulant." Empirical evidence seems to support and is probably responsible for so many juice enthusiasts labeling parsley-containing juices "energy drinks."

NUTRITIONAL ANALYSIS

½ cup chopped parsley (30g)

Nutrients and Units

Water	26.5	g
Calories	10	kcal
Protein	0.66	g
Fat	0.09	g
Carbohydrate	2	g

VITAMINS

Vitamin A	156	RE
Vitamin C	27	mg
Thiamine	0.02	mg
Riboflavin	0.033	mg
Niacin	0.2	mg
Vitamin B6	0.05	mg
Folic acid	55	mcg

MINERALS

Potassium	161	mg
Calcium	39	mg
Iron	1.86	mg
Magnesium	13	mg
Phosphorus	12	mg
Sodium	12	mg

SELECTION

Parsley can be grown at home or purchased fresh from the grocery store. Parsley should be bright, fresh, green, and free from yellowed leaves or dirt. Slightly wilted parsley can be revived to freshness in cold water.

PREPARATION FOR JUICING

Wash organic parsley; soak or spray nonorganic parsley with a biodegradable wash, then rinse. Use a salad spinner to dry. Ball up sprigs of parsley in your hand and then feed into the juicer.

PARSLEY JUICE RECIPES

Parsley juice on its own is quite strong; it is wise to mix it with other juices. See the following recipes above: Beet-Carrot-Parsley, Broccoli-Carrot-Parsley, Cabbage-Carrot-Parsley, Carrot-Celery-Parsley, Carrot-Cucumber-Parsley, Carrot-Leek-Parsley, Carrot-Onion-Parsley, Celery-Cucumber-Parsley, Celery-Cucumber-Parsley-Spinich, Celery-Fennel-Parsley, and Cucumber-Tomato-Parsley.

See the following recipes in Chapter 7: Bone Builder's Cocktail, Cholesterol-Lowering Tonic, Cleansing Cocktail, Cucumber Cooler, The Don Juan, The Energizer, Green Drink,

Immune Power Vegetable, Popeye's Power Drink, Potassium Power, Salad in a Glass, and Super V-7.

Parsley-Spinach-Tomato

½ cup parsley

½ cup spinach

4   tomatoes, quartered

Parsley-Tomato

1 cup parsley

4 tomatoes, quartered

PEPPERS, BELL (SWEET)

Peppers belong to the Solanaceae, or nightshade, family of vegetables that also includes potatoes, eggplant, and tomatoes. Peppers are native to Central and South America. Sweet or bell peppers are available in red, green, yellow, and black. Red bell peppers are actually green peppers that have been allowed to ripen on the vine; hence they are much sweeter. The hotter chili peppers are used in much smaller quantities in the diet.

KEY BENEFITS

Peppers are one of the most nutrient-dense foods and are good sources of a wide number of nutrients, including vitamin C. The red variety will have significantly higher levels of nutrients than the green. Peppers contain substances that have been shown to prevent clot formation and reduce the risk for heart attacks and strokes. Capsaicin from chili peppers is used topically in the treatment of psoriasis and postherpes neuralgia. It should also be pointed out that nightshade-family vegetables may aggravate arthritis in some individuals.

NUTRITIONAL ANALYSIS

1 green bell pepper (74g)

Nutrients and Units

Water	68.65	g
Calories	18	kcal
Protein	0.63	g
Fat	0.33	g
Carbohydrate	3.93	g

VITAMINS

Vitamin A	39	RE
Vitamin C	95	mg
Thiamine	0.063	mg
Riboflavin	0.037	mg
Niacin	0.407	mg
Vitamin B6	0.121	mg
Folic acid	12.5	mcg

MINERALS

Potassium	144	mg
Calcium	4	mg
Iron	0.94	mg
Magnesium	10	mg
Phosphorus	16	mg
Sodium	2	mg

SELECTION

Peppers should be fresh, firm, and bright in appearance.
Avoid peppers that appear dry or wrinkled, or show signs of
decay.

PREPARATION FOR JUICING

Wash organic peppers; soak or spray nonorganic ones with a biodegradable wash, then rinse. Remove the seeds and cut into pieces that will fit into the juicer.

PEPPER JUICE RECIPES

Straight green bell pepper juice is pretty strong; you may want to use only a quarter to a half a pepper in a base of tomato or carrot juice. Larger amounts of the sweet red variety can be used. See the Beet-Carrot-Pepper and Carrot-Pepper recipes above, and the following recipes in Chapter 7: Bone Builder's Cocktail, Everything but the Kitchen Sink, High C, Purple Cow, Salad in a Glass, Some Like It Hot, and Super V-7.

Pepper-Tomato

½ green or red bell pepper
4 tomatoes, quartered

POTATOES

Potatoes are members of the Solanaceae, or nightshade, family and are native to the Andes Mountains of Bolivia and Peru, where they have been cultivated for over 7,000 years. Sometime during the early part of the 16th century, potatoes were brought to Europe by Spanish explorers. Potatoes are a hardy crop and became a particular favorite in Ireland, largely as a result of the tremendous rise in population in the 1800s coupled with a declining economy. Because an acre and a half of land could produce enough potatoes to feed a family of five for a year, most Irish families came to depend on potatoes for sustenance. Several hundred varieties of potatoes are grown worldwide. For juicing, the red and russet varieties may be best.

KEY BENEFITS

Potatoes are an excellent source of many nutrients, including potassium and vitamin C. Potatoes are actually low in calories: a medium-sized potato contains only 115. Unfortunately, most Americans eat the potato in the form of french fries, hash browns, potato chips, or baked potatoes smothered with butter or sour cream. The protein quality of potatoes is actually quite high. Although it is about the same amount as in corn or rice, potatoes contain lysine, an essential amino acid often lacking in grains. Potatoes, like other members of the nightshade family, may aggravate arthritis in some individuals.

As an interesting side note, boiled potato peel dressings may offer effective treatment for skin wounds in some Third World countries where modern skin graft procedures are not available. Preliminary studies conducted at a children's hospital in Bombay, India, using a dressing prepared from boiled potato peelings attached to standard gauze bandages have demonstrated good therapeutic effect in promoting healing and keeping the burn from becoming infected. Patients noted pain relief, and physicians noted reduced levels of bacterial contamination and faster healing.[12]

SELECTION

Use only high-quality potatoes that are firm and display the characteristic features of the variety. Avoid wilted, leathery, or discolored potatoes, especially those with a green tint.

PREPARATION FOR JUICING

Wash organic potatoes; soak or spray nonorganic ones with a biodegradable wash, then scrub and rinse. Cut the potato into pieces that will fit into the juicer.

POTATO JUICE RECIPES

Potato juice on its own is quite stout and will turn black quickly if not consumed immediately. Add 1 potato to the following recipes in Chapter 7, if desired: Basic Carrot-Apple, The Energizer, Ginger Hopper.

SPINACH

Spinach is believed to have originated in southwestern Asia or Persia. It has been cultivated in many areas of the world for hundreds of years, not only as a food but also as an important medicinal plant in many traditional systems of medicine.

KEY BENEFITS

There is much lore surrounding spinach. It was regarded historically as a plant with remarkable abilities to restore energy, increase vitality, and improve the quality of the blood. There are sound reasons for such results, primarily the fact that spinach contains twice as much iron as most other greens. Spinach, like other vegetables that contain chlorophyll and carotene, is a strong protector against cancer.

NUTRITIONAL ANALYSIS

1 cup raw spinach (55g)

Nutrients and Units

Water	51	g
Calories	12	kcal
Protein	1.6	g

Fat	0.2	g
Carbohydrate	2	g

VITAMINS

Vitamin A	376	RE
Vitamin C	16	mg
Thiamine	0.04	mg
Riboflavin	0.1	mg
Niacin	0.4	mg
Vitamin B6	0.11	mg
Folic acid	109.2	mcg

MINERALS

Potassium	312	mg
Calcium	56	mg
Iron	1.52	mg
Magnesium	44	mg
Phosphorus	28	mg
Sodium	22	mg

SELECTION

Fresh spinach should be dark green, fresh-looking, and free from any evidence of decay. Slightly wilted spinach can be revived to freshness in cold water.

PREPARATION FOR JUICING

Wash organic spinach; soak or spray nonorganic spinach with a biodegradable wash, then rinse. Use a salad spinner to dry. Ball up sprigs of spinach in your hand and then feed into the juicer.

SPINACH JUICE RECIPES

Spinach juice on its own is quite strong; it is wise to mix it with other juices, such as carrot, tomato, and apple. See the following recipes above: Beet-Carrot-Spinach, Brussels Sprouts–Carrot-Spinach, Carrot-Dandelions-Spinach, Carrot-Spinach, Celery-Cucumber-Parsley-Spinach, Celery-Lettuce-Spinach, and Parsley-Spinach-Tomato.

See the following recipes in Chapter 7: Everything but the Kitchen Sink, Green Drink, Popeye's Power Drink, Potassium Power, and Super V-7.

Spinach-Tomato

1 cup spinach

4 tomatoes, quartered

SWEET POTATOES AND YAMS

Sweet potatoes belong not to the potato (Solanaceae) family, but to the morning-glory (Convolvulaceae) family. The sweet potato is native to Mexico and Central and South America. In the United States, we tend to call the darker, sweeter sweet potato a yam, which is inaccurate. True yams are native to Southeast Asia and Africa and differ slightly from the sweet potato; for example, true yams have very little carotene.

KEY BENEFITS

Sweet potatoes are exceptionally rich in carotenes. The darker the variety, the higher the concentration. Sweet potatoes are also rich in vitamin C, calcium, and potassium.

NUTRITIONAL ANALYSIS*

1 sweet potato, cooked and peeled (114g)

*No information is available on raw sweet potatoes, but it is estimated that they would have at least 10%–15% more nutritional value than cooked sweet potatoes.

Nutrients and Units

Water	79	g
Calories	160	kcal
Protein	2	g
Fat	1	g
Carbohydrate	37	g

VITAMINS

Vitamin A	923	RE
Vitamin C	25	mg
Thiamine	0.1	mg
Riboflavin	0.08	mg
Niacin	0.8	mg
Vitamin B6	0.06	mg
Folic acid	85	mcg

MINERALS

Potassium	342	mg
Calcium	46	mg
Iron	1	mg
Magnesium	14	mg
Phosphorus	66	mg
Sodium	10	mg

SELECTION

Use only high-quality sweet potatoes that are firm and display the characteristic features of the variety. Remember, the darker the variety, the higher the carotene content. As a bonus, the darker ones are sweeter and taste better. Avoid wilted, leathery, and discolored sweet potatoes, especially those with a green tint.

PREPARATION FOR JUICING

Wash organic sweet potatoes; soak or spray nonorganic ones with a biodegradable wash, then rinse. Slice into pieces that the juicer can accommodate.

SWEET POTATO JUICE RECIPES

If you like to eat sweet potatoes or yams, the flavor of the juice may agree with you. I prefer the Better Red than Dead recipe (see Chapter 7) to straight sweet potato or yam juice. Also, see the Beet–Sweet Potato and Carrot–Sweet Potato recipes above.

TOMATOES

At one time, tomatoes were believed to be poisonous; now they are one of the leading vegetable crops of the world. The tomato, like many other members of the Solanaceae, or nightshade, family, originated in Central and South America. There are numerous varieties of tomatoes, all of which are suitable for juicing.

KEY BENEFITS

The tomato is packed full of nutrition, especially when fully ripe, as red tomatoes have up to four times the amount of beta-carotene as green tomatoes. Tomatoes supply good amounts of vitamin C, carotenes, and potassium. Tomatoes, like other members of the nightshade family, may aggravate arthritis in some individuals.

NUTRITIONAL ANALYSIS

1 raw tomato (123g)

Nutrients and Units

Water	115	g
Calories	24	kcal
Protein	1.09	g
Fat	0.26	g
Carbohydrate	5.34	g

VITAMINS

Vitamin A	239	RE
Vitamin C	21.6	mg
Thiamine	0.07	mg
Riboflavin	0.06	mg
Niacin	0.738	mg
Vitamin B6	0.06	mg
Folic acid	11.5	mcg

MINERALS

Potassium	254	mg
Calcium	8	mg
Iron	0.59	mg
Magnesium	14	mg
Phosphorus	29	mg
Sodium	10	mg

SELECTION

Good-quality tomatoes are well formed and plump, fully red, firm, and free from bruise marks. Avoid tomatoes that are soft and show signs of bruising or decay.

PREPARATION FOR JUICING

Wash organic tomatoes; soak or spray nonorganic ones with a biodegradable wash, then rinse. Cut them in just small enough wedges to feed into the machine.

TOMATO JUICE RECIPES

Tomato juice is refreshing alone, or use it in one of the tomato-based recipes above or in the next chapter. See these recipes above: Cucumber-Tomato-Parsley, Cucumber-Tomato-Watercress, Pepper-Tomato, and Spinach-Tomato. See the following recipes in Chapter 7: Cucumber Cooler, Everything but the Kitchen Sink, Potassium Power, Salad in a Glass, Some Like It Hot, and Tomato Zest.

TURNIP GREENS (SEE KALE)

7

FIFTY FABULOUS
JUICE RECIPES

It is easy to fall into the habit of making the same juice every day. To help you explore, I offer here some of my favorite juice recipes. And I encourage you to develop your own recipes. Don't be concerned about following the recipe exactly. Be flexible. Have fun! My suggestion is to consume as wide an assortment of fresh fruit and vegetable juices as possible. To make it easier, try to consume the fullest possible spectrum of colors of fruits and vegetables each week. More and more evidence is showing us that the plant pigments contain some of the most important properties. Chlorophyll, carotenes, and flavonoids are all being found to possess some truly remarkable health benefits. So drink a rainbow of fresh fruits and vegetable juices!

SOME JUICING GUIDELINES

There are some guidelines that you should try to follow when developing your own recipes. A general rule of thumb is to let your taste buds be your guide. They should steer you in the right direction. For example, it is often recommended that no more than one-fourth of a green juice be composed of greens like parsley, kale, lettuce, wheatgrass, or spinach. Your taste buds should tell you that too strong a green drink doesn't taste all that good; it should be mixed with carrots or apples.

The most important guideline is to enjoy yourself. It's fun to experiment and find a combination that is unusually delicious. I had that experience a few years ago when I invented the Better Red than Dead recipe. It contains carrots, beets, and sweet potatoes. Yes, sweet potatoes—and it is delicious.

Sometimes you may discover a new juice that you don't like. This is great too. Why? Because it shows you are willing to at least try something new. I have made some juices that I won't make again, but at least I tried.

Many people say you should not mix fruits and vegetables, but there is little (if any) scientific information to support

this contention. The belief is based more on philosophy than physiology. Nonetheless, some people do seem to have difficulty with combined fruits and vegetables, complaining of gassy discomfort. If you are one of these people, you should avoid mixing fruits and vegetables together. The exceptions to this rule appear to be carrots and apples, as these foods seem to mix well with either a fruit or a vegetable. Again, let your taste buds be your guide.

It is best to drink the juice as soon as it is made. This offers the greatest possible benefit. However, if this is not possible, store the juice in an airtight container in the refrigerator or in a thermos. You should store the juice for no longer than 12 hours at the absolute maximum. The fresher the juice, the better it is for you.

ABOUT THE RECIPES

Each of the recipes should yield approximately 8 to 12 ounces fresh juice. The actual yield will depend on the size of the fruit or vegetable and the quality of your juicer. Unless otherwise noted, all of the recipes call for medium-size fruits and vegetables. The nutrient content is an approximation based on accepted values. *Note:* Items in **bold** represent more than 35% of the recommended dietary allowance.

APPLE SPICE

This is a delicious zesty apple juice that seems to warm you up. I consider it a fall drink and an alternative to hot apple cider. This drink is good for the liver, as both ginger and cinnamon have been shown to improve liver function. It's also a nice drink before going to bed.

> ¼-inch slice of ginger
> 3 apples, cut into wedges
> ¼ teaspoon cinnamon

Juice the ginger along with the apples, add the cinnamon to the glass of juice, and stir.

Approximate Nutrient Content

Calories	244
Protein	0.92g
Carbohydrate	63 g
Fat	1.52g
Vitamin A	21.3 RE
Vitamin C	**23.6 mg**
Vitamin E	1.2 mg
Thiamine	1.2 mg
Riboflavin	0.07mg
Niacin	0.06mg
Vitamin B6	0.3 mg
Folic acid	11.7 mcg
Sodium	0.3 mg
Calcium	37 mg
Magnesium	18.3 mg
Potassium	480 mg
Iron	1.12mg

APRICOT-MANGO AMBROSIA

This is a fun drink packed full of good nutrition. Apricots and mangoes are extremely good sources of beta-carotenes, while oranges are known as a rich source of vitamin C and flavonoids.

4 apricots, pitted and halved

1 mango, pitted and sliced

1 orange, peeled

Juice the apricots first, then the mango, and finish with the orange. You may need to stir the juice up so that all the flavors mix.

Approximate Nutrient Content

Calories	295	
Protein	5	g
Carbohydrate	73	g
Fat	1.38	g
Vitamin A	**1,220**	**RE**
Vitamin C	**210**	**mg**
Vitamin E	**5.3**	**mg**
Thiamine	0.34	mg
Riboflavin	0.35	mg
Niacin	2.8	mg
Vitamin B6	**0.63**	**mg**
Folic acid	**91**	**mcg**
Sodium	5.3	mg
Calcium	144	mg
Magnesium	54	mg
Potassium	**1,203**	**mg**
Iron	1.28	mg

BASIC CARROT-APPLE

This is a simple "basic" juice, but that doesn't mean it isn't a delicious or supernutrient drink. In fact, this drink is called "The Champ" by Jay Kordich, the Juiceman, as it has been his favorite for over 40 years. And for good reason—Jay believes this juice saved his life. The Basic Carrot-Apple can serve as a base for adding small quantities of more potent vegetables like greens, spinach, radishes, and beets.

   4 carrots
   2 apples, cut into wedges

Alternate the carrots and apple wedges so that the juice mixes well.

Approximate Nutrient Content

Calories	286	
Protein	3.4	g
Carbohydrate	71	g
Fat	1.56	g
Vitamin A	**8,114**	**RE**
Vitamin C	**44**	**mg**
Vitamin E	**2.8**	**mg**
Thiamine	0.33	mg
Riboflavin	0.2	mg
Niacin	2.9	mg
Vitamin B6	**0.64**	**mg**
Folic acid	48	mcg
Sodium	102	mg
Calcium	96	mg
Magnesium	56	mg
Potassium	**1,250**	**mg**
Iron	2.04	mg

BETTER RED THAN DEAD

This is one of my absolute favorite drinks, especially in the fall. It is one of the richest drinks for carotene content, especially the red and orange carotenes. Drinking this juice will give you that George Hamilton look, the year-round tan. I named this drink "Better Red than Dead" because one of my professors, Dr. Ed Madison, gave a lecture on the benefits of carotenes with this title. His lecture really made an impression on me and I have tried to maintain high carotene intake ever since. As noted earlier, there is a strong correlation between carotene levels and life expectancy. This is just a phenomenal drink for raising carotene levels. My wife, Gina, and I will often load up on this drink before we go on vacation to a

sunny location because the carotenes will be deposited in the skin, where they will protect against sunburn.

    1   beet, including top
    ½ medium-size sweet potato, cut into strips
    3   carrots

Juice the beet first, then the yam strips, and then the carrots.

Approximate Nutrient Content

Calories	198	
Protein	4	g
Carbohydrate	46	g
Fat	0.56	g
Vitamin A	**6,076**	**RE**
Vitamin C	**34**	**mg**
Vitamin E	**3.55**	**mg**
Thiamine	0.34	mg
Riboflavin	0.15	mg
Niacin	2.64	mg
Vitamin B6	**0.56**	**mg**
Folic acid	**86**	**mcg**
Sodium	123	mg
Calcium	75	mg
Magnesium	76	mg
Potassium	**1,420**	**mg**
Iron	2	mg

BONE BUILDER'S COCKTAIL

This drink provides the key nutrients required for building bone, such as calcium, boron, magnesium, other minerals, and vitamin K1. This is an extremely nutrient-dense drink in that it provides incredible levels of nutrients per calorie.

> 3 kale leaves
> 2 collard green leaves
>   Handful of parsley
> 3 carrots
> 1 apple, cut into wedges
> ½ green bell pepper

Bunch the greens up to feed them into the juicer; use the carrots and apples to help push the greens through.

Approximate Nutrient Content

Calories	211	
Protein	5.6	g
Carbohydrate	50	g
Fat	1.37	g
Vitamin A	**6,639**	**RE**
Vitamin C	**110**	**mg**
Vitamin E	**6.2**	**mg**
Thiamine	0.33	mg
Riboflavin	0.36	mg
Niacin	3	mg
Vitamin B6	**0.68**	**mg**
Folic acid	**173**	**mcg**
Sodium	143	mg
Calcium	212	mg
Magnesium	**102**	**mg**
Potassium	**1,384**	**mg**
Iron	4.4	mg

BOWEL REGULATOR

Pears and apples are excellent sources of water-soluble fibers like pectin, while prunes contain well-known laxative properties. This mixture has a very good tonifying effect on the bowel. It is very useful in minor cases of constipation.

    2 pitted plums or pitted prunes from a jar or dried
        pitted prunes that have been soaked in 1 cup
        water
    2 apples, cut into wedges
    1 pear, sliced

If using prunes instead of plums, blend the prunes along with 1 cup water in a blender at high speed. Juice apples and pear alternately, add it to the prune juice in a glass, and stir.

Approximate Nutrient Content

Calories	269	
Protein	1.6	g
Carbohydrate	72	g
Fat	1.52	g
Vitamin A	78	RE
Vitamin C	**24.3**	**mg**
Vitamin E	2.1	mg
Thiamine	0.1	mg
Riboflavin	0.23	mg
Niacin	1.1	mg
Vitamin B6	0.23	mg
Folic acid	20	mcg
Sodium	4.8	mg
Calcium	52	mg

Magnesium	32.4	mg
Potassium	**697**	**mg**
Iron	1.35	mg

CHERRY POP

Cherries are an excellent source of flavonoids and have been shown to be of great benefit in cases of arthritis, especially gout. This is a delicious drink that parents can serve their children instead of soft drinks or artificially flavored and colored "fruit" drinks.

> 2 cups pitted cherries
> 1 apple, cut into wedges
> 4 ounces sparkling mineral water

Juice the cherries and the apple. Pour into a glass with some ice, then top it off with the mineral water.

Approximate Nutrient Content

Calories	228	
Protein	2.7	g
Carbohydrate	55	g
Fat	2.6	g
Vitamin A	52	RE
Vitamin C	**22**	**mg**
Vitamin E	1.9	mg
Thiamine	0.12	mg
Riboflavin	0.14	mg
Niacin	1	mg
Vitamin B6	0.17	mg
Folic acid	12.3	mcg
Sodium	1	mg
Calcium	40	mg

Magnesium	30 mg
Potassium	615 mg
Iron	1.2mg

CHOLESTEROL-LOWERING TONIC

If you really want to bring cholesterol levels down quickly, this zesty juice, along with a diet rich in grains, legumes, vegetables, and fruit, can do the trick. It contains a mixture of foods that have been shown to lower cholesterol levels on their own. By combining all of these foods, it is possible that an even greater effect will be produced than if the foods were consumed separately. This is known as a synergistic effect. My personal experience is that this juice can, in fact, be very effective in lowering cholesterol levels. The garlic, ginger, and the capsicum in the Tabasco sauce also work to prevent blood platelets from bunching together, thereby significantly reducing the risk of heart attack and stroke.

¼-inch slice of ginger
1 clove garlic
 Handful of parsley (to absorb some of the odor of the garlic)
4 carrots
1 apple, cut into wedges
 Splash of Tabasco sauce (optional)

Juice the ginger and garlic first by placing them in the center of a handful of parsley and feed it into the juicer. (This reduces much of the garlic's odor.) Follow with the carrots and the apple.

Approximate Nutrient Content

Calories	215
Protein	4g

Carbohydrate	53	g
Fat	1.06	g
Vitamin A	**8,107**	**RE**
Vitamin C	**55**	**mg**
Vitamin E	2.4	mg
Thiamine	0.3	mg
Riboflavin	0.21	mg
Niacin	3	mg
Vitamin B6	0.54	mg
Folic acid	**81**	**mcg**
Sodium	176	mg
Calcium	117	mg
Magnesium	59	mg
Potassium	**1,220**	**mg**
Iron	3.04	mg

CLEANSING COCKTAIL

This is a good drink during a juice fast, because it is nutrient-dense and supports detoxification. If wheatgrass is not available, parsley will suffice. Wheatgrass is extremely rich in chlorophyll and antioxidants; look for it at health food stores if you are not familiar with it. It is very good for you.

½ cup wheatgrass or parsley
4 carrots
1 apple, cut into wedges
2 celery ribs
½ beet with top

Bunch up the wheatgrass or parsley and push through the juicer with the aid of a carrot. Alternate remaining ingredients to ensure proper mixing.

Approximate Nutrient Content

Calories	249	
Protein	5	g
Carbohydrate	60	g
Fat	1.3	g
Vitamin A	**8,118**	**RE**
Vitamin C	**63**	**mg**
Vitamin E	**5.8**	**mg**
Thiamine	0.35	mg
Riboflavin	0.21	mg
Niacin	3.4	mg
Vitamin B6	0.59	mg
Folic acid	**133**	**mcg**
Sodium	221	mg
Calcium	149	mg
Magnesium	**99**	**mg**
Potassium	**1,693**	**mg**
Iron	3.9	mg

COLOR ME PINK

This is a great way to start the day, especially if you are on a weight-loss program. It is low in calories, but the natural fruit sugars will keep your appetite in check. This drink is particularly rich in flavonoids. Make sure you leave as much of the albido (the white pithy part of the peel) as possible on the grapefruit, as this is rich in flavonoids.

    1   cup raspberries
    ½ pink grapefruit, peeled

Juice the raspberries first, then the grapefruit.

Approximate Nutrient Content

Calories	100	
Protein	2	g
Carbohydrate	26	g
Fat	0.9	g
Vitamin A	31	RE
Vitamin C	**73**	**mg**
Vitamin E	0.9	mg
Thiamine	0.08	mg
Riboflavin	0.12	mg
Niacin	1.5	mg
Vitamin B6	0.2	mg
Folic acid	12.2	mcg
Sodium	0	
Calcium	41	mg
Magnesium	32	mg
Potassium	355	mg
Iron	0.8	mg

CRANBERRY CRUSH

Cranberries are fantastic for keeping the bladder free from infection. In this drink the bitter principles of the cranberries are masked by the flavor and natural sweetness of the apples and orange.

> 1 cup cranberries
> 2 apples, cut into wedges
> 1 orange, peeled

Juice the cranberries first, then alternate the apples and the orange.

Approximate Nutrient Content

Calories	306	
Protein	2.8	g
Carbohydrate	78	g
Fat	1.8	g
Vitamin A	56	RE
Vitamin C	**104**	**mg**
Vitamin E	1.7	mg
Thiamine	0.25	mg
Riboflavin	0.24	mg
Niacin	1.1	mg
Vitamin B6	0.4	mg
Folic acid	57	mcg
Sodium	11	mg
Calcium	81	mg
Magnesium	32	mg
Potassium	**684**	**mg**
Iron	0.9	mg

CRUCIFEROUS SURPRISE

The surprise is just how delicious this drink actually tastes. This is a super-nutrient-dense drink that is rich in the sulfur-containing compounds of the cruciferous (cabbage)-family vegetables that have been shown to enhance the body's ability to detoxify cancer-causing chemicals and eliminate heavy metals. It is also rich in calcium, vitamin C, and carotenes. This is a great drink during a juice fast.

> 3 or 4 kale leaves
> ½ cup broccoli florets with stems
> ½ head of cabbage, cut into wedges

2 carrots

2 apples, cut into wedges

Feed the kale first, followed by the broccoli and cabbage. Then alternate the carrots and apple wedges.

Approximate Nutrient Content

Calories	272	
Protein	6.1	g
Carbohydrate	67	g
Fat	1.8	g
Vitamin A	**4,520**	**RE**
Vitamin C	**136**	**mg**
Vitamin E	**7.9**	**mg**
Thiamine	0.31	mg
Riboflavin	0.4	mg
Niacin	2.5	mg
Vitamin B6	**0.79**	**mg**
Folic acid	**126**	**mcg**
Sodium	126	mg
Calcium	183	mg
Magnesium	**104**	**mg**
Potassium	**1,497**	**mg**
Iron	3.9	mg

CUCUMBER COOLER

This drink can be served over ice, or you can juice the tomato the day before and pour into an ice cube tray.

1 tomato, quartered

1 cucumber

2 celery ribs

Parsley sprig for garnish

Juice tomato, followed by the cucumber and celery.

Approximate Nutrient Content

Calories	212	
Protein	2.86g	
Carbohydrate	53	g
Fat	1.64g	
Vitamin A	167	RE
Vitamin C	**47**	**mg**
Vitamin E	2.7	mg
Thiamine	0.17mg	
Riboflavin	0.14mg	
Niacin	1.4	mg
Vitamin B6	0.47mg	
Folic acid	41	mcg
Sodium	84	mg
Calcium	70	mg
Magnesium	48	mg
Potassium	**956**	**mg**
Iron	12	mg

DIGESTIVE DELIGHT

This is a fantastic drink for people who have trouble with indigestion. It is packed full of enzymes, as well as compounds in ginger and mint that help ease spastic intestines and promote the elimination of gas.

¼-inch slice of ginger
½ handful of mint
1 kiwifruit, unpeeled
¼ pineapple with skin, sliced

Juice the ginger and mint first, followed by the kiwifruit and then the pineapple.

Approximate Nutrient Content

Calories	256	
Protein	2.3	g
Carbohydrate	63	g
Fat	2.3	g
Vitamin A	23	RE
Vitamin C	**139**	**mg**
Vitamin E	0.5	mg
Thiamine	**0.51**	**mg**
Riboflavin	0.19	mg
Niacin	2.4	mg
Vitamin B6	0.5	mg
Folic acid	44.5	mcg
Sodium	9	mg
Calcium	50	mg
Magnesium	78	mg
Potassium	**727**	**mg**
Iron	1.8	mg

DIURETIC FORMULA

The diuretic activity of an extract of dandelion greens has been shown to be comparable to that of the drug Lasix. Carrots and celery also have some diuretic activity.

> Handful of dandelion greens (or endive if not available)
> 2 celery ribs
> 4 carrots

Juice the greens first, followed by the celery and carrots.

Approximate Nutrient Content

Calories	148
Protein	5g

Carbohydrate	34	g
Fat	0.96g	
Vitamin A	**8,486**	**RE**
Vitamin C	**49**	**mg**
Vitamin E	**7.2**	**mg**
Thiamine	0.35mg	
Riboflavin	0.38mg	
Niacin	3.3	mg
Vitamin B6	**0.66mg**	
Folic acid	**156**	**mcg**
Sodium	214	mg
Calcium	160	mg
Magnesium	**98**	**mg**
Potassium	**1,472**	**mg**
Iron	3.44mg	

THE DON JUAN

Ginger has been shown to possess some mild aphrodisiac effects and has a long history of use as a sexual aid in the Arabic system of medicine. The parsley will provide increased energy and awareness.

> ¼-inch slice of ginger
> Handful of parsley
> ¼ pineapple with skin, sliced

Place the ginger in the middle of the parsley and feed into the juicer first, followed by the pineapple.

Approximate Nutrient Content

Calories	118
Protein	1.1g
Carbohydrate	29.5g

Fat	1.05g	
Vitamin A	6	RE
Vitamin C	**45**	**mg**
Vitamin E	0.3	mg
Thiamine	0.15mg	
Riboflavin	0.15mg	
Niacin	1.15mg	
Vitamin B6	0.15mg	
Folic acid	46	mcg
Sodium	5.5	mg
Calcium	29.5	mg
Magnesium	35.5	mg
Potassium	317	mg
Iron	1.5	mg

THE ENERGIZER

This drink is a popular replacement for coffee to increase energy and alertness. It is nutrient-packed, yet very low in calories.

> Handful of parsley
> 6 carrots

Bunch the parsley in your hand first, then place in the feeder of the juicer and push it through with a carrot (fat end first).

Approximate Nutrient Content

Calories	192	
Protein	4.6	g
Carbohydrate	45	g
Fat	0.84g	
Vitamin A	**1,215**	**RE**

Vitamin C	60	mg
Vitamin E	3	mg
Thiamine	0.42mg	
Riboflavin	0.24mg	
Niacin	158	mg
Vitamin B6	0.66mg	
Folic acid	97	mcg
Sodium	158	mg
Calcium	140	mg
Magnesium	74	mg
Potassium	1,506	mg
Iron	3.36mg	

ENZYMES GALORE

This drink is packed with enzymes. It is a fantastic way to start the day, a super breakfast. It also tastes great without the banana.

½ mango, pitted
2 oranges, peeled
½ papaya, seeded, sliced
¼ pineapple with skin, sliced
1 banana, peeled

Juice the mango first, followed by one of the oranges, then the papaya, another orange, and finally the pineapple. Pour into a blender, add the banana, and liquefy.

Approximate Nutrient Content

Calories	355
Protein	5.1g
Carbohydrate	90 g
Fat	1.5g

Vitamin A	772	RE
Vitamin C	272	mg
Vitamin E	3	mg
Thiamine	0.4	mg
Riboflavin	0.4	mg
Niacin	2.5	mg
Vitamin B6	1.1	mg
Folic acid	101	mcg
Sodium	7	mg
Calcium	158	mg
Magnesium	84	mg
Potassium	1,476	mg
Iron	0.9	mg

EVERYTHING BUT THE KITCHEN SINK

Have you ever wondered what it would taste like if you mixed all those summer vegetables you have growing in your garden to form one glass of juice? Well, here is your chance. I think it tastes pretty good and I definitely know it is good for me. This drink really seems to wake me up.

Handful of spinach
1 celery rib
3 carrots
2 radishes
1 apple, cut into wedges
½ cucumber
1 tomato, quartered
½ cup broccoli florets with stems
½ green bell pepper

Juice the spinach first, followed by the celery to push it through. Alternate the remaining vegetables with a carrot coming last..

Approximate Nutrient Content

Calories	247	
Protein	7.3	g
Carbohydrate	58	g
Fat	2	g
Vitamin A	**6,522**	**RE**
Vitamin C	**165**	**mg**
Vitamin E	**5.9**	**mg**
Thiamine	**0.52**	**mg**
Riboflavin	0.42	mg
Niacin	4	mg
Vitamin B6	**0.9**	**mg**
Folic acid	**167**	**mcg**
Sodium	169	mg
Calcium	159	mg
Magnesium	**114**	**mg**
Potassium	**1,862**	**mg**
Iron	4.3	mg

FEMME FATALE

A femme fatale is a woman who attracts men with her aura of charm and mystery. This drink supports the female glandular system. Both fennel and celery contain what are known as phytoestrogens. These plant compounds can occupy binding sites for female hormones and exert hormonelike effects. This drink is helpful in a wide range of conditions specific to women, including menopause and PMS, because of these phytoestrogens as well as the important nutrients contained in the juice (such as potassium, magnesium, folic acid, and vitamin B6).

1 small fennel
2 apples, cut into wedges
2 celery ribs

Cut the fennel into narrow wedges and feed it into the juicer, followed by the apples and celery.

Approximate Nutrient Content

Calories	238	
Protein	2.76g	
Carbohydrate	60	g
Fat	1.52g	
Vitamin A	32	RE
Vitamin C	**32.6**	**mg**
Vitamin E	2.2	mg
Thiamine	0.13mg	
Riboflavin	0.09mg	
Niacin	0.82mg	
Vitamin B6	0.22mg	
Folic acid	**83**	**mcg**
Sodium	92	mg
Calcium	108	mg
Magnesium	50	mg
Potassium	**734**	**mg**
Iron	3.2	mg

GINA'S SWEET SUNSHINE

This is the specialty of my wife, Gina. She loves this drink in the morning, and it is one of my favorites as well. It *is* a good morning drink, as well as a good mid-afternoon pick-me-up, because of its rich supply of natural sugars. The effervescent qualities of the mineral water seem to enhance the

aroma of this juice, which makes this an extremely delicious, refreshing drink.

1   cup green grapes
½ lemon, peeled
2   oranges, peeled
4   ounces sparkling mineral water

Juice the grapes first, followed by the lemon and oranges. Mix with mineral water and stir.

Approximate Nutrient Content

Calories	163	
Protein	3	g
Carbohydrate	42	g
Fat	0.66	g
Vitamin A	59	RE
Vitamin C	**157**	**mg**
Vitamin E	2.4	mg
Thiamine	0.25	mg
Riboflavin	0.23	mg
Niacin	0.99	mg
Vitamin B6	0.03	mg
Folic acid	**84**	**mcg**
Sodium	0.5	mg
Calcium	117	mg
Magnesium	28	mg
Potassium	606	mg
Iron	0.54	mg

GINGER ALE

This is a great drink for children, a super replacement for sugary soft drinks. It is also useful in relieving intestinal upset.

¼-inch slice of ginger
1   lemon wedge
1   green apple, cut into wedges
4   ounces sparkling mineral water

Juice the ginger first, followed by the lemon wedge and then the apple. Stir in the mineral water.

Approximate Nutrient Content

Calories	85
Protein	0.45g
Carbohydrate	22.4 g
Fat	0.55g
Vitamin A	7.5 RE
Vitamin C	15.5 mg
Vitamin E	0.4 mg
Thiamine	0.03mg
Riboflavin	0.02mg
Niacin	0.12mg
Vitamin B6	0.12mg
Folic acid	5.4 mcg
Sodium	1.25mg
Calcium	13.8 mg
Magnesium	6 mg
Potassium	179 mg
Iron	0.4 mg

GINGER HOPPER

A good drink to lower cholesterol without using garlic.
¼-inch slice of ginger
1   apple, cut into wedges
4   carrots

Juice the ginger first, followed by the apple, then the carrots.

Approximate Nutrient Content

Calories	205	
Protein	3.1	g
Carbohydrate	50	g
Fat	1.06	g
Vitamin A	**8,107**	**RE**
Vitamin C	**36**	**mg**
Vitamin E	2.4	mg
Thiamine	0.3	mg
Riboflavin	0.18	mg
Niacin	2.8	mg
Vitamin B6	0.54	mg
Folic acid	44	mcg
Sodium	101	mg
Calcium	86	mg
Magnesium	50	mg
Potassium	**1,091**	**mg**
Iron	1.74	mg

GREEN DRINK

Have you ever heard the age-old statement, "When you are green inside, you are clean inside"? I believe there is some truth to that statement. This is probably one of the healthiest juice recipes available.

Handful of parsley or wheatgrass
2 Granny Smith apples, cut into wedges
2 kale leaves
Handful of spinach

Juice the parsley or wheatgrass first, then one of the apples, the kale, spinach, and the second apple.

Approximate Nutrient Content

Calories	189	
Protein	4	g
Carbohydrate	47	g
Fat	1.4	g
Vitamin A	**766**	**RE**
Vitamin C	**56**	**mg**
Vitamin E	**8.4**	**mg**
Thiamine	0.13	mg
Riboflavin	0.44	mg
Niacin	1.1	mg
Vitamin B6	**0.6**	**mg**
Folic acid	**244**	**mcg**
Sodium	94	mg
Calcium	145	mg
Magnesium	**104**	**mg**
Potassium	**996**	**mg**
Iron	4.4	mg

HIGH C

Often we think of citrus fruits as having the highest vitamin C content, but actually several vegetables are higher in vitamin C per serving than citrus.

½ cup broccoli florets with stems
1   green bell pepper
1   sweet red bell pepper
2   apples, cut into wedges

Juice the broccoli first, then the peppers, then the apples.

Approximate Nutrient Content

Calories	210
Protein	3.1 g
Carbohydrate	52 g
Fat	1.75g
Vitamin A	**700 RE**
Vitamin C	**296 mg**
Vitamin E	**3.3 mg**
Thiamine	0.27mg
Riboflavin	0.16mg
Niacin	1.28mg
Vitamin B6	0.47mg
Folic acid	**64 mcg**
Sodium	18 mg
Calcium	49 mg
Magnesium	43 mg
Potassium	**749 mg**
Iron	2.8 mg

IMMUNE POWER FRUIT

This is a drink rich in many nutrients vital to the immune system. It also abounds in flavonoids and other anutrients that have demonstrated antiviral and antioxidant effects. The banana increases the viscosity of the drink and allows for slower absorption of the sugars, an important goal during an active infection.

    1   orange, peeled
    ½ pineapple with skin, sliced
    ½ cup strawberries
    1   banana, peeled

Juice the orange, pineapple, and strawberries; place in a blender with the banana and liquefy.

Approximate Nutrient Content

Calories	246	
Protein	3.6	g
Carbohydrate	56	g
Fat	1.8	g
Vitamin A	71	RE
Vitamin C	**58**	**mg**
Vitamin E	1.5	mg
Thiamine	**0.38mg**	
Riboflavin	0.37mg	
Niacin	2.1	mg
Vitamin B6	**0.84mg**	
Folic acid	**88**	**mcg**
Sodium	4	mg
Calcium	143	mg
Magnesium	96	mg
Potassium	**1,047**	**mg**
Iron	1.6	mg

IMMUNE POWER VEGETABLE

This is a great immune fortifier, especially useful during an active infection. The Jerusalem artichokes, with their high content of inulin, provide additional immune-enhancing benefits.

2   cloves garlic
¼-inch slice of ginger
    Handful of parsley
4   carrots
1   apple, cut into wedges
1   cup Jerusalem artichokes (optional)

Place the garlic and ginger in the center of the parlsey; push it through with a carrot. Alternate the remaining ingredients.

Approximate Nutrient Content

Calories	242	
Protein	5.1	g
Carbohydrate	59	g
Fat	1.16	g
Vitamin A	**8,115**	**RE**
Vitamin C	**51**	**mg**
Vitamin E	2.55	mg
Thiamine	0.34	mg
Riboflavin	0.21	mg
Niacin	3.2	mg
Vitamin B6	0.59	mg
Folic acid	**89**	**mcg**
Sodium	147	mg
Calcium	133	mg
Magnesium	80	mg
Potassium	**1,327**	**mg**
Iron	3.34	mg

IRON PLUS

This is an incredible drink, especially for women prone to anemia and low iron levels. Check out the high content of folic acid, magnesium, vitamins C and E, as well as iron that this drink provides.

- 1 beet with top
- 2 kale leaves
- ½ cup broccoli florets with stems
- 4 carrots
- 1 apple, cut into wedges

Alternate feeding the ingredients into the juicer.

Approximate Nutrient Content

Calories	255	
Protein	6.9	g
Carbohydrate	60	g
Fat	1.45	g
Vitamin A	**8,552**	**RE**
Vitamin C	**97**	**mg**
Vitamin E	**8.7**	**mg**
Thiamine	0.4	mg
Riboflavin	0.4	mg
Niacin	3.7	mg
Vitamin B6	0.84	mg
Folic acid	**229**	**mcg**
Sodium	199	mg
Calcium	172	mg
Magnesium	**136.3**	**mg**
Potassium	**1,812**	**mg**
Iron	**5.5**	**mg**

JICAMA-CARROT-APPLE

This is an example of using carrots and apples as a base to add additional vegetables.

> 1-inch slice of jicama
> 4 carrots
> 1 apple, cut into wedges

Alternate feeding the ingredients into the juicer.

Approximate Nutrient Content

Calories	256
Protein	3.1 g
Carbohydrate	62 g
Fat	1.46g
Vitamin A	**8,107 RE**
Vitamin C	**40 mg**
Vitamin E	2.8 mg
Thiamine	0.33mg
Riboflavin	0.2 mg
Niacin	2.9 mg
Vitamin B6	0.55mg
Folic acid	**97 mcg**
Sodium	92 mg
Calcium	87 mg
Magnesium	51 mg
Potassium	**1,152 mg**
Iron	1.94mg

KIDS' FAVORITE

Kids absolutely love this drink, which can also be frozen. It is a great juice for the dieter (check out the low calories) and the individual with heart troubles, and it gives the immune system a boost.

½ cantaloupe with skin, sliced
1 cup strawberries

Alternate cantaloupe slices with the strawberries.

Approximate Nutrient Content

Calories	139	
Protein	3.2	g
Carbohydrate	33	g
Fat	1.3	g
Vitamin A	**865**	**RE**
Vitamin C	**197**	**mg**
Vitamin E	0.6	mg
Thiamine	0.13	mg
Riboflavin	0.2	mg
Niacin	1.8	mg
Vitamin B6	0.4	mg
Folic acid	72	mcg
Sodium	25	mg
Calcium	49	mg
Magnesium	44	mg
Potassium	**1,072**	**mg**
Iron	1.2	mg

KILL THE COLD

This is a great drink to have when you feel a cold coming on. It is a diaphoretic tea, meaning that it will warm you from the inside and promote perspiration. It's pleasant to drink even when you don't have a cold and just want to warm up and feel good.

    1-inch slice of ginger
    ¼ lemon with skin
    1   cup hot water

Juice the ginger and lemon and add it to the cup of water. You may want to add some nutmeg or cardamom.

LIVER MOVER

This drink is called the Liver Mover because it promotes the flow of bile and fat to and from the liver. This is very useful in promoting weight loss and in liver disorders.

½ beet including top
2 or 3 apples, cut into wedges

Alternate feeding the beets and apple wedges into the juicer.

Approximate Nutrient Content

Calories	188	
Protein	1.5	g
Carbohydrate	48	g
Fat	1.04	g
Vitamin A	15	RE
Vitamin C	**20.3**	**mg**
Vitamin E	**2.85**	**mg**
Thiamine	0.07	mg
Riboflavin	0.05	mg
Niacin	0.43	mg
Vitamin B6	0.23	mg
Folic acid	53	mcg
Sodium	44	mg
Calcium	29	mg
Magnesium	13	mg
Potassium	584	mg
Iron	1.13	mg

LIVER TONIC

A tonic is a substance that improves tone or function. A liver tonic is a substance that specifically improves the tone

and function of the liver, the most important organ of metabolism and detoxification. If dandelion roots cannot be found, you can substitute 4 radishes.

    1   dandelion root
    ½ beet including top
    2   carrots
    1   apple, cut into wedges

Alternate feeding the ingredients into the juicer.

Approximate Nutrient Content

Calories	254	
Protein	3.4	g
Carbohydrate	63	g
Fat	1.56	g
Vitamin A	**7,414**	**RE**
Vitamin C	**44**	**mg**
Vitamin E	2.8	mg
Thiamine	0.33	mg
Riboflavin	0.2	mg
Niacin	2.9	mg
Vitamin B6	**0.63**	**mg**
Folic acid	58	mcg
Sodium	102	mg
Calcium	96	mg
Magnesium	56	mg
Potassium	**1,250**	**mg**
Iron	2.04	mg

MIKE'S FAVORITE

From the name of the recipe, it is obvious that I like this drink. It is my favorite not only for taste, but also for what I

know it can do for my health. It is a great breakfast drink, quite thick and filling.

¼ pineapple with skin, sliced
1 cup blueberries
1 banana, peeled

Juice the pineapple. Pour into a blender, add the blueberries and banana, and liquefy.

Approximate Nutrient Content

Calories	313	
Protein	3.1	g
Carbohydrate	78	g
Fat	2.4	g
Vitamin A	30	RE
Vitamin C	**68**	**mg**
Vitamin E	1.1	mg
Thiamine	**0.5**	**mg**
Riboflavin	0.29	mg
Niacin	2.3	mg
Vitamin B6	**1.1**	**mg**
Folic acid	58	mcg
Sodium	13	mg
Calcium	34	mg
Magnesium	73	mg
Potassium	**865**	**mg**
Iron	1.5	mg

MINT FOAM

This is a great drink that is fun-tasting. Mint has a soothing effect on the intestinal tract and also exhibits some antiviral activity as well.

Handful of mint
2 kiwifruits, peeled
1 green apple, cut into wedges

Juice the mint first, followed by the kiwifruits, then the apple. Pour over ice if desired.

Approximate Nutrient Content

Calories	173	
Protein	1.9	g
Carbohydrate	44	g
Fat	1.1	g
Vitamin A	33	RE
Vitamin C	**157**	**mg**
Vitamin E	0.4	mg
Thiamine	0.05	mg
Riboflavin	0.09	mg
Niacin	0.9	mg
Vitamin B6	0.1	mg
Folic acid	3.9	mcg
Sodium	9	mg
Calcium	50	mg
Magnesium	52	mg
Potassium	**663**	**mg**
Iron	0.9	mg

MONKEY SHAKE

This is another good breakfast drink, filling yet low in calories. It definitely can satisfy a sweet tooth.

½ papaya, peeled, seeded, sliced
1 or 2 oranges, peeled
1 banana, peeled
    Orange twist

Juice the papaya first, then the orange. Pour into a blender, add the banana, and liquefy. Pour it into a glass and garnish with an orange twist.

Approximate Nutrient Content

Calories	226	
Protein	3.35	g
Carbohydrate	57	g
Fat	1	g
Vitamin A	**342**	**RE**
Vitamin C	**174**	**mg**
Vitamin E	0.9	mg
Thiamine	0.25	mg
Riboflavin	0.25	mg
Niacin	1.5	mg
Vitamin B6	**0.85**	**mg**
Folic acid	61	mcg
Sodium	5	mg
Calcium	95	mg
Magnesium	62	mg
Potassium	**1,078**	**mg**
Iron	0.65	mg

ORANGE AID

A variant of orange juice that is quite pleasing to the taste buds.

¼ pineapple with skin, sliced
2 oranges, peeled

Juice the pineapple first, then the oranges.

Approximate Nutrient Content

Calories	224
Protein	2.6g
Carbohydrate	59 g
Fat	1.6g
Vitamin A	48 RE
Vitamin C	**184 mg**
Vitamin E	1.2mg
Thiamine	**0.5mg**
Riboflavin	0.3mg
Niacin	2.3mg
Vitamin B6	**0.7mg**
Folic acid	**124 mcg**
Sodium	4 mg
Calcium	104 mg
Magnesium	61 mg
Potassium	**812 mg**
Iron	1.3mg

PINEAPPLE-GINGER ALE

This drink is absolutely delicious and packed full of therapeutic potential.

¼-inch slice of ginger
½ pineapple with skin, sliced

Juice the ginger, followed by the pineapple.

Approximate Nutrient Content

Calories	252
Protein	1.8g
Carbohydrate	62 g

Fat	2.4	g
Vitamin A	12	RE
Vitamin C	**78**	**mg**
Vitamin E	0.6	mg
Thiamine	**0.6**	**mg**
Riboflavin	0.18	mg
Niacin	2.4	mg
Vitamin B6	**0.6**	**mg**
Folic acid	53	mcg
Sodium	6	mg
Calcium	36	mg
Magnesium	66	mg
Potassium	570	mg
Iron	1.8	mg

POPEYE'S POWER DRINK

Remember the cartoon character Popeye the sailor man? Do you recall how he felt after eating his trusty can of spinach? This drink offers almost the same kind of effect. It is an energizing drink rich in vital nutrients.

> Handful of parsley
> 4 carrots
> Handful of spinach

Juice the parsley first by bunching it up in your hand and pushing it through the juicer with the aid of a carrot. Do the same with the spinach and then feed the remaining carrots through the juicer.

Approximate Nutrient Content

Calories	142
Protein	4.8g

Carbohydrate	32.6 g
Fat	0.76g
Vitamin A	**8,476 RE**
Vitamin C	**62 mg**
Vitamin E	**5.8 mg**
Thiamine	0.32mg
Riboflavin	0.36mg
Niacin	3.3 mg
Vitamin B6	**0.64mg**
Folic acid	**185 mcg**
Sodium	152 mg
Calcium	158 mg
Magnesium	96 mg
Potassium	**1,352 mg**
Iron	4.2 mg

POTASSIUM POWER

This drink provides a whopping 1,834mg potassium and is packed full of carotenes, vitamins, and other minerals.

Handful of parsley
4 carrots
Handful of spinach
2 celery ribs
1 tomato, quartered

Juice the parsley first by bunching it up in your hand and pushing it through the juicer with the aid of a carrot. Do the same with the spinach and then alternate feeding the remaining ingredients into the juicer.

Approximate Nutrient Content

Calories	178
Protein	6.5g

Carbohydrate	41	g
Fat	1.26	g
Vitamin A	**8,625**	**RE**
Vitamin C	**88**	**mg**
Vitamin E	**7.5**	**mg**
Thiamine	**0.42**	**mg**
Riboflavin	**0.44**	**mg**
Niacin	4.2	mg
Vitamin B6	**0.76**	**mg**
Folic acid	**204**	**mcg**
Sodium	232	mg
Calcium	194	mg
Magnesium	**120**	**mg**
Potassium	**1,834**	**mg**
Iron	**5.2**	**mg**

POTASSIUM PUNCH

Thick and delicious, this punch is rich not only in potassium, but also in vitamin C. Another great way to start the day.

1 peach, pitted, sliced
2 oranges, peeled
½ papaya, seeded, sliced
1 banana, peeled

Juice the peach, followed by one of the oranges, the papaya, and another orange. Pour into a blender, add the banana, and liquefy.

Approximate Nutrient Content

Calories	355
Protein	5.1g

Carbohydrate	90	g
Fat	1.5	g
Vitamin A	772	RE
Vitamin C	**272**	**mg**
Vitamin E	2.75	mg
Thiamine	0.4	mg
Riboflavin	0.4	mg
Niacin	7	mg
Vitamin B6	**0.92**	**mg**
Folic acid	32.6	mcg
Sodium	158	mg
Calcium	84	mg
Magnesium	65	mg
Potassium	**1,476**	**mg**
Iron	0.9	mg

PURPLE COW

Like milk, this drink provides calcium. And it also contains some added nutrition not provided by milk.

½ head of red cabbage, cut into wedges
2   kale leaves
1   red bell pepper, quartered
2   red apples, cut into wedges

Juice the cabbage first, followed by the kale, pepper, and apples.

Approximate Nutrient Content

Calories	226	
Protein	4	g
Carbohydrate	55	g
Fat	1.8	g
Vitamin A	**245**	**RE**

Vitamin C	198	**mg**
Vitamin E	6.1	**mg**
Thiamine	0.24	mg
Riboflavin	0.22	mg
Niacin	1.2	mg
Vitamin B6	0.8	**mg**
Folic acid	104	**mcg**
Sodium	42	mg
Calcium	124	mg
Magnesium	64	mg
Potassium	906	**mg**
Iron	3.1	mg

SALAD IN A GLASS

If you have a hard time eating salads, try juicing one. Check out all the nutrition provided in this drink despite its low calorie content.

4 parsley sprigs
3 tomatoes, quartered
½ green bell pepper
½ cucumber
1 scallion
1 lemon wedge

Bunch up parsley and feed into juicer with the tomatoes, green pepper, cucumber, scallion, and lemon. Garnish with lemon if you desire.

Approximate Nutrient Content

Calories	115
Protein	5.4g
Carbohydrate	25.6g

Fat	1.3	g
Vitamin A	**691**	**RE**
Vitamin C	**156**	**mg**
Vitamin E	1.6	mg
Thiamine	0.33	mg
Riboflavin	0.29	mg
Niacin	2.84	mg
Vitamin B6	0.52	mg
Folic acid	**82**	**mcg**
Sodium	39	mg
Calcium	87	mg
Magnesium	73	mg
Potassium	**1,192**	**mg**
Iron	4.05	mg

SOME LIKE IT HOT

If you have a thing for hot and spicy foods, you will love this drink. It is quite invigorating, to say the least.

    2 radishes
    2 tomatoes, quartered
    1 green bell pepper, quartered
    1 sweet red bell pepper, quartered
        Dash of Tabasco sauce (optional)

Feed the ingredients alternately into the juicer.

Approximate Nutrient Content

Calories	91	
Protein	3.8	g
Carbohydrate	20	g
Fat	1.44	g

Vitamin A	896	RE
Vitamin C	**243**	**mg**
Vitamin E	2.6	mg
Thiamine	0.34	mg
Riboflavin	0.23	mg
Niacin	2.34	mg
Vitamin B6	0.43	mg
Folic acid	60	mcg
Sodium	68	mg
Calcium	33	mg
Magnesium	52	mg
Potassium	**904**	**mg**
Iron	3.1	mg

SUPER V-7

If you like V-8, you'll love this drink. It's fresh, it's alive, it's higher in nutrients, and it doesn't taste like a can. This is a great electrolyte replacement drink for athletes and is also a useful diet drink in that it is very nutrient-dense yet calorie-poor.

> Handful of parsley
> 2 carrots
> Handful of spinach
> 2 tomatoes, quartered
> 2 celery ribs
> ½ cucumber
> ½ green bell pepper

Juice the parsley first by bunching it up in your hand and pushing it through the juicer with the aid of a carrot. Do the same with the spinach and then alternate feeding the remaining ingredients into the juicer.

Approximate Nutrient Content

Calories	147	
Protein	5.8	g
Carbohydrate	33.4	g
Fat	1.4	g
Vitamin A	**4,548**	**RE**
Vitamin C	**129**	**mg**
Vitamin E	**5.5**	**mg**
Thiamine	**0.39**	**mg**
Riboflavin	0.35	mg
Niacin	3.6	mg
Vitamin B6	**0.67**	**mg**
Folic acid	**136**	**mcg**
Sodium	168	mg
Calcium	132	mg
Magnesium	**97**	**mg**
Potassium	**1,562**	**mg**
Iron	1.15	mg

TOMATO ZEST

A tomato juice cocktail with a pleasant zing to it. This is a great drink to cool you down.

> 4 tomatoes, quartered
> 2 sweet red bell peppers, quartered
> Dash of Tabasco sauce

Alternate feeding the tomatoes and peppers into the juicer. Pour into a glass (ice optional), pour a dash of Tabasco into the glass, and stir.

Approximate Nutrient Content

Calories	132
Protein	6g

Carbohydrate	29	g
Fat	1.8	g
Vitamin A	**634**	**RE**
Vitamin C	**276**	**mg**
Vitamin E	**3.2**	**mg**
Thiamine	**0.48**	**mg**
Riboflavin	0.34	mg
Niacin	3.6	mg
Vitamin B6	**0.3**	**mg**
Folic acid	**35.5**	**mcg**
Sodium	110	mg
Calcium	40	mg
Magnesium	76	mg
Potassium	**1,314**	**mg**
Iron	2.1	mg

TUMMY TONIC

Fennel, ginger, and peppermint are both carminatives and intestinal antispasmodics. Carminatives are substances that promote digestion and relieve gaseousness; intestinal antispasmodics relieve spastic intestinal muscles. This is an interesting drink worth a try anytime but especially if you have a tummyache.

¼-inch slice of ginger
½ handful of fresh peppermint or spearmint
½ small fennel
2 apples, cut into wedges

Wrap the ginger in the mint and feed it through the juicer, followed by the fennel and apple wedges.

Approximate Nutrient Content

| Calories | 226 |
| Protein | 2.16g |

Carbohydrate	57	g
Fat	1.32g	
Vitamin A	22	RE
Vitamin C	**27.6**	**mg**
Vitamin E	0.8	mg
Thiamine	0.11mg	
Riboflavin	0.07mg	
Niacin	0.62mg	
Vitamin B6	0.2	mg
Folic acid	**76**	**mcg**
Sodium	22	mg
Calcium	80	mg
Magnesium	40	mg
Potassium	506	mg
Iron	2.8	mg

VITAMIN U FOR ULCER

This is one of Dr. Garnett Cheney's recipe recommendations for treating peptic ulcers; another was using 2 carrots instead of the tomatoes.

½ head or 2 cups green cabbage
2   tomatoes, quartered
4   celery ribs

Green cabbage is best, but red cabbage will do. Cut the cabbage into long wedges and feed through the juicer, followed by the tomatoes and then the celery.

Approximate Nutrient Content

Calories	104
Protein	5g
Carbohydrate	24g

Fat	1.24g	
Vitamin A	314	**RE**
Vitamin C	119	**mg**
Vitamin E	5.8	**mg**
Thiamine	0.26mg	
Riboflavin	0.21mg	
Niacin	2.2	mg
Vitamin B6	0.38mg	
Folic acid	117	**mcg**
Sodium	184	mg
Calcium	136	mg
Magnesium	68	mg
Potassium	1,308	**mg**
Iron	2.8	mg

WALDORF SALAD

This drink is delicious and refreshing. It seems to have a relaxing effect and is often recommended for headaches.

> 1 celery rib
> 2 green apples, cut into wedges

Juice the celery, followed by the apples.

Approximate Nutrient Content

Calories	168	
Protein	0.9	g
Carbohydrate	43.5	g
Fat	1.1	g
Vitamin A	19	RE
Vitamin C	18	mg
Vitamin E	1.5	mg
Thiamine	0.06mg	

Riboflavin	0.05mg
Niacin	0.3 mg
Vitamin B6	0.21mg
Folic acid	11.4 mcg
Sodium	37 mg
Calcium	34 mg
Magnesium	17 mg
Potassium	432 mg
Iron	0.8 mg

ZESTY CRAN-APPLE

This is a great drink around the holidays. If you have grown accustomed to commercial cranberry juice, this is a healthy alternative to the sugar-filled cranberry drinks available in cans or bottles. This drink is also useful in urinary tract infections and in individuals prone to kidney stones.

½ cup cranberries
½ lemon, peeled
    Handful of grapes
2   apples, cut into wedges

Juice the cranberries, followed by the lemon, grapes, and apple wedges.

Approximate Nutrient Content

Calories	206
Protein	1.3 g
Carbohydrate	54 g
Fat	1.33g
Vitamin A	21 RE
Vitamin C	**37 mg**
Vitamin E	1.6 mg

Thiamine	0.1	mg
Riboflavin	0.08	mg
Niacin	0.44	mg
Vitamin B6	0.3	mg
Folic acid	14.2	mcg
Sodium	5	mg
Calcium	33	mg
Magnesium	15	mg
Potassium	436	mg
Iron	0.92	mg

8
JUICE AS MEDICINE

Hippocrates, the father of Western medicine, said, "Let your food be your medicine and let your medicine be your food." It is amazing how far we have drifted from this sound advice. I remember a few years ago reading the Sunday paper and noticing one of those "Ask the Doctor" type columns. The doctor was asked, "Does cabbage offer any benefit in the treatment of peptic ulcers?" The doctor's answer was an emphatic no, and he went on to say that in his opinion the promotion of folklore is quackery. His response is most unfortunate for a number of reasons.

First of all, as mentioned earlier, fresh cabbage juice has been well documented in the medical literature as having remarkable success in treating peptic ulcers. Dr. Garnett Cheney at Stanford University's School of Medicine and other researchers in the 1940s and 1950s performed several studies on fresh cabbage juice.[1] The results of these studies clearly demonstrated that fresh cabbage juice is extremely effective in the treatment of peptic ulcers. In fact, the majority of patients experienced complete healing in as little as seven days. Cabbage juice works by increasing the amount of protective substances that line the intestine. A breakdown in the integrity of this lining is what causes most ulcers.

Another disturbing part of the doctor's response was his recommendation of the drugs Tagamet and Zantac. Each year, these two drugs fight it out to see which is going to be the most widely prescribed drug in the United States; in 1989 it was Zantac and in 1990 and 1991 it was Tagamet. The two drugs have combined sales of over $1 billion in the United States alone, and $4 billion worldwide. The companies that produce these drugs consider them "perfect drugs" because they are not only expensive (a full therapeutic dose usually costs about $150 a month), they also have the highest relapse rate (92%) of any antiulcer treatment. The result? A person becomes dependent on a very expensive drug, because without it, the ulcer will likely come back.

Are these really perfect drugs? For most people, the answer is definitely no. Tagamet and Zantac are associated with a number of side effects, including digestive disturbances, nutritional imbalances, liver dysfunction, disruption of bone metabolism, and the development of breasts in men.[2]

The naturopathic approach to peptic ulcers is to first identify and then eliminate or reduce all factors that can contribute to the development of peptic ulcers: food allergy, cigarette smoking, stress, and drugs such as aspirin and other nonsteroidal analgesics. Once the causative factors have been controlled or eliminated, the focus is directed at healing the ulcers and promoting tissue resistance. This includes not only drinking cabbage juice, but eating a diet high in fiber and low in allergenic foods, avoiding those factors known to promote ulcer formation (such as smoking, alcohol, coffee, and aspirin), and incorporating an effective stress-reduction plan. A naturopath may also utilize a special licorice extract known as DGL (short for deglycyrrhizinated licorice), which has been shown to be far superior to Tagamet and Zantac. Like cabbage, DGL works by reestablishing a healthy intestinal lining.

ARE JUICES DRUGS? THE IMPORTANCE OF A TOTAL APPROACH

Many foods and juices do indeed appear to have therapeutic effects, as noted throughout this book. But even though specific juices have been shown to offer benefit in certain health conditions, juices in general should not be viewed as drugs. Rather, juicing should be incorporated as a regular part of a healthy diet and lifestyle. You should remember to juice a wide assortment of fruits and vegetables, rather than rely on any one juice to remedy a specific medical complaint. This ensures that a broad range of beneficial substances are being delivered to the body.

For an example of how fresh juices can be of benefit in a serious health condition, let's look at their use in rheumatoid

arthritis. You may remember bromelain, from fresh pineapple, was mentioned earlier as an anti-inflammatory enzyme that has been used in arthritis. Many people with arthritis may get some relief from fresh pineapple juice, but simply drinking pineapple juice and ignoring other dietary aspects will probably not be very effective in the long run. Juicing must be part of a comprehensive and holistic health program.

Diet has been strongly implicated in many forms of arthritis for several years, in regard to both cause and cure. Various practitioners have recommended all sorts of specific diets for arthritis, especially the most severe form, rheumatoid arthritis. For example, abstaining from allergenic foods has been shown to offer significant benefit to some individuals with rheumatoid arthritis.[3] Fasting or following a diet designed to eliminate food allergy followed by systematically reintroducing foods is often an effective method of isolating offending foods. Virtually any food can result in an aggravation of rheumatoid arthritis, but the most common offending foods are wheat, corn, milk and other dairy products, beef, and nightshade-family foods (tomato, potato, eggplants, peppers, and tobacco).[4]

A recent study highlights the effectiveness of juicing (as part of a healthy diet and lifestyle) in the relief of rheumatoid arthritis. In the 13-month study, conducted in Norway at the Oslo Rheumatism Hospital, two groups of patients suffering from rheumatoid arthritis were compared to determine the effect of diet on their condition. One group (the treatment group) followed a therapeutic diet, and the others (the control group) were allowed to eat as they wished. Both groups started the study by visiting a health spa for four weeks.

The treatment group began their therapeutic diet by fasting for seven to ten days, and then began following a special diet. Dietary intake during the fast consisted of herbal teas,

garlic, vegetable broth, decoction of potatoes and parsley, and the juices of carrots, beets, and celery. Interestingly enough, no fruit juices were allowed.

After the fast, the patients reintroduced a "new" food item every second day. If they noticed an increase in pain, stiffness, or joint swelling within 2 to 48 hours, this item was omitted from the diet for at least seven days before being reintroduced a second time. If the food caused worsening of symptoms after the second time, it was omitted permanently from the diet.

The study indicated that short-term fasting followed by a vegetarian diet led to "a substantial reduction in disease activity" in many patients. The results implied a therapeutic benefit beyond elimination of food allergies alone. The authors suggested that the additional improvements were due to changes in dietary fatty acids.[5]

Fatty acids are important mediators of inflammation. Manipulation of dietary fat intake can significantly increase or decrease inflammation, depending on the type of fat or oil being manipulated. Arachidonic acid, a fatty acid derived almost entirely from animal sources (such as meat and dairy products), contributes greatly to the inflammatory process through its conversion to inflammatory prostaglandins and leukotrienes. The benefit of a vegetarian diet to those suffering inflammatory conditions like rheumatoid arthritis and asthma presumably results from the decrease in the availability of arachidonic acid for conversion to inflammatory compounds.[6]

Rheumatoid arthritis is a prime example of a very complex "multifactorial" disease. While fresh pineapple juice may be effective in the treatment of some people with rheumatoid arthritis, if we simply use foods or juices for their "druglike" effects we may not be addressing many of the underlying causes of the disease. Instead of looking for a specific juice to

cure a specific health condition, we should focus on adopting a diet and a lifestyle that will address the contributing factors of these diseases.

JUICING WITH FRESH HERBS AND SPICES

Supplementing your juices with medicinal herbs and spices can provide additional benefits. For example, as noted in Chapter 6, garlic has many health-promoting properties—including antibiotic, immune-enhancing, anticancer, cholesterol-lowering, blood-pressure-reducing, and detoxification-enhancement activities.[7] Fresh garlic is much more potent than cooked, dried, or prepared garlic.

Fresh garlic can be added to a number of vegetable juices to make a delicious and healthy drink. To reduce the strong odor of garlic, it is a good idea to juice the garlic by placing a clove or two in the middle of a handful of parsley or other chlorophyll-rich green leafy vegetable and feed it through the juicer, then follow that with carrots, celery, or other vegetables to dilute some of the flavor.

Another popular addition to juice is fresh ginger. This is a great idea if a little zest is desired or if an individual is suffering from intestinal spasms, arthritis, or motion sickness (see Chapter 6). Although most scientific studies have used powdered gingerroot, fresh gingerroot at an equivalent dosage is believed to yield even better results because it contains active enzymes. Most studies utilized 1g of powdered gingerroot. This would be equivalent to approximately 10g or one-third ounce fresh gingerroot. Fresh ginger is available at most grocery stores.

The addition of ginger and garlic are great examples of supplementing your juice with a medicinal herb or spice. Other examples include parsley, peppermint, capsicum (red pepper), onions, and dandelion greens or root.

JUICE RECOMMENDATIONS FOR
COMMON HEALTH CONDITIONS

The following recommendations are for nutritional support only. Again, juices should not be viewed as drug substitutes for proper medical treatment. Nonetheless, these recommendations may prove beneficial in many instances. For a more complete discussion of the natural approach to common health conditions, please consult *The Encyclopedia of Natural Medicine,* which I coauthored with Dr. Joseph Pizzorno, president of Bastyr College. The *Encyclopedia* is available at most bookstores or directly from Prima Publishing, (916) 786-0426.

ACNE

Carrot
Green Drink
Purple Cow
Better Red than Dead

Additional recommendations: Enzymatic Therapy's Derma-Klear Acne Treatment Program, available at independent health food stores, is an excellent comprehensive nutritional support and skin-cleansing plan. Zinc supplementation (45mg per day) is almost always indicated.

AIDS (SEE CHAPTER 11)

ANEMIA (IRON DEFICIENCY)

Iron Plus
Everything but the Kitchen Sink
Green Drink

Additional recommendations: Some people may respond only to a type of iron known as heme-iron. Heme-iron is found in liver and other animal products. For B12- and folic-acid-deficiency anemias, supplementation may be necessary.

ANGINA

Cholesterol-Lowering Tonic

Pineapple-Ginger Ale

Kids' Favorite

Additional recommendations: Try coenzyme Q10 (60mg a day), a vitaminlike compound that has been shown to be quite useful in heart problems.

ANXIETY

Potassium Punch

Potassium Power

Waldorf Salad

Additional recommendations: Regular exercise is the best prescription for relieving stress and anxiety. Also, regular deep breathing exercises are often helpful.

ARTHRITIS

Pineapple-Ginger Ale

Ginger Hopper

Color Me Pink

Additional recommendations: Reduce stress on joints by achieving ideal body weight. Try eliminating nightshade-family vegetables (tomatoes, potatoes, peppers, tobacco), as these foods can often aggravate arthritis.

ASTHMA AND HAYFEVER

Cholesterol-Lowering Tonic

Salad in a Glass

High C

Additional recommendations: Food allergies often play a major role, especially in childhood asthma. The most common allergens are wheat, corn, milk and dairy products, citrus, and eggs. A vegetarian diet has been shown to be extremely effective in severe cases. For immediate relief, try herbal products that contain ephedra.

ATHEROSCLEROSIS AND HIGH CHOLESTEROL LEVELS

Cholesterol-Lowering Tonic

Cherry Pop

Pineapple-Ginger Ale

Additional recommendations: Along with diet and exercise, try herbal products containing gugulipid, a natural cholesterol-lowering agent long used in India. Gugulipid products are available at health food stores.

BLADDER INFECTION (CYSTITIS)

Cranberry Crush

Zesty Cran-Apple

Immune Power Vegetable

Additional recommendations: The herb uva-ursi is commonly used for urinary tract infections. Avoid refined carbohydrates and drink at least eight glasses of liquids a day.

BOILS (FARUNCLES)

Green Drink
Cleansing Cocktail
Immune Power Vegetable

Additional recommendations: Australian tea tree oil ointment applied topically may be useful.

BRONCHITIS AND PNEUMONIA

Immune Power Vegetable
Orange Aid
Kill the Cold

Additional recommendations: The herb goldenseal has profound immune-enhancing and antibiotic activity. Also, additional vitamin C (up to 1g every hour) may be beneficial.

BRUISING

Mike's Favorite
Color Me Pink
Orange Aid

Additional recommendations: Extra vitamin C (1–3g a day) may prove helpful.

CANKER SORES

Green Drink
Vitamin U for Ulcer
Potassium Punch

Additional recommendations: Allergies to milk and wheat are often the triggering factor. Try DGL (deglycyrrhizinated licorice) for recurrent canker sores.

CARPAL TUNNEL SYNDROME

Potassium Power

Pineapple-Ginger Ale or Orange Aid

Ginger Hopper

Additional recommendations: 200mg vitamin B6 a day has been shown to be very effective in many cases.

CATARACTS

Blueberry-apple juice

High C

Color Me Pink

Additional recommendations: High doses of vitamin C (1–3g daily) and other antioxidants like selenium may be necessary to prevent further damage in individuals with existing cataracts.

COMMON COLD

Immune Power Vegetable

Immune Power Fruit

Kill the Cold

Additional recommendations: Rest and drink plenty of liquids. The herb echinacea is often used to bolster the immune system during a cold. Also, 1g vitamin C every two hours, and the use of lozenges that contain zinc may be quite helpful in reducing the severity of symptoms and the course of the cold.

CONSTIPATION

Bowel Regulator

Green Drink

Enzymes Galore

Additional recommendations: Bulk-forming laxatives like powdered psyllium seed husks, guar, and oat bran may be quite helpful. Increase consumption of whole foods like grains, legumes, fruits, and vegetables.

CROHN'S DISEASE AND ULCERATIVE COLITIS

Green Drink

Cleansing Cocktail

Enzymes Galore

Additional recommendations: These are serious disorders. Follow additional recommendations outlined in *The Encyclopedia of Natural Medicine.*

DIABETES

Shot of bitter melon juice

Jerusalem artichoke juice in vegetable-based juices

Super V-7

Salad in a Glass

Additional recommendations: Achieve ideal body weight; being overweight leads to diabetes. Follow a high-fiber complex-carbohydrate diet. The trace mineral chromium may help improve blood sugar control.

DIARRHEA

Monkey Shake

Potassium Punch

Tummy Tonic

Additional recommendations: If diarrhea lasts more than 24 hours or is quite profuse, consult a physician.

ECZEMA (ATOPIC DERMATITIS)

Digestive Delight

Cleansing Cocktail

Immune Power Vegetable

Additional recommendations: Food allergies often play a major role. The most common allergens are wheat, corn, milk and dairy products, citrus, and eggs. A vegetarian diet has been shown to be extremely effective in severe cases. Also, essential fatty acids such as flaxseed oil and evening primrose oil are often helpful.

FIBROCYSTIC BREAST DISEASE

Liver Mover

Liver Tonic

Cleansing Cocktail

Additional recommendations: Constipation is a contributing factor in many. Iodine, vitamin E, and eliminating caffeine have all been shown to be helpful.

GALLSTONES

Liver Tonic

Color Me Pink

Digestive Delight

Additional recommendations: Low-fat, high-fiber diet. Drink an additional four to six glasses of water a day. Try a special herbal product known as silymarin phytosome.

GLAUCOMA (CHRONIC OPEN-ANGLE)

Mike's Favorite

Blueberry-apple juice

Orange juice

Additional recommendations: Extra vitamin C (1–3g daily) is required.

GOUT

Cherry Pop
Pineapple-Ginger Ale
Green Drink

Additional recommendations: Gout is easily controlled by diet. Eliminate alcohol, and foods high in purines (organ meats, meats, shellfish), reduce fat and refined sugar intake, and increase the consumption of water and liquids to include four to six glasses of water and three or four glasses of fresh juice a day.

HAYFEVER (SEE ASTHMA)

HEADACHE

Potassium Power
Femme Fatale
Ginger Hopper

Additional recommendations: Food allergies often play a major role. The most common allergens are wheat, corn, milk and dairy products, citrus, and eggs.

HEPATITIS

Liver Tonic
Cholesterol-Lowering Tonic
Immune Power Vegetable

Additional recommendations: Silymarin, a compound from the herb milk thistle, has been shown to be extremely effective. Silymarin phytosome, available at health food

stores, is the best form. Also, nutritional liver support is recommended; see *The Encyclopedia of Natural Medicine.*

HERPES (SEE CHAPTER 11)

HIGH BLOOD PRESSURE

Cholesterol-Lowering Tonic
Potassium Power
Salad in a Glass

Additional recommendations: Eliminate alcohol, caffeine, and tobacco use. Achieve ideal body weight, exercise, and employ stress-reduction techniques.

HYPOGLYCEMIA

Jerusalem artichoke juice in vegetable-based juices
Super V-7
Salad in a Glass

Additional recommendations: Dilute fruit juices with an equal amount of water. Eat frequent, smaller meals.

INDIGESTION

Digestive Delight
Pineapple-Ginger Ale
Tummy Tonic

Additional recommendations: Eat frequent, smaller meals in a relaxed atmosphere. Chew your food thoroughly.

INSOMNIA

Waldorf Salad
Immune Power Fruit
Potassium Punch

Additional recommendations: Eliminate caffeine and alcohol, as these substances disrupt normal sleep processes. Frequent exercise is associated with better sleep habits. If additional support is needed, try products containing valerian, or chamomile tea.

IRRITABLE BOWEL SYNDROME

Tummy Tonic
Ginger Hopper
Digestive Delight

Additional recommendations: Eliminate food allergies, increase fiber content of diet, and supplement the diet with a gel-forming fiber like psyllium or oat bran. If additional support is required, try enteric coated peppermint oil capsules from the health food store.

KIDNEY STONES

Zesty Cran-Apple
Cranberry Crush
Diuretic Formula

Additional recommendations: Additional amounts of vitamin B6 (100mg) and magnesium (300mg) may also help prevent recurrences.

MACULAR DEGENERATION

Blueberry-apple juice
High C
Color Me Pink

Additional recommendations: Ginkgo biloba extract (24% ginkgoflavoglycosides) or a concentrated bilberry extract is strongly recommended due to the serious nature of the condition. Please consult *The Encyclopedia of Natural Medicine* for additional information.

MENOPAUSE (SEE ALSO OSTEOPOROSIS)

Femme Fatale
Bone Builder's Cocktail
Color Me Pink

Additional recommendations: Herbal support is often helpful, especially formulas containing *Angelica sinensis* or Dong Quai.

MENSTRUAL BLOOD LOSS, EXCESSIVE (MENORRHAGIA)

Iron Plus
Everything but the Kitchen Sink
Green Drink

Additional recommendations: Low thyroid function is a frequent cause of excessive menstrual blood flow. Key nutrients for thyroid hormone manufacture include the amino acid tyrosine, iodine, and vitamin C.

MENSTRUAL PAIN (DYSMENORRHEA)

Femme Fatale
Pineapple-Ginger Ale
Potassium Power

Additional recommendations: Restrict intake of animal fats, with the exception of fish oils, and increase intake of vegetable oils such as flaxseed, canola, and sunflower.

MORNING SICKNESS (NAUSEA AND VOMITING OF PREGNANCY)

Ginger Hopper
Tummy Tonic
Digestive Delight

Additional recommendations: Frequent small meals are typically handled better. Vitamin B6, 25mg three times daily, has recently been shown to be of benefit.

OSTEOPOROSIS

> Bone Builder's Cocktail
> Green Drink
> Super V-7

Additional recommendations: Refined sugars, soft drinks, and too much protein can increase calcium excretion. If bone loss is already apparent, use OsteoPrime, a bone-building supplement developed by Jonathan Wright, M.D., and Alan Gaby, M.D. OsteoPrime is made by Enzymatic Therapy and is available from health food stores.

PERIODONTAL DISEASE

> Bone Builder's Cocktail
> High C
> Color Me Pink

Additional recommendations: Proper dental hygiene (regular brushing, flossing, and cleaning) is imperative. Refined sugars, especially sticky candies and chocolates, should be eliminated.

PROSTATE ENLARGEMENT (BPH)

> Cholesterol-Lowering Tonic
> The Don Juan
> Super V-7

Additional recommendations: Pumpkin seeds provide zinc and essential fatty acids that support prostate function. The liposterolic extract of saw palmetto berries (*Serenoa*

repens) has been shown to be extremely effective. Serenoa extracts are available at health food stores.

PSORIASIS

Liver Tonic

Immune Power Vegetable

Pineapple-Ginger Ale

Additional recommendations: Restrict intake of animal products, except fish. Increase fiber content of diet. Omega-3 oils like flaxseed oil and EPA (eicosa pentanoic acid) have also been shown to be effective.

RHEUMATOID ARTHRITIS

Pineapple-Ginger Ale

Cleansing Cocktail

Ginger Hopper

Additional recommendations: See section above, "Are Juices Drugs?" Also, read *The Encyclopedia of Natural Medicine,* as this is a very complex disease.

SPORTS INJURIES (SEE ARTHRITIS)

ULCER

Vitamin U for Ulcer

Green Drink

Potassium Punch

Additional recommendations: Eliminate causative factors such as stress, smoking, and ulcer-causing drugs like aspirin and corticosteroids. Allergies to milk can be a triggering factor. Use DGL (deglycyrrhizinated licorice), available at health food stores.

VARICOSE VEINS

Orange-Aid

Mike's Favorite

Color Me Pink

Additional recommendations: Avoid standing in one place for prolonged periods of time, wear support hose, and get regular exercise.

WATER RETENTION

Diuretic Formula

Potassium Power

Watermelon juice

Additional recommendations: Reduce sodium intake.

9
THE JUICE FAST

Substances toxic to our bodies are everywhere—in the air we breathe, the food we eat, and the water we drink. Even our bodies and the bacteria in the intestines produce toxic substances. It can be strongly said that the health of an individual is largely determined by the ability of the body to "detoxify." This ability is based almost entirely on the function of one important organ: the liver.

Our environment is deteriorating as industrialization continues to spread. More and more chemicals that did not exist before are being dumped into the ecosystem and eventually absorbed into our bodies. Our health is not so much being threatened by one individual chemical as it is being undermined by a constant barrage of chemicals: pesticides, herbicides, food additives, lead, mercury, synthetic fertilizers, air pollutants, solvents, and thousands of other compounds.

Now, perhaps more than ever, it is critical for us to support the body's detoxification systems if we desire health. Periodic juice fasting is a healthy way to support your body's ability to deal with toxins.

TYPES OF TOXIC SUBSTANCES

HEAVY METALS

Included in this category are lead, mercury, cadmium, arsenic, nickel, and aluminum. These metals tend to accumulate in the brain, kidneys, and immune system, where they can severely disrupt normal function.[1]

The typical person has more lead and other heavy metals in his or her body than is compatible with health. It is conservatively estimated that up to 25% of the U.S. population suffers from heavy metal poisoning to some extent. Hair mineral analysis is a good screening test for heavy metal toxicity.[2]

Most of the heavy metals in the body are a result of industrial contamination. For example, in the United States alone, industrial sources and cars burning leaded gasoline dump more than 600,000 tons of lead into the atmosphere to be inhaled or, after landing on food crops, in fresh water, and soil, to be ingested.

Common sources of heavy metals, in addition to industrial sources, include: lead from the solder in tin cans, pesticide sprays, and cooking utensils; cadmium and lead from cigarette smoke; mercury from dental fillings, contaminated fish, and cosmetics; and aluminum from antacids and cookware.

Early signs of heavy metal poisoning are vague or associated with other problems. They can include headache, fatigue, muscle pains, indigestion, tremors, constipation, anemia, pallor, dizziness, and poor coordination. The person with even mild heavy metal toxicity will experience impaired ability to think or concentrate. As toxicity increases, so do the severity of signs and symptoms.[3]

Numerous studies have demonstrated a strong relationship between childhood learning disabilities (and other disorders, including criminal behavior) and body stores of heavy metals.[4] In general, learning disabilities seem to correlate with a general pattern of high hair levels of mercury, cadmium, lead, copper, and manganese. Poor nutrition and elevation of heavy metals usually go hand in hand, due to decreased consumption of food factors known to chelate these heavy metals or decrease their absorption.

More and more information is accumulating that indicates chronic heavy metal toxicity is a major problem in our modern society. Every effort should be made to reduce heavy metal levels. This is particularly true for individuals who are exposed to high levels. Some professions with extremely high exposure include battery makers, gasoline station attendants, printers, roofers, solderers, dentists, and jewelers.

TOXIC CHEMICALS, DRUGS, ALCOHOL, SOLVENTS, FORMALDEHYDE, PESTICIDES, HERBICIDES, AND FOOD ADDITIVES

Exposure to food additives, solvents (cleaning materials, formaldehyde, toluene, benzene), pesticides, herbicides, and other toxic chemicals can give rise to a number of symptoms. Most common are psychological and neurological conditions such as depression, headaches, mental confusion, mental illness, tingling in extremities, abnormal nerve reflexes, and other signs of impaired nervous system function. The nervous system is extremely sensitive to these chemicals. Respiratory tract allergies and increased rates for many cancers are also noted in people chronically exposed to chemical toxins.[5]

The importance of reducing our toxic load by consuming organic produce cannot be overstated. In the United States, each year over 1.2 billion pounds of pesticides and herbicides are sprayed or added to our crops. Most pesticides in use are synthetic chemicals of questionable safety. The major long-term health risks include the potential to cause cancer and birth defects, while the major health risks of acute intoxication include vomiting, diarrhea, blurred vision, tremors, convulsions, and nerve damage.

MICROBIAL COMPOUNDS

Toxins produced by bacteria and yeast in the gut can be absorbed, causing significant disruption of body functions. Examples of these types of toxins include endotoxins, exotoxins, toxic amines, toxic derivatives of bile, and various carcinogenic substances.

Gut-derived microbial toxins have been implicated in a wide variety of diseases, including liver diseases, Crohn's disease, ulcerative colitis, thyroid disease, psoriasis, lupus erythematosis, pancreatitis, allergies, asthma, and immune disorders.[6]

In addition to toxic substances being produced by microorganisms, antibodies formed against microbial antigens can cross-react with the body's own tissues, thereby causing autoimmunity. The list of autoimmune diseases that have been linked to cross-reacting antibodies includes rheumatoid arthritis, myasthenia gravis, diabetes, and autoimmune thyroiditis.

To reduce the absorption of toxic substances, a fiber-rich diet is recommended. The water-soluble fibers, such as those found in guar gum, pectin, oat bran, and other vegetables, are particularly valuable. Fiber has an ability to bind to toxins within the gut and promote their excretion. The immune system as well as the liver is responsible for dealing with the toxic substances that are absorbed from the gut.

BREAKDOWN PRODUCTS OF PROTEIN METABOLISM

The kidneys are largely responsible for the elimination of toxic waste products of protein breakdown (such as ammonia and urea). The kidneys can be supported in their important function by drinking adequate amounts of liquids (especially fresh juices) and avoiding excessive protein intake.

Most Americans consume far greater amounts of protein than their bodies require. The recommended daily allowance for protein is 56g and 44g for the average man and woman, respectively, or approximately 8%–9% of the total daily calories. Most Americans consume almost twice this amount. As a point of reference, approximately four ounces of lean cuts of meat, chicken, or fish and two cups of legumes or nuts along with a varied, healthy diet will usually provide more than the RDA for protein.

THE DIAGNOSIS OF TOXICITY

A number of special laboratory techniques are useful in detecting toxins in the body. For heavy metals, the most reliable measure of chronic exposure is the hair mineral analysis. Reliable results of hair analysis are dependent on: (1) a properly collected, cleaned, and prepared sample of hair and (2) experienced personnel using appropriate analytical methods in a qualified laboratory.

For determining exposure to the second category of toxins, toxic chemicals, a detailed medical history by an experienced physician in these matters is essential. When appropriate, the laboratory analysis for this group of toxins can involve measuring blood and fatty tissue for suspected chemicals. It is also necessary to measure the effect that these chemicals have on the liver. The most sensitive test is the serum bile acid assay. Other tests for liver function (serum bilirubin and liver enzymes) are also important, but are less sensitive.

Physicians use a number of special laboratory techniques to determine the presence of microbial compounds, including tests for the presence of: (1) abnormal microbial concentrations and disease-causing organisms (stool culture); (2) microbial byproducts (urinary indican test); and (3) endotoxins (microclot generation test).

The determination of the presence of high levels of breakdown products of protein metabolism and kidney function involves both blood and urine measurement of these compounds.

FASTING

Fasting is defined as abstinence from all food and drink except water for a specific period of time, usually for a therapeutic or religious purpose. It is often used as a detoxification method, as it is one of the quickest ways to increase elimination of wastes and enhance the healing processes of the body. This process spares essential tissue (vital organs) while utilizing nonessential tissue (fatty tissue and muscle) for fuel.

Although therapeutic fasting is probably one of the oldest known therapies, it has been largely ignored by the scientific community. The most recent development in the study and promotion of fasting has been the formation of the International Association of Professional Natural Hygienists (IAPNH, 204 Staumbaugh Building, Youngstown, OH 44503). This organization comprises doctors specializing in therapeutic fasting as an integral part of total health care.

Research into fasting has been reported since 1880. Since then, medical journals have carried articles on the use of fasting in the treatment of obesity, chemical poisoning, arthritis, allergies, psoriasis, eczema, thrombophlebitis, leg ulcers, irritable bowel syndrome, impaired or deranged appetite, bronchial asthma, depression, neurosis, and schizophrenia.[7]

A most encouraging use of fasting was published in the *American Journal of Industrial Medicine* in 1984. This study involved patients who had ingested rice oil contaminated with polychlorinated biphenyls, or PCBs. All patients reported improvement in symptoms, and some observed "dramatic" relief, after undergoing seven-to-ten-day fasts.[8] This research supports past studies of PCB-poisoned patients and indicates the therapeutic effects of fasting. Caution must be used, however, when fasting after significant contamination with fat-soluble toxins like pesticides. The pesticide DDT has been shown to be mobilized during a fast and may reach blood levels toxic to the nervous system.[9] For this reason, it is a good idea to include those guidelines given below for supporting detoxification reactions while fasting.

THE SHORT FAST OR FRESH JUICE ELIMINATION DIET

By strict definition, during a fast only water is consumed. If you are drinking fresh fruit or vegetable juice, this is technically known as an elimination diet rather than a fast, but we will call it a "juice fast." Most healthy people do not need to go on a strict water fast to aid in detoxification. Instead, a three-fo-five-day fresh fruit and vegetable juice fast actually provides the greatest benefit. It is important to emphasize that only fresh fruit or vegetable juice be used to aid elimination. As we have noted, fresh juice provides valuable enzymes to our system.

Drinking fresh juice for cleansing reduces some of the side effects associated with a water fast, such as light-headedness, fatigue, and headaches. While on a fresh juice fast, individuals typically experience an increased sense of well-being, renewed energy, clearer thought, and a sense of purity.

Although a short juice fast can be started at any time, it is best to begin on a weekend or during a time period when adequate rest can be assured. The more rest, the better the results, as energy can be directed toward healing instead of toward other body functions.

Prepare for a fast on the day before solid food is stopped by making the last meal one of only fresh fruits and vegetables (some authorities recommend a full day of raw food to start a fast, even a juice fast).

Only fresh fruit and vegetable juices (ideally prepared from organic produce) should be consumed for the next three to five days, four 8- to 12-ounce glasses throughout the day. Virtually any fresh juice provides support for detoxification; however, some of the better juices to consume during a fast include Pineapple-Ginger Ale, Zesty Cran-Apple, Green Drink, Cleansing Cocktail, Cruciferous Surprise, and Potassium Power. In addition to the fresh juice, pure water should also be consumed. The quantity of water should be dictated by thirst, but at least four 8-ounce glasses should be drunk every day during the fast.

Other Important Guidelines

No coffee, soft drinks, cigarettes, or anything else should be taken except water or fresh juice. Herbal teas can be quite supportive of a fast, but they should not be sweetened.

Exercise is not usually encouraged while fasting. It is a good idea to conserve energy and allow maximal healing. Short walks or light stretching are useful, but heavy workouts tax the system and inhibit repair and elimination.

Cleansing the skin with lukewarm water is encouraged, but extremes of temperature can be tiring. Deodorants, soaps, sprays, detergents, synthetic shampoos, and exposure to other chemicals should be avoided. These only hinder elimination and add to the body's detoxification and elimination burden.

Sunlight is essential for healthy cells, but excessive exposure will strain the body's protective systems. At least 10 to 20 minutes of direct sun exposure a day is beneficial while fasting.

Rest is one of the most important aspects of a fast. A nap or two during the day is recommended. Less sleep will usually be required at night, since daily activity is lower.

Enemas are usually not necessary, but this will depend on an individual's health. If constipation is a usual problem, a longer prefast period of fresh fruits and vegetables will assist elimination.

Body temperature usually drops during a fast, as do blood pressure, pulse, and respiratory rate—all measures of the slowing of the metabolic rate of the body. It is important, therefore, to stay warm.

In breaking a fast, as outlined below, an individual is encouraged to eat slowly, chew thoroughly, limit quantities, and eat foods at room temperature. While breaking a fast and in the days that follow, it can be very helpful to carefully record what is eaten and note any adverse effects. Many of today's health problems result from food allergies and overeating.

BREAKING YOUR FAST

DAY 1

Breakfast	Lunch	Dinner
One of the following: melon, nectarine, or pineapple	a different fruit from the breakfast list	8 oz of any other fruit

DAY 2

Breakfast	Lunch	Dinner
12 oz of one type of fresh fruit	14 oz of whole pears, papaya, or citrus fruit	Raw vegetable salad with leafy greens, tomato, celery, and cucumber or 2 pears, 2 apples, and ¼ avocado

DAY 3

Resume healthy diet (raw fresh fruits, raw/steamed vegetables, whole grains, nuts, seeds, and legumes)

SUPPORTING DETOXIFICATION REACTIONS WHILE FASTING

If a person is particularly toxic, it is a good idea to support detoxification reactions while fasting. This is partly done by electing to go on a fresh juice fast over a water fast, but many people may need additional support. The reason is that during a fast, stored toxins in our fat cells are released into the system. Here are some suggestions:

1. Take a high-potency multiple vitamin and mineral formula to provide general support.
2. Take a lipotropic formula, a special formula for supporting the liver that is available at health food stores. These formulas are typically rich in choline and methionine, two important nutrients for the liver. Your dosage of the lipotropic formula should provide 1g of each of these nutrients.
3. Take 1g vitamin C three times daily.
4. Take 1–2 tablespoons of a fiber supplement at night before retiring. The best fiber sources are

the water-soluble fibers such as powdered psyllium seed husks, guar gum, and oat bran.

5. If you need additional liver support, you can take a special extract of milk thistle known as silymarin. The dosage is 70–210mg three times daily.

THE LONG-TERM APPROACH

Detoxification of harmful substances is a continual process in the body. Detoxification does not have to be an unpleasant experience and does not have to be performed only while on a fast. Actually, the best approach may be to detoxify gradually.

A rational approach to aiding the body's detoxification mechanisms can include the use of periodic short juice fasts (three to five days) or longer medically supervised fasts. However, to truly support the body's detoxification processes, a long-term detoxification program is recommended. This involves adopting: (1) a healthy diet that focuses on fresh fruits and vegetables, whole grains, legumes, nuts, and seeds; (2) a healthy lifestyle including regular exercise; and (3) a healthy attitude or positive mental outlook.

The key factors in the battle against heavy metals and other environmental toxins are nutrients like sulfur-containing compounds, vitamins, minerals, and antioxidants.[10] The better your diet, the better equipped your body is to deal with the environment.

SUMMARY

The ability to detoxify is one of the critical factors for health. It is amazing just how well the body handles the constant onslaught of modern living. Periodic juice fasting, as well as a long-term approach to detoxification, can be used to support the body's detoxification mechanisms.

10
JUICING FOR WEIGHT LOSS

Why do some people gain weight so easily, while others eat all they want and never seem to put on a pound? And why do so many people find it extremely difficult to lose weight, while others have difficulty keeping weight on? What is the best approach for permanent results? What is the best diet? Researchers have worked for decades to provide answers to the growing number of overweight Americans. How many Americans are overweight? Estimates range from 30% to 50% of the adult population.[1]

There are numerous myths and misconceptions about obesity. Many individuals, including many physicians, falsely believe that obesity is just a matter of poor eating habits or lack of proper nutrition education. In addition, in recent years the psychological aspects of obesity have been overstated. The result is that a tremendous stigma is attached to being overweight.

More and more research is supporting a biological basis for obesity. The signals of whether to eat or not appear to be tied directly to the biochemical activity of the fat cells themselves. This increased understanding of what causes obesity offers renewed hope for individuals who have tried diets, behavioral modification, and myriad other approaches without much success. This increased understanding is leading to more effective methods to not only lose weight but, more important, keep the weight off.

OBESITY DEFINED

The simplest definition of obesity is an excessive amount of body fat. It must be distinguished from the term *overweight,* which refers to an excess of body weight relative to height. For example, a muscular athlete may be overweight, yet have a very low body fat percentage. What causes him or her to be overweight is muscle or lean body mass. Despite the fact that body weight alone does not always reflect body fat percentage,

obesity is often defined as a weight greater than 20% more than the average desirable weight for men and women of a given height.

Many physicians and nutritionists utilize more precise estimations of body fat percentage, such as skinfold thickness, bioelectric impedance, and ultrasound. With these sophisticated techniques, obesity is better defined as a body fat percentage greater than 30% for women and 25% for men.[2]

The best-known height and weight charts are the tables of "desirable weight" provided by the Metropolitan Life Insurance Company. The most recent edition of these tables, published in 1983, gives weight ranges for men and women at one-inch increments of height for three body frame sizes. It should be pointed out that many nutrition experts have been reluctant to use the 1983 table because of the higher weight range as compared to earlier tables. Figure 10.1 provides the 1983 Metropolitan height and weight tables.

1983 METROPOLITAN HEIGHT AND WEIGHT TABLE

HEIGHT	SMALL FRAME	MEDIUM FRAME	LARGE FRAME
MEN			
5'2"	128–134	131–141	138–150
5'3"	130–136	133–143	140–153
5'4"	132–138	135–145	142–156
5'5"	134–140	137–148	144–160
5'6"	136–142	139–151	146–164
5'7"	138–145	142–154	149–168
5'8"	140–148	145–157	152–172
5'9"	142–151	148–160	155–176
5'10"	144–154	151–163	158–180
5'11"	146–157	154–166	161–184
6'0"	149–160	157–170	164–188

6'1"	152–164	160–174	168–192
6'2"	155–168	164–178	172–197
6'3"	158–172	167–182	176–202
6'4"	162–176	171–187	181–207

WOMEN

4'10"	102–111	109–121	118–131
4'11"	103–113	111–123	120–134
5'0"	104–115	113–126	122–137
5'1"	106–118	115–129	125–140
5'2"	108–121	118–132	128–143
5'3"	111–124	121–135	131–147
5'4"	114–127	124–138	134–151
5'5"	117–130	127–141	137–155
5'6"	120–133	130–144	140–159
5'7"	123–136	133–147	143–163
5'8"	126–139	136–150	146–167
5'9"	129–142	139–153	149–170
5'10"	132–145	142–156	152–173
5'11"	135–148	145–159	155–176
6'0"	138–151	148–162	158–179

Weights for adults age 25 to 59 years based on lowest mortality. Weight in pounds according to frame size in indoor clothing (five pounds for men and three pounds for women) wearing shoes with one-inch heels.

DETERMINING FRAME SIZE

To make a simple determination of your frame size: Extend your arm and bend the forearm upward at a 90-degree angle. Keep the fingers straight and turn the inside of your wrist away from your body. Place the thumb and index finger of your other hand on the two prominent bones on either side of your elbow. Measure the space between your fingers with a tape measure. Compare the measurement with the following measurements for medium-framed individuals. A reading lower indicates a small frame; readings higher indicate a large frame.

Men

HEIGHT IN 1" HEELS	ELBOW BREADTH
5'2" to 5'3"	2½" to 2⅞"
5'4" to 5'7"	2⅝" to 2⅞"
5'8" to 5'11"	2¾" to 3"
6'0" to 6'3"	2¾" to 3⅛"
6'4"	2⅞" to 3¼"

Women

HEIGHT IN 1" HEELS	ELBOW BREADTH
4'10" to 5'3"	2¼" to 2½"
5'4" to 5'11"	2⅜" to 2⅝"
6'0"	2½" to 2¾"

CLASSIFICATION AND TYPES OF OBESITY

Obesity is often classified into three major categories based on the size and number of fat (adipose) cells. Hyperplastic obesity is when fat cells are increased in number; hypertrophic obesity is when fat cells are increased in size; hyperplastic-hypertrophic obesity is when they are increased in both number and size.

The development of too many fat cells (hyperplastic obesity) usually begins in childhood. Although it predisposes an individual to a lifelong battle with overweight, this form of obesity tends to be associated with fewer health risks than obesity resulting from an increase in the size of the fat cells. That form of obesity (hypertrophic obesity) usually develops later on in life and is generally associated with weight gain in the torso, or male-patterned (android) obesity. Hypertrophic obesity is associated more with the metabolic complications of obesity, such as diabetes, high blood pressure, and high cholesterol and triglyceride levels. When there is both an increased number and increased size of fat cells, it is extremely difficult to achieve ideal body weight.

Male-patterned (android) and female-patterned (gynecoid) obesity refer to a classification of obesity based on fat distribution. In android obesity, fat is deposited primarily in the upper body and abdomen. This type of obesity is typically seen in obese men, hence the term male-patterned. A waist girth greater than the hip girth is diagnostic.

In female-patterned, or gynecoid, obesity, the fat is distributed primarily in the buttocks and thighs. This obesity pattern is most typically observed in women, hence the term female-patterned.[3]

In general, android obesity is associated with more serious metabolic disorders, especially diabetes. In addition to this link to diabetes, android obesity, whether in men or women, has been shown to significantly increase the risk for heart disease. Android obesity is often associated with high blood pressure and high cholesterol levels, as well as gallstones and endocrine diseases.[4]

PSYCHOLOGICAL ASPECTS OF OBESITY

The current psychological view of obesity assumes that excessive eating for psychological or emotional reasons is the primary cause of obesity. The main belief of the psychological approach is that obese individuals eat in response to external cues (sight, smell, and taste) and stimuli, even if they are satisfied.[5]

There is some evidence to support this. For example, television watching has been linked very strongly to obesity. In fact, the number of hours spent watching television is the strongest predictor for becoming obese.[6] This fits very nicely with the psychological theory (increased sensitivity to external cues), as watching TV has been shown to result in increased food consumption. However, there are also several biological effects of watching TV that promote obesity,

such as reducing physical activity and the actual lowering of the metabolic rate to a level similar to that experienced during trancelike states. These factors clearly support the biological view.

Psychological therapy is designed to offer different stimuli that will reduce food intake. Unfortunately, this approach when used alone has not had a great deal of success.[7] In addition, many obese individuals consume far fewer calories than their lean counterparts and still put on weight. This suggests a deeper biological role than previously thought.

An important psychological factor that must also be considered is the stigma attached to being obese. A group of children were once asked what they would rather be if given the choice of being fat or physically disabled. The results of the study were clear: Children would rather be physically disabled than fat.

Obese individuals have experienced much damage to their self-esteem. Fashion trends, insurance programs, college placements, employment opportunities—all discriminate against the obese. Consequently, they learn many self-defeating and self-degrading attitudes. They are made to believe that fat is "bad," which often results in a vicious cycle of low self-esteem, depression, overeating for consolation, increased fatness, social rejection, and further lowering of self-esteem. Counseling is often necessary to change attitudes about being obese and to aid in the improvement of self-esteem. If this psychological element is not dealt with, even the most perfect diet and exercise plan will fail. Improving the way overweight people feel about themselves assists them in changing their eating behaviors. This is a key goal of any effective psychological support system.

A BIOLOGICAL VIEW OF OBESITY

Whereas the psychological theory proposes that obese individuals are insensitive to internal cues of hunger and

satiety, the biological theory states almost the opposite: Obese individuals appear to be extremely sensitive to specific internal clues. More and more research is supporting a biological basis for obesity.[8]

The biological/biochemical models of obesity are tied to the metabolism of the fat cells. These models support the notion that obesity is not just a matter of overeating, and explain why some people can eat very large quantities of calories and not increase their weight substantially, while for the obese just the reverse is the case.

Research with animals and humans has found that each person has a programmed "set point" weight. It has been postulated that individual fat cells control this set point: When the fat cell becomes smaller, it sends a message to the brain to eat. Since many obese individuals have both more and larger fat cells, the result is an overpowering urge to eat.

This explains why most diets don't work. While the obese individual can fight off the impulse for a time, eventually the signal becomes too strong to ignore. The result is rebound overeating, with individuals often exceeding their previous weight. In addition, their set point is now set at a higher level, making it even more difficult to lose weight.[9] This is known as the "yo-yo" or "ratchet" effect.

The set point seems to be tied to the sensitivity of fat cells to the hormone insulin. Obesity leads to insulin insensitivity and vice versa. Both obesity and diabetes are strongly linked to the so-called Western diet, presumably because of the harmful effects refined sugar has on insulin and blood sugar control mechanisms.[10]

The key to overcoming the fat cells' set point appears to be increasing their sensitivity to insulin. The set point theory suggests a weight-loss plan that does not improve insulin sensitivity will most likely fail to provide long-term results. Insulin sensitivity can be improved, and the set point lowered, by exercise and slow, gradual weight loss.

HOW TO LOSE WEIGHT

Weight loss is perhaps one of the most challenging health goals. Few people want to be overweight, yet only 5% of markedly obese individuals and only 66% of people just a few pounds or so overweight are able to attain and maintain "normal" body weight.[11]

Successful permanent weight loss must incorporate high nutrition, adequate exercise, and a positive mental attitude. All the components are critical and interrelated; no single component is more important than another. Improving one facet may be enough to result in some positive changes, but improving all three yields the greatest results.

There are literally hundreds of diets and weight-loss programs that claim to be the answer to the problem of obesity. Dieters are constantly bombarded with new reports of "wonder" diets. The basic equation for losing weight never changes, however. In order to lose weight, calorie intake must be less than the amount of calories burned. This can be done by decreasing food intake and/or by exercising.

To lose one pound of fat, a person must take in 3,500 fewer calories than he or she expends. To lose three pounds of fat each week, there must be a negative caloric balance of 1,000 calories a day. This can be achieved by decreasing the amount of calories ingested and/or by exercise. To reduce one's caloric intake by 1,000 calories a day by exercise (a person would need to jog for 90 minutes, play tennis for 2 hours, or take a brisk 2½-hour walk). The most sensible approach to weight loss is to simultaneously eat less and exercise more.

A successful weight-loss program should provide about 1,200–1,500 calories a day. This, along with aerobic exercise for 15–20 minutes three or four times a week, will produce optimum weight loss at a rate of approximately one to three pounds a week. Crash diets usually result in rapid

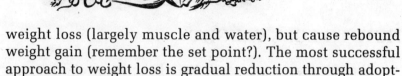

weight loss (largely muscle and water), but cause rebound weight gain (remember the set point?). The most successful approach to weight loss is gradual reduction through adopting long-standing dietary and lifestyle modifications.

THE FRESH JUICE ADVANTAGE

Juicing fresh fruits and vegetables provides numerous nutritional advantages that are extremely important to weight loss. Fresh juice offers concentrated nutrition that is easily absorbed, a rich supply of protein, carbohydrate, essential fatty acids, vitamins, and minerals.

As mentioned in Chapter 1, diets containing a high percentage of uncooked foods are significantly associated with weight loss, improved blood sugar control, and lower blood pressure. Researchers seeking to determine why raw-food diets produce these effects have concluded that:

1. A raw-food diet is much more satisfying to the appetite. Cooking can cause the loss of up to 97% of water-soluble vitamins (A, D, E, and K). Since uncooked foods such as juices contain more vitamins and other nutrients, they are more satisfying to the body. If the body is not fed, it feels that it is starving. The result: Metabolism will slow down. This means less fat will be burned.

2. The blood-pressure-lowering effect of raw foods is most likely due to healthier food choices, fiber, and potassium. However, the effect of cooking the food cannot be ruled out. When patients are switched from a raw-food diet to a cooked diet (without the content of calories or sodium), there is a rapid increase of blood pressure to prestudy values.

3. A diet in which 60% of the calories ingested come from raw foods reduces stress on the body.

Specifically, the presence of enzymes in raw foods, the reduced allergenicity of raw foods, and the effects of raw foods on our gut-bacteria ecosystem are thought to be much more healthful than the effects of cooked foods.

Juicing helps the body's digestive process and allows for quick absorption of high-quality nutrition. The result: increased energy levels. This is one of the great advantages of achieving weight loss through improved nutrition. Unlike other plans that leave you feeling tired and lifeless, fresh juices along with sensible eating will provide you with energy: energy to burn more calories with physical activity.

THE IMPORTANCE OF FIBER TO WEIGHT LOSS

Although it is the juice that nourishes us, fiber is still very important. It is well established that a fiber-deficient diet is a significant factor in the development of obesity.[12] Dietary fiber plays a role in preventing obesity by: (1) slowing the eating process, (2) increasing excretion of calories in the feces, (3) altering digestive-hormone secretion, (4) improving glucose tolerance, and (5) inducing satiety by increasing gastric filling, stimulating the release of appetite-suppressing hormones like cholecystokinin, and enhancing intestinal bulking action.

Perhaps the prime effects of fiber on obesity are related to improving glucose metabolism. Blood sugar problems (hypoglycemia and diabetes) appear to be among those most clearly related to inadequate dietary fiber intake.[13] Numerous clinical trials have demonstrated the beneficial effects of several water-soluble fibers, such as guar gum, gum karaya, and pectin, on blood sugar control. In the treatment of obesity, dietary fiber supplementation has been shown to promote weight loss.[14] Its main action appears to be reducing caloric consumption by increasing the feeling of

fullness and decreasing the feeling of hunger. Utilize mix-
tures of fiber sources, especially water-soluble fibers, for the
maximum benefit.

PREPARING YOUR BODY
FOR WEIGHT LOSS

During the first week of a weight-loss program it is often
recommended that an individual prepare the body by going
on a juice fast consisting of three or four 8- to 12-ounce juice
meals spread throughout the day. During this week your
body will begin ridding stored toxins. If your body needs
support, follow the recommendations given in Chapter 9, or
use a product like Trillium's Juice + Four Super-Nutrient
Meal Replacement Formula to provide key nutrients that
will help your body deal with and eliminate these harmful
substances. As the program progresses, your body will continue to eliminate these stored toxins and will continue to
need the protection of fresh juice and a high-fiber diet.

After week 1, take two juice meals (I recommend breakfast and a mid-afternoon snack), plus two meals of whole-
some foods, including additional juices. Choose meals from
the New Four Food Groups (grains, legumes, fruits, and vegetables), as they will give your body important fiber and nutrients. They will also provide continued support for
enhanced detoxification. The following dietary guidelines
are important to the success of the program.

HEALTHY FOOD CHOICES

Permanent results require permanent changes in choosing what foods to eat and when to eat them. The healthy-
diet component of an effective weight-loss program must
stress the New Four Food Groups. A healthy-diet weight-loss
program must provide adequate, but not excessive, quantities of protein.

Avoiding food components detrimental to health, such as sugar, saturated fats, cholesterol, salt, food additives, alcohol, and agricultural residues like pesticides and herbicides, is strongly recommended. The healthy foods recommended are divided into the following categories:

> Vegetables
> Fruits
> Breads, cereals, and starchy vegetables
> Legumes (beans)
> Protein sources
> Fats
> Sweeteners

VEGETABLES

Vegetables are fantastic "diet" foods because they are very high in nutritional value but low in calories. Vegetables are excellent sources of vitamins, minerals, and health-promoting fiber compounds. In addition to being juiced and mixed with Juice + Four, the following vegetables can be eaten in their raw state, in salads, or steamed. The vegetables noted with an asterisk (*) are termed "free foods" and can be eaten in any desired amount because the calories they contain are offset by the number of calories your body burns in the process of digestion. Another effect of these free foods is they help keep you feeling satisfied between meals.

In addition to the vegetables being consumed as juice, you should eat (or juice) at least four cups of vegetables daily with one of these cups being a dark leafy vegetable. Additional amounts can be eaten if they are chosen from those marked by an asterisk. Buy vegetables that are in season and eat a variety for nutrient diversity. Starchy vegetables like potatoes are included in the Breads, Cereals, and Starchy Vegetables category below.

VEGETABLE	CALORIES PER CUP
*Alfalfa sprouts	20
Artichokes	44, steamed heart and leaves
Asparagus	21 per 6 medium spears
Beets	54
*Bell peppers	22
*Bok choy	20
Broccoli	40
Brussels sprouts	54
*Cabbage (green or red)	24 raw, 31 cooked
Carrots	46
*Celery	17
*Cauliflower	27
Chard	30
*Cucumber	16
Daikon radish	26
Eggplant	38 cooked
*Endive	10
*Escarole	10
Garlic	10 (per clove)
Greens:	
Beet	36
Collard	40
Mustard	40
Turnip	29
Jicama	49
Kale	37
Kohlrabi	40

Leeks	53
*Lettuce	10
*Mushrooms	20
Okra	36 (per 8 pods)
Onions	50–60
Parsley	26
Peas	106
*Radishes	20
Rhubarb	50
*Spinach	41
*Sprouted mung beans	21
String beans (green or yellow)	31
Summer squash (yellow)	40
Tomatoes	23
*Turnips	36
Watercress	7
Zucchini	25

FRUITS

Fruits make excellent snacks, because they contain fructose, or fruit sugar, which is absorbed slowly into the bloodstream, thereby allowing the body time to utilize it. Fruits are also excellent sources of vitamins and minerals as well as health-promoting fiber compounds. However, fruits are typically higher in calories than vegetables, so their intake should be restricted somewhat on a weight-loss plan. Two of the following servings of fruit can be eaten during the day or utilized in juice form:

FRUIT	PORTION	CALORIES
Apple	1 large or 2 small	125
Applesauce (unsweetened)	1 cup	100
Apricots, dried	8 halves	70
Apricots, fresh	4 medium	70
Banana	1 small	100
Berries		
Blackberries	1 cup	85
Blueberries	1 cup	90
Cranberries	1 cup	90
Raspberries	1 cup	70
Strawberries	1 cup	55
Cherries	10 large	45
Dates	4	100
Figs, dried	2	100
Figs, fresh	2	100
Grapefruit	1	50
Grapes	20	70
Mango	1 small	125
Melons		
Cantaloupe	½ small	80
Honeydew	¼ medium	110
Watermelon	2 cups	110
Nectarines	2 small	80
Oranges	2 small	110
Papaya	1 small	110
Peaches	2 medium	80

Persimmons, native	2 medium	130
Pineapple	1 cup	80
Plums	4 medium	80
Prunes	4 medium	110
Raisins	¼ cup	105
Tangerines	2 medium	80

BREADS, CEREALS, AND STARCHY VEGETABLES

Breads, cereals, and starchy vegetables are classified as complex carbohydrates. Chemically, complex carbohydrates are made up of long chains of simple carbohydrates or sugars. This means the body has to digest or break down the large sugar chains into simple sugars. Therefore, the sugar from complex carbohydrates enters the bloodstream more slowly. This means blood sugar levels and appetite are better controlled.

Complex-carbohydrate foods like breads, cereals, and starchy vegetables are higher in fiber and nutrients but lower in calories than foods high in simple sugars like cakes and candies. Two of the following servings of a complex carbohydrate can be eaten per day:

Breads

Bagel, small 1
Dinner roll 2
English muffin, small 1
Tortilla (6-inch) 2
Whole wheat, rye, or pumpernickel bread
2 slices

Cereals

Bran flakes 1 cup
Cornmeal (dry) ¼ cup
Cereal (cooked) 1 cup
Flour 5 tablespoons
Grits (cooked) 1 cup
Pasta (cooked) 1 cup
Puffed cereal (unsweetened) 2 cups
Rice or barley (cooked) 1 cup
Wheat germ ½ cup
Other unsweetened cereal 1½ cups

Crackers

Arrowroot 6
Graham (2½" square) 4
Matzo (4" × 6") 1
Rye wafers (2" × 3½") 6
Saltines 12

Starchy Vegetables

Corn ⅔ cup
Corn on cob 2 small
Parsnips 2 cups
Potato, mashed 1 cup
Potato, white 1 medium
Squash, winter, acorn, or butternut 1 cup
Yam or sweet potato ½ cup

LEGUMES

Legumes are fantastic weight-loss foods. They are rich
in important nutrients for proper metabolism. Legumes help
improve liver function, as evidenced by their cholesterol-

lowering actions. Legumes have also been shown to be effective in improving blood sugar control. Since obesity has been linked to loss of blood sugar control (insulin insensitivity), legumes appear to be extremely important in a weight-loss plan.

One cup of the following cooked beans can be eaten per day:

> Black-eyed peas
> Chickpeas or garbanzo beans
> Kidney beans
> Lentils
> Lima beans
> Pinto beans
> Split peas
> Tofu
> Other dried beans and peas

ANIMAL PRODUCTS

To prevent breakdown of muscle during weight loss, it is important that protein intake be adequate. The plant foods recommended above, especially if supplemented with a meal replacement formula like Trillium's Juice + Four, will provide more than enough protein. Although I stress the importance of the New Four Food Groups, I realize it is necessary to give you some guidelines if you choose to eat some animal protein sources, especially during the transition phase. Certainly you should limit this to no more than twice a week. If one of the following food choices is made, it will be necessary to reduce the fat selection to a half serving and reduce by half the breads, cereals, and starchy vegetables selection and eliminate the legume selection.

> Fish: 6 oz of cod, sole, halibut, salmon, tuna
> packed in water, red snapper, or perch

Beef: 4 oz lean cuts of veal, chipped beaf, chuck, steak (flank, plate), tenderloin plate ribs, round (bottom, top), all cuts rump, spare ribs, or tripe

Lamb: 4 oz lean cuts of leg, rib, sirloin, loin (roast and chops), shank, or shoulder

Poultry: 4 oz chicken or turkey without skin

Dairy: 2 cups nonfat milk, 1 cup 2% milk, 1 cup low-fat yogurt, or ½ cup low-fat cottage cheese

FATS

Fat intake should be reduced to a minimum, since fats are very dense in calories. If you can do without it, this is the best. One of the following may be consumed each day:

Avocado (4" diameter) ⅛

Vegetable oil (olive, corn, safflower, soy, sunflower, canola) 1 teaspoon

Olives 5 small

Almonds 10 whole

Pecans 2 large

Peanuts
    Spanish 20 whole
    Virginia 10 whole

Walnuts 6 small

Butter 1 teaspoon

Salad dressings 2 teaspoons

Mayonnaise 1 teaspoon

SWEETENERS

Sweetener intake should also be restricted. Again, if you can do without it, this is best. One of the following can be eaten each day:

Honey 1 tablespoon
Jams, jellies, preserves 1 tablespoon

EXERCISE

The health benefits of regular exercise cannot be overstated. The immediate effect of exercise is stress on the body; however, with a regular exercise program the body adapts. The body's response to this regular stress is that it becomes stronger, functions more efficiently, and has greater endurance. Exercise is a vital component in a successful permanent weight-loss plan.[15]

Physical inactivity may be a major cause of obesity in the United States. Indeed, childhood obesity seems to be associated more with inactivity than overeating, and strong evidence suggests that 80%–86% of adult obesity begins in childhood. In the adult population, obese adults are less active than their leaner counterparts.[16] Regular exercise is a necessary component of a weight-loss program because:

1. When weight loss is achieved by dieting without exercise, a substantial portion of the total weight loss comes from the lean tissue, primarily as water loss.[17]

2. When exercise is included in a weight-loss program, there is usually an improvement in body composition due to a gain in lean body weight because of an increase in muscle mass and a concomitant decrease in body fat.[18]

3. Exercise helps counter the reduction in basal metabolic rate (BMR) that usually accompanies calorie restriction alone.[19]

4. Exercise increases the BMR for an extended period of time following the exercise session.[20]

5. Moderate to intense exercise may have an appetite suppressant effect.[21]

6. Those subjects who exercise during and after weight reduction are better able to maintain the weight loss than those who do not exercise.[22]

PHYSICAL BENEFITS OF EXERCISE

The entire body benefits from regular exercise, largely as a result of improved cardiovascular and respiratory function. Simply stated, exercise enhances the transport of oxygen and nutrients into cells. At the same time, exercise enhances the transport of carbon dioxide and waste products from the body tissues to the bloodstream and ultimately to eliminative organs.

Regular exercise is particularly important in reducing the risk of heart disease. It does this by lowering cholesterol levels, improving blood and oxygen supply to the heart, increasing the functional capacity of the heart, reducing blood pressure, reducing obesity, and exerting a favorable effect on blood clotting.

PSYCHOLOGICAL AND SOCIAL BENEFITS OF EXERCISE

Regular exercise makes people not only look better, but feel better. Tensions, depressions, feelings of inadequacy, and worries diminish greatly with regular exercise. The value of an exercise program in the treatment of depression cannot be overstated. Exercise alone has been demonstrated to have a tremendous impact on improving mood and the ability to handle stressful life situations.

A recent study published in the *American Journal of Epidemiology* found that increased participation in exercise, sports, and physical activities is strongly associated with decreased symptoms of depression (feelings that life is not worthwhile, low spirits), anxiety (restlessness, tension), and malaise (rundown feeling, insomnia).[23]

HOW TO START AN EXERCISE PROGRAM

Before you start an exercise program, make sure you are fit enough. If you have been mostly inactive for a number of years or have a previously diagnosed illness, see your physician first.

If you are fit enough to begin, select an activity that you feel you would enjoy. The best exercises are the kind that get your heart moving. Aerobic activities such as walking briskly, jogging, bicycling, crosscountry skiing, swimming, aerobic dance, and racquet sports are good examples. Brisk walking (five miles an hour) for approximately 30 minutes may be the very best form of exercise for weight loss. Walking can be done anywhere; it doesn't require any expensive equipment, just comfortable clothing and shoes that fit well; and the risk for injury is extremely low.

The concept of "spot reduction" is a myth.[24] Exercise draws from all the fat stores of the body, not just from local deposits. While aerobic exercise generally enhances weight-loss programs, weight-training programs can also substantially alter body composition, by increasing lean body weight and decreasing body fat.[25] Thus, weight training may be just as effective as or more effective than aerobic exercise in maintaining or increasing lean body weight and, therefore, the metabolic rate of individuals undergoing weight reduction.

INTENSITY OF EXERCISE

Exercise intensity is determined by measuring your heart rate (the number of times your heart beats per minute). This can be quickly done by placing your index and middle finger of one hand on the side of the neck just below the angle of the jaw or on the opposite wrist. Beginning with zero, count the number of heartbeats for six seconds. Simply add a

zero to this number and you have your pulse. For example, if you counted 14 beats, your heart rate would be 140. Would this be a good number? It depends on your training zone.

A quick and easy way to determine your maximum training heart rate is to simply subtract your age from 185. For example, if you are 40 years old, your maximum heart rate would be 145. To determine the bottom of the training zone, simply subtract 20 from this number. In the case of a 40-year-old, this would be 125. So the training range would be between 125 and 145 beats per minute. For maximum health benefits you must stay in this range and never exceed it.

DURATION AND FREQUENCY

A minimum of 15 to 20 minutes of exercising at your training heart rate at least three times a week is necessary to gain any significant benefits from exercise. It is better to exercise at the lower end of your training zone for longer periods of time than it is to exercise at a higher intensity for a shorter period of time. It is also better if you can make exercise a part of your daily routine.

AFTER THE WORK-OUT

After exercising, your body needs to replace fluids and electrolytes (potassium, magnesium, sodium, and calcium). Fresh juice is the absolute best way to replenish lost water and electrolytes. Virtually any fresh juice is suitable; perhaps the best are the Potassium Punch and Potassium Power recipes (see Chapter 7).

SUMMARY

Permanent weight loss is possible, but it requires a comprehensive system that addresses the underlying factors contributing to obesity. The plan described in this chapter

focuses on giving the body the quality of nutrition it truly desires rather than depriving it. The central feature of the plan is fresh fruit and vegetable juice along with a highly nutritious high-fiber diet. By supplying your body with improved quality of nutrition, the quantities of calories you consume will be reduced, energy levels will skyrocket, and you will feel like exercising. With improved quality of nutrition, it is possible for you to improve the quality of your life.

11

JUICING, IMMUNE FUNCTION, AND THE CANCER PATIENT

Although juicing provides benefit to nearly everyone, there are several groups for whom it should be viewed as essential: people undergoing chemotherapy or radiation therapy for cancer and people with severely decreased immune functions resulting from AIDS. In addition to dealing with their disease, these individuals are often subjected to a tremendous increase in their free-radical load as a side effect of their medical treatment. They desperately need the nutritional support and protection offered by fresh fruit and vegetable juices. One of the ways these juices offer support to these individuals is through enhancing the immune system.

THE IMMUNE SYSTEM: A QUICK OVERVIEW

The immune system is perhaps one of the most complex and fascinating systems of the human body. While the workings of other bodily systems (respiratory, cardiovascular, digestive, muscular/skeletal) have been well known for some time, it has only been relatively recently that researchers, scientists, and physicians have understood the basic structure and functions of our immune system. Immunology, the study of the immune system, is one of the most dynamic fields of study involving the human body.

The immune system is composed of the lymphatic vessels and organs (thymus, spleen, tonsils, and lymph nodes), white blood cells (lymphocytes, neutrophils, basophils, eosinophils, monocytes), specialized cells residing in various tissue (macrophages, mast cells), and specialized serum factors. The immune system's prime functions are protecting the body against infection and cancer.

THE THYMUS GLAND: THE MASTER GLAND OF THE IMMUNE SYSTEM

The thymus is composed of two soft pinkish-gray lobes lying in a biblike fashion just below the thyroid gland and above the heart. The thymus gland shows maximum development immediately after birth. During the aging process the thymus gland undergoes shrinkage, or involution. The reason for this involution is that the thymus gland is extremely susceptible to free-radical and oxidative damage caused by stress, drugs, radiation, infection, and chronic illness. When the thymus gland becomes damaged, its ability to control the immune system is severely compromised.

The thymus is responsible for many immune system functions, including the production of T lymphocytes, a type of white blood cell responsible for "cell-mediated immunity." Cell-mediated immunity refers to immune mechanisms not controlled or mediated by antibodies. Cell-mediated immunity is extremely important in the resistance to infection by moldlike bacteria, yeast (including *Candida albicans*), fungi, parasites, and viruses (including herpes simplex and Epstein-Barr). Cell-mediated immunity is also critical in protecting against the development of cancer and allergies.

The thymus gland also releases several hormones, such as thymosin, thymopoeitin, and serum thymic factor, which regulate many immune functions. Low levels of these hormones in the blood are associated with depressed immunity and an increased susceptibility to infection. Typically, thymic hormone levels will be very low in the elderly, those prone to infection, cancer and AIDS patients, and individuals exposed to undue stress.

Ensuring optimal thymus gland activity, thymic hormone levels, and cell-mediated immunity depends on: (1) prevention of thymic shrinkage, (2) use of nutrients that act as

cofactors for the thymic hormones, and (3) stimulation of thymus gland activity. Fresh juices can be helpful in achieving all three of these goals, although usually a comprehensive approach involving herbs, nutritional supplements, special nutritional factors, and other supportive therapies is indicated in the more seriously ill.

FACTORS THAT IMPAIR
THE IMMUNE SYSTEM

STRESS

Stress causes increases in the adrenal gland hormones, including corticosteroids and catecholamines. Among other things, these hormones inhibit white blood cells and cause the thymus gland to shrink. This leads to a significant suppression of immune function, leaving the individual susceptible to infections, cancer, and other illnesses. The level of immune suppression is usually proportional to the level of stress.

Stress results in stimulation of the sympathetic nervous system, which is responsible for the fight-or-flight response. The immune system functions better under parasympathetic nervous system tone. This portion of our autonomic nervous system assumes control over bodily functions during periods of rest, relaxation, visualization, meditation, and sleep. During the deepest levels of sleep, potent immune-enhancing compounds are released and many immune functions are greatly increased. The value of good-quality sleep, exercise, and relaxation techniques for counteracting the effects of stress and enhancing the immune system cannot be overemphasized.

Numerous studies have clearly demonstrated that stress, personality, attitude, and emotion are causative factors in many diseases. Reaction to stress is entirely individual, reinforcing the fact that people differ significantly in their perceptions and responses to various life events. The variations

in response help account for the wide diversity of stress-induced illnesses.

Perhaps the most important factor in maintaining or attaining a healthy immune system is a consistent positive mental attitude. How do you develop a positive mental attitude? It usually happens by degrees, subtle changes accumulating one by one. The first step is to take personal responsibility for your own mental state, your life, your current situation, your immune system, and your health. The next step is to take action to make the changes you desire in your life.

NUTRITIONAL DEFICIENCIES

Undernourishment is generally regarded as the most frequent cause of immunodeficiency in the world. Although, historically, research relating nutritional status to immune function has concerned itself with severe malnutrition states (such as kwashiorkor and marasmas), attention is now shifting toward marginal deficiencies of single or multiple nutrients and the effects of overnutrition. There is ample evidence to support the conclusion that any single nutrient deficiency can profoundly impair the immune system.

Nutrient deficiency is not limited to Third World countries. Nutrition surveys of the U.S. population have shown that most Americans are deficient in at least one nutrient. Several studies have estimated that 19% to 66% of the elderly population in parts of North America consume two-thirds or less of the RDA for various nutrients.[1] The significance of these findings to the immune system is substantial, as virtually any nutrient deficiency will result in an impaired immune system, putting an individual at risk for cancer and infections.

SUGAR

Studies in the 1970s showed that the ingestion of 100g (roughly 3½-ounce) portions of carbohydrate as glucose,

fructose, sucrose, honey, and pasteurized orange juice all significantly reduced the ability of white blood cells (neutrophils) to engulf and destroy bacteria.[2] In contrast, the ingestion of 100g starch had no effect. These effects started in less than 30 minutes after ingestion and lasted for over five hours. Typically there was at least a 50% reduction in neutrophil activity two hours after ingestion. Since neutrophils constitute 60% to 70% of the total circulating white blood cells, impairment of their activity leads to depressed immunity.

In addition, ingestion of 75g glucose has also been shown to depress lymphocyte activity.[3] Other aspects of immune function are also undoubtedly affected by sugar consumption. It has been suggested that the ill effects of high glucose levels are a result of competition between blood glucose and vitamin C for membrane transport sites into the white blood cells.[4] This is based on evidence that vitamin C and glucose appear to have opposite effects on immune function and the fact that both require insulin for membrane transport into many tissues.

Considering that the average American consumes 150g sucrose, plus other refined simple sugars, each day, the inescapable conclusion is that most Americans have chronically depressed immune systems. It is clear, particularly during an infection or chronic illness like cancer or AIDS, that the consumption of refined sugars is deleterious to immune status.

OBESITY

Obesity is associated with such conditions as atherosclerosis, hypertension, diabetes mellitus, and joint disorders. It is also associated with decreased immune status, as evidenced by the decreased bacteria-killing activity of neutrophils, and increased morbidity and mortality from infections.[5] Cholesterol and lipid levels are usually elevated in

obese individuals, which may explain their impaired immune function (see below).

FATS IN THE BLOOD

Increased blood levels of cholesterol, free fatty acids, triglycerides, and bile acids inhibit various immune functions, including the ability of lymphocytes to proliferate and produce antibodies, and the ability of neutrophils to migrate to areas of infections and engulf and destroy infectious organisms.[6] Optimal immune function therefore depends on control of these serum components.

ALCOHOL

Alcohol increases the susceptibility to experimental infections in animals, and alcoholics are known to be more susceptible to pneumonia and other infections. Studies of white blood cells (neutrophils) show a profound depression after alcohol ingestion in even nutritionally normal people. Obviously, alcohol ingestion should be eliminated entirely in the severely ill and anyone seeking a strong immune system.

BUILDING OPTIMAL IMMUNE FUNCTION

Optimal immune function requires the active pursuit of good health, through a positive mental attitude, a healthy diet, and exercise. A healthy diet is one that (1) is rich in whole, natural foods, such as fruits, vegetables, grains, beans, seeds, and nuts, (2) is low in fats and refined sugars, and (3) contains adequate, but not excessive, amounts of protein. On top of this, an individual should consume 16 to 24 ounces of fresh fruit and vegetable juice a day, drink five or six 8-ounce glasses of water a day (preferably pure), take a good basic multivitamin-mineral supplement, engage in at least 30 minutes of aerobic exercise and 5 to 10 minutes of

passive stretching daily, perform daily deep breathing and
relaxation exercises (such as meditation or prayer), take time
each day to play and enjoy family and friends, and still get at
least six to eight hours of sleep daily.

JUICING AND THE CANCER PATIENT

There is perhaps no greater need for the benefits of fresh
fruit and vegetable juice than in cancer. In many cases the
body must deal not just with the stress of cancer, but with the
side effects of medical treatment. Specifically, chemotherapy
and radiation expose healthy cells, as well as cancer cells,
to free-radical damage. The result is a great stress to antioxidant mechanisms and depletion of valuable antioxidant enzymes and nutrients. Cancer patients need higher quantities
of antioxidant nutrients.

Supporting the cancer patient with antioxidant nutrients like coenzyme Q10, vitamin C, selenium, vitamin E, and
sulfur compounds is gaining respect in orthodox cancer research. Studies are showing that these nutrients can help
reduce some of the side effects of the chemotherapy drugs
and radiation, thereby increasing their effectiveness.[7]

Juicing not only provides important antioxidant nutrients that can protect against some of the damaging effects of
chemotherapy and radiation, it provides a wide range of anutrients as well (see Chapter 3). These anutrients may exert direct anticancer effects as well as stimulate the immune
system.

Furthermore, juicing can help deal with some of the nutritional problems that develop as a result of the cancer or
the chemotherapy and radiation. About two-thirds of all people with cancer develop a condition known as cachexia,
which is characterized by a loss of appetite, resulting in decreased nutrient intake. This in turn leads to malnutrition,
muscle wasting, and impaired immune function. This condition is quite serious, as it greatly reduces the quality of

life and contributes greatly to the development of further illness or even the death of the patient. Juicing is used as part of the nutritional support program for the cancer patient at several orthodox cancer treatment centers across the country as well as being featured in many alternative cancer treatments.

CAROTENE-RICH JUICES

As mentioned in Chapter 3, considerable research is currently examining the relationship between both vitamin A and carotenes and the incidence of epithelial cancer, that is, cancer of the lungs, gastrointestinal tract, genitourinary tract, and skin. Studies have consistently demonstrated an inverse relationship between carotene intake and cancer incidence: the higher the intake of carotenes, the lower the incidence of cancer. Most of the research has focused on beta-carotene.

Although it is generally accepted that carotenes offer significant protection against many cancers, it is not known whether carotenes offer any therapeutic benefit in existing cancers. There are ample animal studies to support the use of carotenes, especially beta-carotene, not only in the prevention of cancer, but also in the treatment of cancer. Unfortunately, studies in humans have not been performed.

Some human studies in precancerous conditions have shown oral beta-carotene to reverse the condition.[8] For example, beta-carotene has been found to have "substantial" activity in reversing a precancerous condition known as leukoplakia, a white plaquelike lesion occurring on the lips or oral cavity. It is generally a reaction to irritation, such as cigarette smoking or tobacco chewing. Leukoplakia almost invariably leads to cancer. In one study, 17 of 24 patients with leukoplakia responded to a relatively low dose of beta-carotene (30mg a day) within a three-month period.[9] These

results are encouraging to cancer researchers because of beta-carotene's total lack of side effects.

Beta-carotene has also been shown to exert many beneficial effects on the immune system. For example, a study in normal human volunteers demonstrated that oral beta-carotene (180mg a day, approximately 300,000 I.U. or 30,000 RE) significantly increased the frequency of a type of white blood cell known as the helper T-cell by approximately 30% after seven days.[10] As helper T-cells play a critical role in determining immune status, this study indicates that oral beta-carotene may be effective in increasing immune status even in healthy individuals, as well as raising the helper T-cells in conditions like AIDS and cancer, two conditions characterized by low helper T-cells.

The effects of carotenes on the immune system go well beyond the thymus and T-cells. Carotenes have been shown to enhance the function of several types of white blood cells as well as increase the antiviral and anticancer properties of our own immune system mediators, such as interferon.

Simply stated, carotene-rich drinks appear to boost antitumor immunity in cancer patients. They should consume a minimum of 24 ounces of carotene-rich drinks each day. It is a good idea to rely on a variety of juices rather than simply carrot. Figure 3.3 lists the carotene contents of common fruits and vegetables.

VITAMIN C

Many claims have been made about the role of vitamin C (ascorbic acid) in enhancing the immune system, especially in regard to the prevention and treatment of the common cold. Despite numerous positive clinical and experimental studies, for some reason this effect is still hotly debated.[11] From a biochemical viewpoint, there is considerable evidence that vitamin C plays a vital role in many im-

mune mechanisms. The high concentration of vitamin C in white blood cells, particularly lymphocytes, is rapidly depleted during infection, and a relative vitamin C deficiency may ensue if vitamin C is not regularly replenished.

Vitamin C has been shown to increase many different immune functions, including white blood cell activity, interferon levels, antibody responses, antibody levels, secretion of thymic hormones, and integrity of ground substance.[12] Vitamin C has many biochemical effects very similar to interferon, the body's natural antiviral and anticancer compound.

It is a good idea for cancer patients to supplement their diet with additional vitamin C (3–8g daily) and consume juices high in vitamin C, especially the vegetable juices, because they are also rich sources of carotenes. The High C juice in Chapter 7 is an excellent source of natural vitamin C and other antioxidants.

CRUCIFEROUS VEGETABLES

The anticancer effects of the cruciferous, or cabbage, family of vegetables (cabbage, brussels sprouts, broccoli, cauliflower) have been mentioned in Chapter 3 and 6. The American Cancer Society is recommending the regular consumption of these foods to prevent cancer. Animal studies are showing that sulfur-containing compounds in cruciferous vegetables, in addition to enhancing the detoxification of cancer-causing compounds, may have some therapeutic potential in cancer as well. Specifically, compounds are being shown to inhibit the progression of many types of tumors and cancers, including breast cancer. Cruciferous vegetables are also very good sources of carotenes and vitamin C. The cancer patient should try to consume two cups of cruciferous vegetables a day in their whole or juiced form. The Cruciferous Surprise recipe in Chapter 7 is an excellent drink for getting your quota of these vegetables.

GARLIC

The ancient Greek physician Hippocrates prescribed eating garlic as treatment for cancers. Judging from animal research and some human studies, this recommendation may have been extremely wise. Several garlic components have displayed significant antitumor effects and are known to inhibit formation of cancer-causing compounds as well as enhance the immune system.

Human studies showing garlic's anticancer effects are largely based on population studies. They indicate an inverse relationship between cancer rates and garlic consumption, that is, cancer rates are lowest where garlic consumption is greatest. For example, a study in China comparing populations in different regions found that death from gastric cancers in regions where garlic consumption was high was significantly less than in regions with lower garlic consumption.[13]

Many of the therapeutic compounds in garlic have not been found in cooked, processed, and commercial garlic preparations; the broad range of beneficial effects attributed to garlic are best obtained from fresh, raw garlic. Consistently, the most potent garlic component is allicin. Unfortunately, this component is also the factor responsible for the odor. Juicing the garlic with chlorophyll-rich foods like parsley and kale may reduce the odor. The Immune Power Vegetable recipe in Chapter 7 is an excellent drink for the immune system.

JUICING AND THE AIDS PATIENT

Juicing is an important aspect of nutritional support for the individual with acquired immunodeficiency syndrome, or AIDS. The individual with AIDS or the human immunodeficiency virus (HIV) has an immune system that is severely compromised and in need of extra support. HIV-

infected patients are in a precarious position, as there is no current universally effective treatment. They have an increased need for antioxidant nutrients, because they are in a state of oxidative imbalance.[14] Specifically, AIDS patients have a greater number of pro-oxidants in their system than antioxidants. Furthermore, the development of AIDS in a symptom-free HIV-infected individual may depend on the cumulative effects of oxidative damage. If this is true, antioxidant therapy holds great promise.

Specific antioxidant therapy, such as N-acetyl-cysteine, is showing great promise in AIDS, but a more comprehensive approach, including the use of fresh fruit and vegetable juices, is indicated.[15] Specific juice recommendations mirror those given above for the cancer patient. (For more information on the natural approach to AIDS, please consult *The Encyclopedia of Natural Medicine.*

JUICING AND OTHER CHRONIC VIRAL ILLNESSES

Juicing may provide exceptional benefit in patients with herpes, Epstein-Barr, or other chronic viral illness through its delivery of large quantities of immune-enhancing antioxidants.

SUMMARY

The immune system is responsible for fighting off infection and cancer. The thymus gland is the major gland of the immune system, controlling many aspects of immune function. The health of the thymus gland is largely determined by the status of stress and nutrition. Antioxidant nutrients are critical in protecting the thymus gland from damage as well as enhancing its function. Alcohol, sugar, stress, and high cholesterol levels all inhibit immune function. Fresh fruit and vegetable juices offer nutritional

support to the immune system, largely as a result of their high content of antioxidants such as vitamin C, carotenes, and trace minerals. Cancer and AIDS patients are examples of individuals who appear to desperately need the nutritional support offered by fresh fruit and vegetable juices.

12

ANSWERS TO COMMON QUESTIONS ABOUT JUICING

I hope I have answered all your questions about juicing before this chapter. So why am I including this chapter in the book? In my live lectures I have noticed that no matter how many times I would answer some of the more common questions, I would still get asked the same questions during the question-and-answer period. More often than not, I would get asked some of these questions more than once. Sometimes we need to hear things several times or hear them in a new light before they sink in. I will also answer some questions on topics that were not covered in the preceding chapters.

Q. When I juice fruits and vegetables, I throw away the fiber, but isn't the fiber an important part of my diet?

A. Definitely, yes. Fiber is an important part of your diet and you should juice too. Think about it—fiber refers to indigestible material found in plants; it is the juice that nourishes us. Our body actually converts the food we eat into juice so that it can be absorbed. Juicing helps the body's digestive process and allows for quick absorption of high-quality nutrition. Juicing quickly provides the most easily digestible and concentrated nutritional benefits of fruits and vegetables. The result is increased energy levels.

Juicing fresh fruits and vegetables does provide some fiber, particularly the soluble fiber. And it is the soluble fiber that has been shown to lower cholesterol levels and exert other beneficial effects beyond improved bowel function.

Q. Can I do anything with the pulp?

A. Yes. The pulp from many vegetable juices, such as Salad in a Glass and Immune Power Vegetable (see Chapter 7), can make a great soup stock. Carrot or apple pulp can be added to bran muffin or healthy carrot cake recipes to increase the fiber content. Perhaps the

best use of the pulp is adding it to your compost pile and returning it to the earth.

Q. What is the difference between a juicer and a blender?

A. A juicer separates the liquid from the fiber. A blender is designed to blend or liquefy food by chopping it up at high speeds. It doesn't separate the juice from the pulp, so the result is a mushy, globby mess that really doesn't taste very good in most cases.

Blenders can be quite useful in tandem with the juicer. For example, bananas contain very little juice but taste delicious in drinks. You can mix freshly extracted juice, such as pineapple juice, along with banana or unsweetened frozen fruits to create a delicious smoothie.

Q. I have heard that you shouldn't mix fruits and vegetables. Why?

A. There is little (if any) scientific information to support this contention. The belief is based more on philosophy than physiology. Nonetheless, some people do seem to have difficulty with combined fruits and vegetables, complaining of gassy discomfort. If you are one of these people, you should avoid mixing fruits and vegetables. The exceptions to this rule appear to be carrots and apples, as these foods seem to be able to mix with either a fruit or a vegetable. My advice is to let your body and taste buds be your guide.

Q. How much juice should I drink each day?

A. I recommend up to 16 ounces of fresh fruit juice and up to 24 ounces of fresh vegetable juice a day for most people. I also recommend that people try to drink an assortment of juices. We are learning more and more that the pigments of fruits and vegetables—the carotenes, flavonoids, and chlorophyll—are responsible for many of the benefits, so I tell people to eat a

rainbow assortment of fruits and vegetables. Try to consume a variety of colors in your diet.

Q. I am confused. I know that vitamin A is stored in the liver, where it can accumulate to toxic levels, and disrupt normal liver function. Vitamin A toxicity can also lead to severe headaches, nausea and vomiting, and dry skin. Since beta-carotene is converted to vitamin A in the body, why isn't beta-carotene toxic?

A. Vitamin A is available in the diet either as "preformed" vitamin A, as found in dairy and other animal products, or as "provitamin A" carotenes, as found in plant foods. Over 400 carotenes have been characterized, but only about 30 to 50 are believed to have vitamin A activity. Beta-carotene has been termed the most active of the carotenes, due to its higher provitamin A activity. However, other carotenes exhibit far greater antioxidant and anticancer activities.

The conversion of a provitamin A carotene, like beta-carotene, to vitamin A depends on several factors: level of vitamin A in the body, protein status, thyroid hormones, zinc, and vitamin C. The conversion diminishes as carotene intake increases and when serum vitamin A levels are adequate. Simply stated, if vitamin A levels are sufficient, the beta-carotene is not converted to vitamin A. Instead, it is delivered to body tissues for storage.

Vitamin A and carotenes differ in how they are absorbed by the body and where they are stored. Specifically, vitamin A is stored primarily in the liver, while carotenes may be stored in fat cells, other organs (the adrenals, testes, and ovaries have the highest concentrations), and epithelial cells. Epithelial cells are found in the skin and the linings of the internal organs, including the respiratory tract, gastrointestinal tract, and genitourinary tract.

There have not been any reports of vitamin A toxicity from the ingestion of foods rich in carotenes or supplemental beta-carotene. In addition, beta-carotene has not been shown to possess any significant toxicity despite its use in very high doses in the treatment of numerous medical conditions. Unlike vitamin A, carotene is safe during pregnancy. In fact, carotenes have been shown to prevent genetic damage.

It should be pointed out that though there have been no reports of toxicity due to beta-carotene, some evidence indicates that too much carrot juice over a long period of time—one to two quarts of fresh carrot juice a day for several years—may cause a decrease in the number of white blood cells and cessation of menstruation. These effects may be attributable to some other factor in the diet or possibly in carrots themselves. Neither of these effects nor any others have been observed in subjects with severe sun sensitivity consuming very high doses of pure beta-carotene—for example, 300,000–600,000 I.U. per day (which is equivalent to four to eight pounds of raw carrots) over long periods of time.

This possible effect of daily consumption of more than a quart of carrot juice over several years can be avoided by utilizing other juices in addition to carrot juice on a regular basis. A wide range of carotene-rich foods should be consumed in the diet. This will provide the greatest benefit.

Q. Why does my skin turn orange when I drink a lot of carrot juice? Is this a sign of toxicity?

A. The storage of carotenes in the skin results in carotenodermia, or the appearance of yellow-orange-colored skin. This is nothing to be alarmed about; it is not associated with any toxicity. In fact, it is probably a very beneficial sign. It simply indicates that the body

has a good supply of carotenes. Carotenodermia that is not directly due to dietary intake or supplementation of carotenes, however, may be a sign of a deficiency in a necessary conversion factor, such as zinc, thyroid hormone, vitamin C, or protein.

Q. Does juicing provide greater benefit than beta-carotene supplements or intact carotene-rich foods?

A. Definitely. Juicing ruptures cell membranes, thereby liberating important nutritional compounds like carotenes for easier absorption. Beta-carotene supplementation, while beneficial, only provides one particular type of carotene, whereas juicing a wide variety of carotene-rich foods will provide a broad range of carotenes, many of which have properties more advantageous than beta-carotene.

Q. If I juice, do I need to take vitamin or mineral pills?

A. The question whether Americans need to supplement their diet with vitamins and minerals is hotly debated. Many experts say supplementation is necessary; others say diet alone can provide all the essential nutrition. Which side is right? They both are right to an extent. It all boils down to what their view of "optimum" nutrition is.

An expert who believes optimum nutrition simply means no obvious signs of nutrient deficiency or impaired health will answer differently from an expert who thinks of optimum nutrition as the degree of nutrition that will allow an individual to function at the highest level possible with vitality, energy, and enthusiasm for living.

Can an individual get all the nutrition he or she needs from diet alone? Possibly, but highly unlikely. During recent years, the U.S. government has sponsored a number of comprehensive studies to detemine

the nutritional status of the population. These studies indicate the chances of consuming a diet that meets the recommended dietary allowance (RDA) for all nutrients are extremely remote for most Americans, especially children and the elderly. These studies suggest dietary supplementation may be extremely beneficial. I am a firm believer in the need for vitamin and mineral supplementation for most people. Even the most dedicated health advocate, like myself, cannot possibly meet the tremendous nutritional requirements for optimum health through diet alone. In my view, supplementation is essential.

There is a large body of information to support my view. For example, a recent study, published in a major medical journal, demonstrated that a multiple vitamin-mineral supplement increased intelligence even in children who were not malnourished. In another study from a well-respected medical journal, a formula containing vitamins and minerals, as well as carbohydrate, protein, and fat, was shown to have a tremendously beneficial effect on the immune system. These are just two of the tens of thousands of articles from the medical literature demonstrating the health benefits of dietary supplements.

Additional research is rapidly accumulating to support the contention that dietary supplements do, in fact, exhibit health-promoting activity. It may be many years, however, before the evidence is sufficient to satisfy many research groups. With the information available at this time, many experts feel that dietary supplements may be of great benefit to a large number of individuals, especially when combined with a healthy diet and lifestyle. I am in agreement with this position.

Q. When can a baby start drinking juice?

A. My recommendation of no juice until at least six months of age is shared by many experts. After six months of age, fresh juices can be introduced slowly. Pay attention for any possible signs of intolerance, like diarrhea or gas. It is recommended that the juices be diluted with an equal amount of water. Good juices for children are the sweeter ones, such as carrot, apple, cantaloupe, and orange. Never let the baby go to sleep with a bottle of juice in his or her mouth or suck on a bottle for prolonged periods of time. Too much sugar, including that of fresh juices, can lead to problems in tooth development.

Q. Can I freeze the juices?

A. Yes. You will lose some of the nutritional benefits and enzymes, but it is better than letting the juice go to waste. Also, you can make delicious homemade popsicles. Try freezing the Kids' Favorite recipe (see Chapter 7) in an ice tray with some toothpicks.

Q. Do I have to follow the juice recipes exactly?

A. Absolutely *not*. Juicing is meant to be fun. Recipes are only designed to point you in the right direction. Have fun. Create your own favorites.

Q. Should I juice if I am hypoglycemic?

A. Too much of any simple sugar, including the sugars found in fruit and vegetable juices, can lead to stress of blood sugar control mechanisms, especially if you are hypoglycemic or diabetic. The advantage of the assortment of natural simple sugars in fruits and vegetables over sucrose (white sugar) and other refined sugars is that they are balanced by a wide range of nutrients that aid in the utilization of the sugars. The real problems with carbohydrates begin when they are refined and stripped of these nutrients. Virtually all the vitamin content has been removed from white

sugar, white breads and pastries, and many breakfast cereals. Nonetheless, it is often recommended that individuals with faulty blood sugar control consume no more than eight ounces of juice at any one time. It is also a good idea to focus on vegetable juices and drink the juice with a meal to delay the absorption of the sugars.

Q. I suffer from recurrent kidney stones. Should I avoid juices because many are high in calcium?

A. Avoid juices containing spinach, because spinach is rich in both calcium and oxalate, but your diet should include other fresh juices. In fact, there are several juices that you should be consuming on a regular basis.

The high rate of kidney stones in the United States has been directly linked to the following dietary factors: low fiber, refined sugar, alcohol, large amounts of animal protein, high fat, high calcium, salt, and vitamin D–enriched foods like milk. The best dietary advice for individuals prone to developing recurrent kidney stones is to adopt a vegetarian diet. As a group, vegetarians have shown a decreased risk of developing kidney stones. However, studies have also shown that even among meat eaters, those who ate higher amounts of fresh fruits and vegetables had a lower incidence of stones. Fiber supplementation, as well as the simple change from white to whole wheat bread, has resulted in lowering urinary calcium excretion.

As for a specific juice for an individual prone to recurrent kidney stones, cranberry juice has been shown to reduce the amount of ionized calcium in the urine by over 50% in patients with kidney stones. High urinary calcium levels greatly increase the risk of developing a kidney stone.

Q. I am concerned about osteoporosis. Can I get the calcium my bones require without drinking milk?

A. Osteoporosis literally means porous bone. It affects more than 20 million people in the United States. Many factors can result in excessive bone loss, and different variants of osteoporosis exist. Postmenopausal osteoporosis is the most common form.

Osteoporosis involves both the mineral (inorganic) and the nonmineral (organic matrix composed primarily of protein) components of bone. This is the first clue that there is more to osteoporosis than a lack of dietary calcium. Recently there has been an incredible push for increasing dietary calcium to prevent osteoporosis. While this appears to be sound medical advice for many, osteoporosis is much more than a lack of dietary calcium. It is a complex condition involving hormonal, lifestyle, nutritional, and environmental factors.

Rather than being obsessed with calcium, it would be better to focus on other lifestyle and dietary factors, such as exercise, sugar, protein, and fresh fruit and vegetable juices.

In fact, physical fitness, not calcium intake, is the major determinant of bone density. One hour of moderate activity three times a week has been shown to prevent bone loss. In fact, this type of exercise has actually been shown to increase the bone mass in postmenopausal women. Walking is probably the best exercise to start with. In contrast to exercise, immobility doubles the rate of calcium excretion, resulting in an increased likelihood of developing osteoporosis.

Coffee, alcohol, and smoking induce a negative calcium balance (more calcium is lost than absorbed) and are associated with an increased risk of osteoporosis. Obviously, these lifestyle factors must be eliminated.

Many general dietary factors have been suggested as a cause of osteoporosis: low calcium–high phosphorus intake, high protein diet, high acid-ash diet, and trace mineral deficiencies, to name a few. To help slow down bone loss, foods high in calcium are often recommended. You do not need dairy products to meet your body's calcium requirement. Calcium is found in high amounts in many green leafy vegetables and other plant foods (see p. 318).

A vegetarian diet, both lacto-ovo and vegan, is associated with a lower risk of osteoporosis. Vegans do not consume dairy products, yet they have a lowered risk for osteoporosis? How can this be? Several factors are probably responsible for this decrease in bone loss observed in vegetarians. Perhaps most important is a reduced intake of protein. A high-protein diet and a diet high in phosphates are associated with increasing the excretion of calcium in the urine. Raising daily protein from 47g to 142g doubles the excretion of calcium in the urine. A diet this high in protein is common in the United States and may be a significant factor in the growing number of people suffering from osteoporosis in this country.

Another culprit in inducing bone loss is refined sugar. Following sugar intake, there is an increase in the urinary excretion of calcium. Considering that the average American consumes in one day 150g sucrose, plus other refined simple sugars, and a glass of a carbonated beverage loaded with phosphates, along with the high protein, it is little wonder that there are so many suffering from osteoporosis in this country. When lifestyle factors are also taken into consideration, it is very apparent why osteoporosis has become a major medical problem.

Juicing offers significant benefit in an osteoporosis-prevention plan. Fresh fruit and vegetable juices

Calcium Content of Selected Foods

Milligrams (mg) per 100 grams edible portion (100 grams = 3.5 oz.)

Kelp	1,093	Globe artichokes	51
Cheddar cheese	750	Dried prunes	51
Carob flour	352	Pumpkin/squash seeds	51
Dulse	296	Cooked dry beans	50
Collard greens	250	Common cabbage	49
Kale	249	Soybean sprouts	48
Turnip greens	246	Hard winter wheat	46
Almonds	234	Oranges	41
Brewer's yeast	210	Celery	41
Parsley	203	Cashews	38
Dandelion greens	187	Rye grain	38
Brazil nuts	186	Carrots	37
Watercress	151	Barley	34
Goat milk	129	Sweet potatoes	32
Tofu	128	Brown rice	32
Dried figs	126	Garlic	29
Buttermilk	121	Summer squash	28
Sunflower seeds	120	Onions	27
Yogurt	120	Lemons	26
Wheat bran	119	Fresh green peas	26
Whole milk	118	Cauliflower	25
Buckwheat, raw	114	Cucumbers	25
Sesame seeds, hulled	110	Lentils, cooked	25
Ripe olives	106	Sweet cherries	22
Broccoli	103	Asparagus	22
English walnuts	99	Winter squash	22
Cottage cheese	94	Strawberries	21
Soybeans, cooked	73	Millet	20
Pecans	73	Pineapple	17
Wheat germ	72	Grapes	16
Peanuts	69	Beets	15
Miso	68	Cantaloupe	14
Romaine lettuce	68	Tomatoes	13
Dried apricots	67	Eggplant	12
Rutabagas	66	Chicken	12
Raisins	62	Avocados	10
Black currants	60	Beef	10
Dates	59	Bananas	8
Green snap beans	56	Apples	7

Source: "Nutritive Value of American Foods in Common Units,"
U.S.D.A Agriculture Handbook No. 456

provide a rich source of a broad range of vitamins and minerals, such as calcium, vitamin K1, and boron, that are being shown to be equally important as calcium in bone health.

Vitamin K1 is the form of vitamin K found in green leafy vegetables (such as kale, collard greens, parsley, lettuce). A function of vitamin K1 that is often overlooked is its role in converting inactive osteocalcin to its active form. Osteocalcin is the major noncollagen protein in bone. Its role in bone is to anchor calcium molecules and hold them in place within the bone.

A deficiency of vitamin K leads to impaired mineralization of the bone due to inadequate osteocalcin levels. Very low blood levels of vitamin K1 have been found in patients with fractures due to osteoporosis. The severity of fracture strongly correlated with the level of circulating vitamin K. The lower the level of vitamin K, the more severe the fracture. Since vitamin K is found in green leafy vegetables, they may be one of the key protective factors of a vegetarian diet against osteoporosis.

In addition to vitamin K1, the high levels of many minerals such as calcium and boron in plant foods, particularly green leafy vegetables, may also be responsible for this protective effect. Boron is a trace mineral gaining attention as a protective factor against osteoporosis. It has been shown to have a positive effect on calcium and active estrogen levels in postmenopausal women, the group at highest risk for developing osteoporosis. In one study, supplementing the diet of postmenopausal women with 3mg boron a day reduced urinary calcium excretion by 44% and dramatically increased the levels of the most biologically active estrogen. It appears boron is required to activate certain hormones involved in bone health, including estrogen and vitamin D. Since fruits and

vegetables are the main dietary sources of boron, diets low in these foods may be deficient in boron. Supplementation with boron is not necessary if the diet is rich in fruits and vegetables.

If you have already experienced some bone loss, I would recommend that you take OsteoPrime, by Enzymatic Therapy. This comprehensive formula for bone health is available at health food stores.

Q. I smoked for many years, and even though I quit four years ago, I still have trouble breathing. Will fresh juices help restore my ability to breathe?

A. Perhaps. As you know, the risks of smoking include emphysema and other chronic obstructive pulmonary diseases, such as asthma and chronic bronchitis. Of these, emphysema is the most severe. Cigarette smoking causes emphysema by (1) blocking key enzymes that can prevent damage to the lungs and (2) depleting tissue stores of key antioxidant nutrients like vitamin C.

In Britain and the United States, several studies have shown that individuals who smoke consume less fresh fruit and vegetables than nonsmokers. This greatly increases their risk not only for emphysema, but other diseases as well, such as heart disease, cancer, and strokes.

A group of British researchers sought to determine the effect of fresh fruits and fresh fruit juices on respiratory function in both smokers and nonsmokers. They studied the reported frequency of consumption of fresh fruit and juice among 1,502 lifelong nonsmokers and 1,357 current smokers aged 18–69 with no history of chronic respiratory disease. The amount of air expelled in one second (forced expiratory volume in one second, or FEV1) into a turbine spirometer was used as a measurement. Winter fruit

consumption was used as an indicator of year-round consumption.

The results were as expected in smokers: Those who ate fresh fruit or juice had much better respiratory function than those who never drank fresh juice or ate fresh fruit less than once a week (FEV1 values were on average 78ml lower in the latter group). In nonsmokers, something was discovered that was not expected: Respiratory function was greatest in those who ate fresh fruit or drank fresh fruit juice on a regular basis.

The researchers felt that the observed effects of improved respiratory tract function with fresh fruit and juice consumption may be related more to dietary habits during childhood than to a direct influence of diet on airway function in adult life. They believed the effect of fresh fruit consumption in childhood is even more pronounced than in adults, as fresh fruits may promote improved lung growth and lung capacity.

The results of this study imply that fresh fruit and juice consumption not only protects against chronic respiratory diseases such as emphysema and asthma, but that it can improve lung function in healthy individuals and may promote improved lung growth and capacity if consumed during childhood. From this study, I conclude that fresh fruit and vegetable juices may be of great benefit in helping you restore your health.

Q. I've heard that cabbage-family vegetables can cause goiters, yet everybody is telling me to eat them. Should I be concerned?

A. Cabbage-family vegetables do contain compounds that can interfere with thyroid hormone action by blocking the utilization of iodine. However, there is

no evidence that these compounds cause any problems when dietary iodine levels are adequate. Therefore, it is a good idea if large quantities of cruciferous vegetables are being consumed that the diet also contain adequate amounts of iodine. Iodine is found in kelp and other seaweeds, vegetables grown near the sea, iodized salt, and in food supplements.

Q. Can you juice sprouts?

A. Yes. In fact, you can juice virtually any edible plant or food as long as it has a high water content, sprouts included. Sprouts provide a wide range of nutrients and can add flavor to any vegetable juice.

Q. Why should I juice?

A. It was my goal in writing this book to answer this question. Let me summarize the key benefits of fresh juice.

Improved energy

Improved nutritional quality

Increased intake of health-promoting anutrients

It's fun and tastes great

One final note: As I was finishing up this book, I came across an article entitled "Glutathione in foods listed in the National Cancer Institute's health habits and history food frequency questionnaire" that appeared in the medical journal *Nutrition and Cancer*.[1] Glutathione is an important antioxidant in the body. It is also an important anticancer agent and aids in the detoxification of heavy metals such as lead as well as in the elimination of pesticides and solvents. When researchers measured the glutathione levels in foods, what do you suppose they found? Fresh fruits and vegetables provided excellent levels of glutathione.

COMPARISON OF GLUTATHIONE IN FRESH VS. CANNED OR BOTTLED JUICE

Foood	Glutathione mg/100mg Dry Weight	
	FRESH	CANNED OR BOTTLED
Apples	21	0.0
Carrots	74.6	0.0
Grapefruit	70.6	0.0
Spinach	166	27.1
Tomatoes	169	0.0

This is additional evidence that to get the greatest benefit from our foods, we should be consuming them in their fresh form.

PERSONAL MESSAGE

I hope the information presented in this book not only has made it clear that juicing is an integral part of a healthy diet and lifestyle, but has inspired you to get started. Being healthy takes commitment. The reward is often difficult to see or feel. It is usually not until the body fails us in some manner that we realize we haven't taken care of it. Ralph Waldo Emerson said, "The first wealth is health." Don't wait until you have lost your health to realize how important it is to you. Get started right now on living a healthy life.

The reward for most people maintaining a positive mental attitude, eating a healthy diet, and exercising regularly is a life filled with very high levels of energy, joy, vitality, and a tremendous passion for living. This is my wish for you.

REFERENCES

CHAPTER 1 WHY JUICE?

1. Block G, Dietary guidelines and the results of food consumption surveys, *Am J Clin Nutr* 53:356S–7S, 1991.
2. National Research Council, *Diet and health: Implications for reducing chronic disease risk* (Washington, DC: National Academy Press, 1989); Trowell H, Burkitt D, and Heaton K, *Dietary fibre, fibre-depleted foods and disease* (New York: Academic Press, 1985).
3. Resnicow K, Barone J, Engle A et al., Diet and serum lipids in vegan vegetarians: A model for risk reduction, *J Am Diet Soc* 91:447–53, 1991; Phillips RL, Role of lifestyle and dietary habits in risk of cancer among Seventh-Day Adventists, *Cancer Res* 35:3513–22, 1975.
4. Robbins J, *Diet for a new America* (Walpole, NH: Stillpoint Publishing, 1987).
5. Physicians Committee for Responsible Medicine, P.O. Box 6322, Washington, DC, 20015.
6. American Cancer Society, *Nutrition and cancer: Cause and prevention* (New York: American Cancer Society, 1984).
7. Wald NJ, Thompson SG, Densem JW et al., Serum beta-carotene and subsequent risk of cancer: Results from the

BUPA study, *Br J Cancer* 57:428–33, 1988; Harris RWC, Key TJA, Silcocks PB et al., A case-control study of dietary carotene in men with lung cancer and in men with other epithelial cancers, *Nutr Canc* 15:63–68, 1991; Peto R, Doll R, Buckley JD et al., Can dietary beta-carotene materially reduce human cancer rates? *Nature* 290:201–8, 1981; Rogers AE and Longnecker MP, Biology of disease: Dietary and nutritional influences on cancer: A review of epidemiologic and experimental data, *Lab Invest* 59:729–59, 1988.

8. Konowalchuk J and Speirs JI, Antiviral effect of apple beverages, *Appl Envir Microbiol* 36:798–801, 1978.

9. Shils ME and Young VR, *Modern nutrition in health and disease,* 7th ed. (Philadelphia: Lea and Febiger, 1988).

10. White PL and Selvey N, Nutritional qualities of fresh fruits and vegetables (Mount Kisco, NY: Futura Publishing, 1974).

11. Douglass JM, Rasgon, IM, Fleiss PM et al., Effects of a raw food diet on hypertension and obesity, *Southern Med J* 78:841–44, 1985.

12. Chow CK, ed., *Cellular antioxidant defense mechanisms,* vol. 1, 2, & 3. (Boca Raton, FL: CRC Press, 1988).

13. Rosa GD, Keen CL, Leach RM, and Hurley LS, Regulation of superoxide dismutase activity by dietary manganese, *J Nutri* 110:795–804, 1980; Levine M, New concepts in the biology and biochemistry of ascorbic acid, *New Eng J Med* 314:892–902, 1986; Burton G and Ingold K, Beta-carotene: An unusual type of antioxidant, *Science* 224:569–73, 1984; Cody V, Middleton E, and Harborne JB, *Plant flavonoids in biology and medicine: Biochemical, pharmacological, and structure-activity relationships* (New York: Alan R. Liss, 1986).

CHAPTER 2 WHAT'S IN JUICE?
THE NUTRIENTS

1. American Medical Association, *Drinking water and human health* (Chicago: American Medical Association, 1984).

2. See Ch. 1, note 2.
3. *Nutritive value of foods.* Home and Garden Bulletin Number 72. (Washington, DC: U.S. Department of Agriculture, 1981).
4. Hart JP, Shearer MJ, Klenerman L et al., Electrochemical detection of depressed circulating levels of vitamin K1 in osteoporosis, *J Clin Endocrinol Metabol* 60:1268–69, 1985; Bitensky L, Hart JP, Catterall A et al., Circulating vitamin K levels in patients with fractures, *J Bone Joint Surg* 70-B:663–64, 1988.
5. See note 3.
6. Nielsen FH, Boron: An overlooked element of potential nutrition importance, *Nutrition Today* Jan/Feb:4–7, 1988.
7. See note 3.
8. Khaw KT and Barrett-Connor E, Dietary potassium and stroke-associated mortality, *N Engl J Med* 316:235–40, 1987; Jansson B, Dietary, total body, and intracellular potassium-to-sodium ratios and their influence on cancer, *Cancer Detect Prevent* 14:563–65, 1991.
9. Iimura O, Kijima T, Kikuchi K et al., Studies on the hypotensive effect of high potassium intake in patients with essential hypertension, *Clin Sci 61*(Supplement 7):77s–80s, 1981.
10. See note 8; Ch. 1, notes 2 and 9.

CHAPTER 3 WHAT'S IN JUICE?
THE ANUTRIENTS

1. Steinmetz KA and Potter JD, Vegetables, fruit, and cancer. II. Mechanisms, *Canc Causes Control* 2:427–42, 1991. See also Ch. 1, notes 2, 6, and 7.
2. See note 1 above; Ch. 1, note 2.
3. See note 1 above.
4. See Ch. 1, note 6.
5. Howell E, *Enzyme nutrition* (Wayne, NJ: Avery Publishing, 1985); Grossman MI, Greengard H, and Ivy AC, The effect of diet on pancreatic enzymes, *Am J Physiol* 138:676–82, 1943.

6. Kenton L and Kenton S, *Raw energy* (London: Century Publishing, 1984).

7. Taussig S and Batkin R, Bromelain: The enzyme complex of pineapple (Ananas comosus) and its clinical application. An update, *J Ethnopharmacol* 22:191–203, 1988.

8. Murray MT, *Healing power of herbs* (Rocklin, CA: Prima, 1991).

9. Miller J and Opher A, The increased proteolytic activity of human blood serum after oral administration of bromelain, *Exp Med Surg* 22:277–80, 1964; Izaka K, Yamada M, Kawano T, and Suyama T, Gastrointestinal absorption and anti-inflammatory effect of bromelain, *Jap J Pharmacol* 22:519–34, 1972; Seifert J, Ganser R, and Brendel W, Absorption of a proteolytic enzyme of plant origin from the gastrointestinal tract into the blood and lymph of adult rats, *Z Gastroenterol* 17:1–18, 1979.

10. Olson JA, Chapter 11. Vitamin A, in MB Brown, ed. *Present knowledge in nutrition,* 6th ed. (Washington, DC: Nutrition Foundation, 1990), pp 96–107.

11. Bendich A and Olson JA, Biological actions of carotenoids, FASEB J 3:1927–32, 1989; see also note 10 above.

12. See note 10 above.

13. Ziegler RG, A review of epidemiologic evidence that carotenoids reduce the risk of cancer, *J Nutr* 119:116–22, 1989; see also note 10 above; Ch. 1, note 2.

14. Krinsky NI, Carotenoids and cancer in animal models, *J Nutr* 119:123–6, 1989; Bendich A, Carotenoids and the immune response, *J Nutr* 119:112–15, 1989; Alexander M, Newmark H, and Miller RG, Oral beta-carotene can increase the number of OKT4+ cells in human blood, *Immunol Letters* 9:221–24, 1985; see also notes 10 and 11 above.

15. Cutler RG, Carotenoids and retinol: Their possible importance in determining longevity of primate species, *Proc Natl Acad Sci* 81:7627–31, 1984.

16. See note 11 above.
17. Bendich A, The safety of beta-carotene, *Nutrition and Cancer* 11:207–14, 1988.
18. Kuhnau J, The flavonoids: A class of semi-essential food components: Their role in human nutrition, *Wld Rev Nutr Diet* 24:117–91, 1976.
19. Cody V, Middleton E, Harborne JB, and Beretz A, *Plant flavonoids in biology and medicine II: Biochemical, pharmacological, and structure-activity relationships* (New York: Alan R. Liss, 1988); Havsteen B, Flavonoids, a class of natural products of high pharmacological potency, *Biochem Pharmacol* 32:1141–48, 1983; see also note 18 above, and Ch. 1, note 13, Cody.
20. Blau LW, Cherry diet control for gout and arthritis, *Texas Report on Biology and Medicine* 8:309–11, 1950; Wegrowski J, Robert AM, and Moczar M, The effect of procyanidolic oligomers on the composition of normal and hypercholesterolemic rabbit aortas, *Biochem Pharmacol* 33:3491–97, 1984.
21. Amella M, Bronner C, Briancon F et al., Inhibition of mast cell histamine release by flavonoids and biflavonoids, *Planta Medica* 51:16–20, 1985; Busse WW, Kopp DE, and Middleton E, Flavonoid modulation of human neutrophil function, *J Aller Clin Immunol* 73:801–9, 1984; see also Ch. 1, note 13, Cody.
22. Rafsky HA and Krieger CI, The treatment of intestinal diseases with solutions of water-soluble chlorophyll. *Rev Gastroenterol* 15:549–53, 1945; Smith L and Livingston A, Chlorophyll: An experimental study of its water soluble derivatives in wound healing, *Am J Surg* 62:358–69, 1943.
23. Nahata MC, Sleccsak CA, and Kamp J, Effect of chlorophyllin on urinary odor in incontinent geriatric patients, *Drug Intel Clin Pharm* 17:732–34, 1983; Young RW and Beregi JS, Use of chlorophyllin in the care of geriatric patients, *J Am Ger Soc* 28:46–47, 1980.
24. Patek A, Chlorophyll and regeneration of the blood, *Arch*

Int Med 57:73–76, 1936; Gubner R and Ungerleider HE, Vitamin K therapy in menorrhagia, *South Med J* 37:556–58, 1944.

25. Ong T, Whong WZ, Stewart J, and Brockman HE, Chlorophyllin: A potent antimutagen against environmental and dietary complex mistures, *Mutation Research* 173:111–15, 1986.

26. Ohyama S, Kitamori S, Kawano H et al., Ingestion of parsley inhibits the mutagenicity of male human urine following consumption of fried salmon, *Mutation Research* 192:7–10, 1987.

CHAPTER 4 HOW TO JUICE: GETTING STARTED

1. Sterling T and Arundel AV, Health effects of phenoxy herbicides, *Scand J Work Environ Health* 12:161–73, 1986; Fan AM and Jackson RJ, Pesticides and food safety, *Regulatory Toxicol Pharmacol* 9:158–74, 1989; Mott L and Broad M, *Pesticides in Food* (San Francisco: National Resources Defense Council, 1984); see Ch. 3, notes 25 and 26; see Ch. 5, note 2.

2. See Ch. 4, note 1, Sterling.

3. See Ch. 4, note 1, Sterling, Fan, and Mott.

4. See Ch. 4, note 1, Mott.

5. See Ch. 4, note 1, Fan.

CHAPTER 5: A JUICER'S GUIDE TO FRUITS

1. See Ch. 3, note 18.

2. Smart RC, Huang MT, Chang RL et al., Effect of ellagic acid and 3-O-decylellagic acid on the formation of benzo[a]pyrene in mice, *Carcinogenesis* 7:1669–75, 1986.

3. Majid S, Khanduja KL, Gandhi RK et al., Influence of ellagic acid on antioxidant defense system and lipid peroxidation in mice *Biochem Pharmacol* 42:1441–45, 1991.
4. Best R, Lewis DA, and Nasser N, The anti-ulcerogenic activity of the unripe plantain banana (Musa species), *Br J Pharmacol* 82:107–16, 1984.
5. Murray, *Herbs* (see Ch. 3, note 8).
6. Pinski SL and Maloney JD, Adenosine: A new drug for acute termination of supraventricular tachycardia, *Clev Clin J Med* 57:383–88, 1990.
7. Sobota AE, Inhibition of bacterial adherence by cranberry juice: Potential use for the treatment of urinary tract infections, *J Urology* 131:1013–16, 1984.
8. Ofek I, Goldhar J et al., Anti-escherichia activity of cranberry and blueberry juices, *New England Journal of Medicine* 324, 1599, 1991.
9. Masquelier J, Pycnogenols: Recent advances in the therapeutic activity of procyanidins, in *Natural products as medicinal agents,* vol. 1 (Stuttgart: Hippokrates-Verlag, 1981) pp 243–56.
10. Robbins RC, Martin FG, and Roe JM, Ingestion of grapefruit lowers elevated hematocrits in human subjects, *Int J Vit Nutr Res* 58:414–17, 1988.
11. Kodama R, Yano T, Furukawa et al., Studies on the metabolism of d-limonene, *Xenobiotica* 6:377–89, 1976; Wattenberg LW, Inhibition of neoplasia by minor dietary constituents, *Cancer Res* 43 (Suppl):2448s–53s, 1983.
12. Carper J, *The food pharmacy* (New York: Bantam, 1989).
13. Leung A, *Encyclopedia of common natural ingredients used in food, drugs, and cosmetics* (New York: John Wiley, 1980).
14. Taussig SJ, Szekerczes J, and Batkin S, Inhibition of tumour growth in vitro by bromelain, an extract of the pineapple plant (Ananas comosus), *Planta Medica* 52: 538–39. 1985.

CHAPTER 6 A JUICER'S GUIDE TO VEGETABLES

1. Manousos O, Day NE, Trichopoulus D et al., Diet and colorectal cancer: A case-control study in Greece, *Int J Cancer* 32:1–5, 1983.
2. Welihinda J, Karunanaya EH, Sheriff MHR, and Jayasinghe KSA, Effect of Momardica charantia on the glucose tolerance in maturity onset diabetes, *J Ethnopharmacol* 17:277–82, 1986; Welihinda J, Arvidson G, Gylfe E et al., The insulin-releasing activity of the tropical plant Momordica charantia, *Acta Biol Med Germ* 41:1229–40, 1982; Jifka C, Strifler B, Fortner GW et al., In vivo antitumor activity of the bitter melon (Momardica charantia), *Acta Biol Med Germ* 41:5151–55, 1983.
3. American Cancer Society, *Nutrition and cancer* (see Ch. 1, note 6).
4. See Ch. 1, notes 2 and 7; Ch. 3, note 1; Ch. 5, note 12.
5. Cheney G, Rapid healing of peptic ulcers in patients receiving fresh cabbage juice, *Cal Med* 70:10–14, 1949; Antipeptic ulcer dietary factor, *J Am Diet Assoc* 26:668–72, 1950.
6. See Ch. 1, note 7; Ch. 3, note 13; Ch. 5, note 12.
7. Sainani GS, Desai DB, Gohre NH et al., Effect of dietary garlic and onion on serum lipid profile in Jain community, *Ind J Med Res* 69:776–80, 1979.
8. Mowrey D and Clayson D, Motion sickness, ginger, and psychophysics, *Lancet* i:655–57, 1982; Grontved A, Brask T, Kambskard J, and Hentzer E, Ginger root against seasickness: A controlled trial on the open sea, *Acta Otolaryngol* 105:45–49, 1988.
9. Fischer-Rasmussen W, Kjaer SK, Dahl C, and Asping, U, Ginger treatment of hyperemesis gravidarum, *Eur J Ob Gyn Reproductive Biol* 38:19–24, 1990.

10. Srivastava KC and Mustafa T, Ginger (Zingiber officinale) and rheumatic disorders, *Med Hypothesis* 29:25–28, 1989.
11. Cooper PD and Carter M, The anti-melanoma activity of inulin in mice, *Molecular Immunol* 23:903–18, 1986.
12. Keswani MH, Vartak AM, Patil A, and Davies JWL, Histological and bacteriological studies of burn wounds treated with boiled potato peel dressings, *Burns* 16:137–43, 1990.

CHAPTER 8 JUICE AS MEDICINE

1. See Ch. 6, note 5.
2. *Physicians' desk reference,* 45th ed. Medical Economics Company (Oradell, NJ: Medical Economics Company, 1991).
3. See Ch. 4, note 1, Sterling, Fan, and Mott.
4. Darlington LG, Ramsey NW, and Mansfield JR, Placebo-controlled, blind study of dietary manipulation therapy in rheumatoid arthritis, *Lancet* i:236–38, 1986; Hicklin JA, McEwen LM, and Morgan JE, The effect of diet in rheumatoid arthritis, *Clinical Allergy* 10:463–67, 1980; Panush RS, Delayed reactions to foods: Food allergy and rheumatic disease, *Annals of Allergy* 56:500–3, 1986; Kjeldsen-Kragh J, Haugen M, Borchgrevink CF et al., Controlled trial of fasting and one-year vegetarian diet in rheumatoid arthritis, *Lancet* 338:899–902, 1991; Ziff M, Diet in the treatment of rheumatoid arthritis, *Arthritis Rheumatism* 26:457–61, 1983.
5. See note 4, Kjeldsen-Kragh et al.
6. Lindahl O, Lindwall L, Spangberg A et al., Vegan diet regimen with reduced medication in the treatment of bronchial asthma. *J Asthma* 22:45–55, 1985. See also note 4, Kjeldsen-Kragh et al. and Ziff.
7. Dausch JG and Nixon DW, Garlic: A review of its relationship to malignant disease, *Preventive Medicine* 19:346–61, 1990; Lau BH, Adetumbi MA, and Sanchez A, Allium

sativum (garlic) and atherosclerosis: A review, *Nutri Research* 3:119–28, 1983.

CHAPTER 9 THE JUICE FAST

1. Passwater RA and Cranton FM, *Trace elements, hair analysis and nutrition.* (New Canaan, CT: Keats, 1983); Rutter M and Russell-Jones R, (eds), *Lead versus health: Sources and effects of low level lead exposure.* (New York: John Wiley, 1983); Yost KJ, Cadmium, the environment and human health: An overview, *Experentia* 40:157–64, 1984; Gerstner BG and Huff JE, Clinical toxicology of mercury, *J Toxicol Environ Health* 2:471–526, 1977; Editorial: Toxicologic consequences of oral aluminum, *Nutrition Reviews* 45:72–74, 1987.
2. See note 1, Passwater and Cranton.
3. See note 1.
4. Marlowe M, Coissairt A, Welch I, and Errera J, Hair mineral content as a predictor of learning disabilities, *J Learn Disabil* 17:418–21, 1977; Pihl R and Parkes M, Hair element content in learning disabled children, *Science* 198: 204–6, 1977; David O, Clark J, and Voeller K, Lead and hyperactivity, *Lancet* ii:900–3, 1972; David O, Hoffman S, and Sverd J, Lead and hyperactivity: Behavioral response to chelation: a pilot study, *Am J Psychiatry* 133:1155–88, 1976; Benignus V, Otto D, Muller K, and Seipple K, Effects of age and body lead burden on CNS function in young children: EEG spectra, *EEG and Clin Neurophys* 52:240–48, 1981; Rimland B and Larson G, Hair mineral analysis and behavior: An analysis of 51 studies, *J Learn Disabil* 16:279–85, 1983.
5. Hunter B, Some food additives as neuroexcitors and neurotoxins, *Clinical Ecology* 2:83–89, 1984; Cullen MR (ed), *Workers with multiple chemical sensitivities* (Philadelphia: Hanley & Belfus, 1987); Stayner LT, Elliott L, Blade L et al., A retrospective cohort mortality study of workers

exposed to formaldehyde in the garment industry, *Am J Ind Med* 13:667–81, 1988; Lindstrom K, Riihimaki H, and Hannininen K, Occupational solvent exposure and neuropsychiatric disorders, *Scan J Work Environ Health* 10:321–23, 1984.

6. Donovan P, Bowel toxemia, in Pizzorno JE, and Murray MT, *A textbook of natural medicine.* (Seattle: JBC Publications, 1985).

7. Salloum TK, Therapeutic fasting, in Pizzorno JE and Murray MT, *A textbook of natural medicine;* Duncan GG, Duncan TG, Schless GL, and Cristofori FC, Contraindications and therapeutic results of fasting in obese patients, *Ann NY Acad Sci* 131:632–36, 1965; Sorbis R, Aly KO, Nilsson-Ehle P et al., Vegetarian fasting of obese patients: A clinical and biochemical evaluation, *Scand J Gastroenterol* 17:417–24, 1982; Suzuki J, Yamauchi Y, Horikawa M, and Yamagata, S, Fasting therapy for psychosomatic disease with special reference to its indications and therapeutic mechanism, *Tohoku J Exp Med* 118(Suppl):245–59, 1976; Imamura M and Tung T, A trial of fasting cure for PCB poisoned patients in Taiwan, *Am J Ind Med* 5:147–53, 1984; Lithell H, Bruce A, Gustafsson IB et al., A fasting and vegetarian diet treatment trial on chronic inflammatory disorders, *Acta Derm Venereol* 63:397–403, 1983; Boehme DL, Preplanned fasting in the treatment of mental disease: Survey of the current Soviet literature, *Schizophr Bull* 3:2:388–96, 1977.

8. See note 7, Imamura and Tung.

9. Shakman RA, Nutritional influences on the toxicity of environmental pollutants: A review, *Arch Env Health* 28: 105–33, 1974.

10. Flora SJS, Jain VK, Behari JR, and Tandon SK, Protective role of trace metals in lead intoxication, *Toxicology Letters* 13:51–56, 1982; Papaioannou R, Sohler A, and Pfeiffer CC, Reduction of blood lead levels in battery workers by zinc and vitamin C, *J Orthomol Psychiatry* 7:94–106, 1978;

Flora SJS, Singh S, and Tandon SK, Role of selenium in protection against lead intoxication, *Acta Pharmacol et Toxicol* 53:28–32, 1983; Tandon SK, Flora SJS, Behari JR, and Ashquin M, Vitamin B complex in treatment of cadmium intoxication, *Annals Clin Lab Sci* 14:487–92, 1984; Bratton GR, Zmudzki J, Bell MC, and Warnock LG, Thiamin (vitamin B1) effects on lead intoxication and deposition of lead in tissue: Therapeutic potential, *Toxicol Appl Pharmacol* 59:164–72, 1981; Flora SJS, Singh S, and Tandon SK, Prevention of lead intoxication by vitamin B complex, *Z Ges Hyg* 30:409–11, 1984; Ballatori N and Clarkson TW, Dependence of biliary excretion of inorganic mercury on the biliary transport of glutathione, *Biochem Pharmacol* 33:1093–98, 1984; Murakami M and Webb MA, A morphological and biochemical study of the effects of L-cysteine on the renal uptake and nephrotoxicity of cadmium, *Br J Exp Pathol* 62:115–30, 1981; Cha CW, A study on the effect of garlic to the heavy metal poisoning of rat, *J Korean Med Sci* 2:213–23, 1987.

CHAPTER 10 JUICING FOR WEIGHT LOSS

1. Shils ME and Young VR, *Modern nutrition in health and disease,* 7th ed. (Philadelphia: Lea and Febiger, 1988); Bray GA, Obesity: Definition, diagnosis and disadvantages, *Med J Australia* 142:52–58, 1985; Raymond CA, Biology, culture, dietary changes conspire to increase incidence of obesity, *JAMA* 256:2157–58, 1986; Bjorntorp P, Classification of obese patients and complications related to the distribution of surplus fat, *Am J Clin Nutr* 45:1120–25, 1987.
2. See note 1, Shils and Young; Bray.
3. Ashwell M, Cole TJ, and Dixon AK, Obesity: New insight into the anthropometric classification of fat distribution shown by computed tomography, *Br Med J* 290:1692–94, 1985; see also note 1, Bjorntorp.
4. Gillum RF, The association of body fat distribution with hypertension, hypertensive heart disease, coronary heart disease, diabetes and cardiovascular risk factors in men and

women aged 18–79 years, *J Chron Dis* 40:421–28, 1987; Contaldo F, di Biase G, Panico S et al., Body fat distribution and cardiovascular risk in middle-aged people in southern Italy, *Atherosclerosis* 61:169–72, 1986; Williams PT, Fortmann SP, Terry RB et al., Associations of dietary fat, regional adiposity, and blood pressure in men, *JAMA* 257:3251–56, 1987; Haffner SM, Stern MP, Hazuda HP et al., Role of obesity and fat distribution in non-insulin-dependent diabetes mellitus in Mexican Americans and non-Hispanic whites, *Diabetes Care* 9:153–61, 1986.

5. See note 3.
6. Dietz WH and Gortmaker SL, Do we fatten our children at the television set? *Pediatrics* 75:807–12, 1985.
7. Foreyt JP, Mitchell RE, Garner DT et al., Behavioral treatment of obesity: Results and limitations, *Behavioral Therapy* 13:153–61, 1982.
8. Kolata G, Why do people get fat? *Science* 227:1327–28, 1985.
9. Bennett W and Gurin J, *The dieter's dilemma* (New York: Basic Books, 1982).
10. Anderson JW and Bryant CA, Dietary fiber: diabetes and obesity, *Am J Gastroenterol* 81:898–906, 1986.
11. See note 1.
12. See Ch. 1, note 2.
13. See note 10.
14. Rossner S, Zweigbergk DV, Ohlin A, and Ryttig K, Weight reduction with dietary fibre supplements: Results of two double-blind studies, *Acta Med Scand* 222:83–88, 1987; Shearer RS, Effect of bulk producing tablets on hunger intensity and dieting pattern, *Curr Ther Res* 19:433–41, 1976; Hylander B and Rossner S, Effects of dietary fiber intake before meals on weight loss and hunger in a weight-reducing club, *Acta Med Scand* 213:217–20, 1983; see also note 10.
15. Thompson JK, Jarvie GJ, Lahey BB, and Cureton KJ, Exercise and obesity: Etiology, physiology, and intervention, *Psychol Bull* 91:55–79, 1982.

16. Pollack ML, Wilmore JH, and Fox SM, *Exercise in health and disease* (Philadelphia: W. B. Saunders, 1984), pp 131, 141–47, 219–21, 228–34, 378, 382, 384–85, 457–58.
17. American College of Sports Medicine, Position statement on proper and improper weight loss programs, *Med Sci Sports and Exerc* 15:ix–xiii, 1983.
18. Oscai LB and Holloszy JO, Effects of weight changes produced by exercise, food restriction or overeating on body composition, *J Clin Invest* 48:2124–28, 1969.
19. Lennon D, Nagle F, Stratman F et al., Diet and exercise training effects on resting metabolic rate, *Int J Obes* 9:39–47, 1988.
20. American College of Sports Medicine, *Guidelines for graded exercise testing and prescription,* 3rd ed. (Philadelphia: Lea and Febiger, 1986), pp 1–4, 22, 36, 48–49, 74–78, 80–83, 456–59.
21. See note 20.
22. Hill JO, Schlundt DG, and Sbrocco T et al., Evaluation of an alternating-calorie diet with and without exercise in the treatment of obesity, *Am J Clin Nutr* 50:238–54, 1989.
23. Farmer ME, Locke BZ, Mosciki EK et al., Physical activity and depressive symptomatology: The NHANES 1 epidemiologic follow-up study, *Am J Epidemiol* 1328:1340–51, 1988.
24. Gwinup G, Chelvam R, and Steinberg T, Thickness of subcutaneous fat and activity of underlying muscles, *Am Int Med* 74:408–11, 1971.
25. Wilmore JH, Alterations in strength, body composition and anthropometric measurements consequent to a 10-week training program, *Med Sci Sports* 6:133–8, 1974; Ballor DL, Katch VL, Becque MD, and Marks CR, Resistance weight training during calorie restriction enhances lean body weight maintenance, *Am J Clin Nutr* 47:19–25, 1988.

CHAPTER 11 JUICING, IMMUNE FUNCTION, AND THE CANCER PATIENT

1. Leevy C, Cardi L, Frank O et al., Incidence and significance of hypovitaminemia in a randomly selected municipal hospital population, *Am J Clin Nutr* 17:259–71, 1965.
2. Sanchez A, Reeser J, Lau H et al., Role of sugars in human neutrophilic phagocytosis, *Am J Clin Nutr* 26:1180–84, 1973; Ringsdorf W, Cheraskin E, and Ramsay R, Sucrose, neutrophil phagocytosis and resistance to disease, *Dent Surv* 52:46–48, 1976.
3. Bernstein J, Alpert S, Nauss K, and Suskind R, Depression of lymphocyte transformation following oral glucose ingestion, *Am J Clin Nutr* 30:613, 1977.
4. Mann G and Newton P, The membrane transport of ascorbic acid, *Ann N Y Acad Sci* 258:243–51, 1975.
5. Palmblad J, Hallberg D, and Rossner S, Obesity, plasma lipids and polymorphonuclear (PMN) granulocyte functions, *Scand J Hematol* 19:293–303, 1977.
6. See note 5.
7. Sundstrom H, Korpela H, Sajanti E, and Kauppila A, Supplementation with selenium, vitamin E and their combination in gyneacological cancer during cytotoxic chemotherapy, *Carcinogenesis* 10:273–78, 1989; Hoffman FA, Micronutrient requirements of cancer patients, *Cancer* 55: 295–300, 1985; Judy WV, Hall JH, Dugan W et al., Coenzyme Q10 reduction of adriamycin cardiotoxicity. In: Folkers K and Yamamura Y, eds, *Biomedical and clinical aspects of coenzyme Q*, vol. 4. (Amsterdam: Elsevier Science, 1984), pp 231–41.
8. Stich H, Stich W, Rosin M, and Vallejera M, Use of the micronucleus test to monitor the effect of vitamin A, beta-carotene and canthaxanthin on the buccal mucosa of betal nut/tobacco chewers, *Int J Cancer* 34:745–50, 1984;

Garewal HS, Potential role of beta-carotene in prevention of oral cancer, *Am Clin Nutr* 53:294S–7S, 1991; Garewal HS, Meyskens FL, Killen D et al., Response of oral leuko-plakia to beta-carotene, *J Clin Oncol* 8:1715–20, 1990.

9. See note 8, Stich et al.
10. See Ch. 3, note 14, Alexander et al.
11. Baird I, Hughes R, Wilson H et al., The effects of ascorbic acid and flavonoids on the occurrence of symptoms normally associated with the common cold, *Am J Clin Nutr* 32:1686–90, 1979; Anderson T, Reid D, and Beaton G, Vitamin C and the common cold: A double blind trial, *Can Med Assoc J* 107:503–8, 1972; Cheraskin E, Ringsdorf WM, and Sisley EL, *The vitamin C connection* (New York: Bantam Books, 1983); Anderson TW, Large scale trials of vitamin C, *Ann NY Acad Sci* 258:494–505, 1975.
12. Scott J, On the biochemical similarities of ascorbic acid and interferon, *J Theor Biol* 98:235–38, 1982; Schwerdt P and Scherdt C, Effect of ascorbic acid on rhinovirus replication in WI-38 cells, *Proc Soc Exp Biol Med* 148:1237–43, 1975.
13. See Ch. 8, note 7, Dausch and Nixon.
14. Fuchs J, Ochsendorf F, Schofer H et al., Oxidative imbalance in HIV infected patients, *Med Hypothesis* 36:60–64, 1991.
15. Wu J, Levy EM, and Black PH, 2-mercaptoethanol and n-acetylcysteine enhance T cell colony formation in AIDS and ARC, *Clin Exp Immunol* 77:7–10, 1989.

CHAPTER 12 ANSWERS TO COMMON QUESTIONS ABOUT JUICING

1. Jones DP, Coates RJ, Flagg EW et al., Glutathione in foods listed in the National Cancer Institute's health habits and history food frequency questionnaire, *Nutr Cancer* 17:57–75, 1992.

INDEX

Michael T. Murray, N.D.

One of the most respected authorities in the field of natural healing, Michael Murray, N.D., is a graduate and faculty member of Bastyr College in Seattle, Washington. In addition to maintaining a private naturopathic medical practice, Dr. Murray is an accomplished writer, educator, and lecturer. He is co-author of *The Textbook of Natural Medicine* and the *Encyclopedia of Natural Medicine,* and sole author of *The Healing Power of Herbs.*

Dr. Murray serves on many editorial boards and advisory panels and is a consultant to the health food industry. Since 1985, he has served as Science Director for Enzymatic Therapy, a leading manufacturer of nutritional and herbal supplements. In 1991, Dr. Murray was appointed Director of Nutrition for Trillium Health Products.

The **JUICEMAN II**—the very best automatic juice extractor on the market today! Here's why:

- New technology that extracts the purest, most delicious pulp-free juice.
- New, innovatively designed components that twist together quickly and securely—with no clamps! —for even easier, fumble-free use and assembly.
- Non-stop, continuous action, so you can juice as much as you desire.

- Power to spare—tough one-half horsepower with an integrated circuit for maximum level of efficiency.
- New, razor-sharp, surgical stainless steel blade basket —tough enough to handle skins, stems, rinds and all, without bogging down under heavy loads.
- Even easier clean-up and longer-lasting wear.

Plus with your **JUICEMAN II** order, you also get:

- Vidoo Operations Guide and Manual
- Recipe and Menu Planner
- Friend Get a Friend Coupon Book

- Juiceman Audio Cassette or Album
- Nutrition Hotline
- 16-oz. Juice Glass

ALL THIS FOR ONLY $199.00
To order your JUICEMAN II, or for free information,
CALL 1–800–233–9054